Information Systems Management:
Analytical Tools and Techniques

Phillip Ein-Dor
Tel-Aviv University

Carl R. Jones
Naval Postgraduate School

Elsevier
New York • Amsterdam • Oxford

Elsevier Science Publishing Co., Inc.
52 Vanderbilt Avenue, New York, New York 10017

Sole distributions outside the U.S.A. and Canada:

Elsevier Science Publishers B.V.
P.O. Box 211, 1000 AE Amsterdam, The Netherlands

© 1985 by Elsevier Science Publishing Co., Inc.

This book has been registered with the Copyright Clearance Center, Inc. For further information, please contact the Copyright Clearance Center, Salem, Massachusetts

Library of Congress Cataloging in Publication Data

Ein-Dor, Phillip.
    Information systems management.

    Includes index.
    1. Electronic data processing—Management.
2. Management information systems.   3. System analysis.
I. Jones, Carl R.   II. Title.
QA76.9.M3E4   1985   004'.068   85-13013
ISBN 0-444-00957-4

Current printing (last digit):
  10   9   8   7   6   5   4   3   2   1

Manufactured in the United States of America

Information Systems Management:
Analytical Tools and Techniques

Contents

Preface		ix
Acknowledgments		xi
List of Symbols		xiii

Chapter 1 Information System Management: An Overview — 1

    1.1 Information Systems and Information Resources — 2
    1.2 Describing an Information System — 4
    1.3 The Structure of Information Systems Management — 6
    1.4 External Markets — 11
    1.5 Summary of the Analytical Approach — 11
    1.6 Organization of the Book — 11
    References — 12

Chapter 2 The Cost and Value of Information — 13

    2.1 Value of Information — 13
    2.2 Statistical Decision Theory — 15
    2.3 Team Theory — 21
    2.4 Simulation: Industrial Dynamics — 28
    2.5 Subjective Evaluation of Information — 30
    2.6 Costs of Information — 32
    2.7 Summary — 34
    References — 35

Chapter 3 Economic Foundations for Information System Management: Part 1 — 36

    3.1 The Information System Life Cycle — 37
    3.2 The Role of Time in Economic Decisions — 38
    3.3 Production Plans — 40

3.4 Scale of Operations: The Decision Problem and Decision Rules	44
3.4.1 The Production Function Approach	44
3.4.2 The Cost Function Approach	45
3.5 Scale of Operation and Resource Mix	47
3.6 The Two-Resource Decision Problems and Decision Rules	49
3.6.1 The Production Function Approach	49
3.6.2 The Two-Resource Problem: Cost Function Approach	52
References	52

Chapter 4   Economic Foundations for Information System Management: Part 2   53

4.1 The Production Function Formulation	53
4.1.1 The Product Mix Decision Problem	55
4.1.2 The Decision Rules	55
4.2 The Multiple-Product Cost Function	58
4.2.1 Ray Cost Behavior	60
4.2.2 Incremental Product Cost	67
4.2.3 Economies of Scope	69
4.2.4 Isocost Contours	72
4.2.5 A Realistic Picture	72
4.3 Analysis of Two Resources—Two Information Products	74
4.4 Summary of Chapters 3 and 4	75
4.5 Postscript	76
References	76

Chapter 5   Information System Management   77

5.1 Physical Flows in an Information System	77
5.2 The Organizational Structure	80
5.3 The Information System Planning, Coordinating, and Control Structure	83
5.3.1 The Software Activity	84
5.3.2 The Computer Center	88
5.3.3 The Users	90
5.3.4 The System Manager	92
5.4 The Information System Planning, Coordinating, and Control Data Flows	93
5.5 Information System Behavior	95
5.6 The Capital Budgeting System for Nonroutine Activities	100
5.7 Summary: The Generalized Information System Design Problem	103
References	104

Contents

Chapter 6	**The Computer Center**	**105**
	6.1 The Computer Center as an Information Resource	105
	6.2 The Production Model	109
	6.2.1 Stage 1 of the Production Model	110
	6.2.2 Stage 2 of the Production Model	111
	6.3 The Computer Center Decision Problem	112
	6.3.1 The Profit Function	112
	6.3.2 The Constraints	114
	6.3.3 The Decision Variables	114
	6.3.4 The Computer Center Manager's Decision Problem	115
	6.4 The Computer Center Manager's Decision Rules	116
	6.4.1 The Computer System Capacity Decisions	116
	6.4.2 The Product Decisions	118
	6.4.3 The Choice of Technology	121
	6.4.4 The Allocation Decisions	126
	6.5 The Short-Run Utilization Decision Problem	128
	6.5.1 The Profit Function	128
	6.5.2 The Constraints	129
	6.5.3 The Decision Variables	129
	6.5.4 The Manager's Decision Problem	129
	6.5.5 The Manager's Decision Rules	130
Chapter 7	**Computer Center Management: Special Topics and Practical Techniques**	**133**
	7.1 System Initiation, Termination, and Replacement Decisions	133
	7.2 Rent or Buy Decisions	138
	7.3 Pricing Computer Services—The Supply Side	140
	7.4 Financing Considerations	141
	7.5 Performance Evaluation	142
	7.5.1 Hardware Monitors	142
	7.5.2 Software Monitors	143
	7.5.3 Software Optimizers	144
	7.5.4 System Accounting	145
	7.5.5 Kiviat Charts	146
	7.5.6 Configuration Management	147
	7.6 The Computer Cost Function	151
	7.7 The Economics of Centralization and Dispersion of Computers	156
	7.8 Establishing Transfer Prices	162
	7.9 Capacity Management	165
	References	170
Chapter 8	**The Software Development and Maintenance Activity**	**172**
	8.1 Software Development and Maintenance in the Information System	172

	8.2	Software Development and Maintenance Technology	174
	8.3	The Manager's Long-Run Decision Problem	180
	8.4	The Manager's Long-Run Decision Rules	181
		8.4.1 The Decision Rule for the Mix of CPU Time and Memory in the Development of Applications Software Product a	181
		8.4.2 The Decision Rule for the Allocation of CPU Time Between the Development of Application Software Product a and Systems Software Product b	184
		8.4.3 The Decision Rule for the Allocation of Labor Between Development and Maintenance	184
		8.4.4 The Cost-Minimizing Level of Each Resource to Employ	184
		8.4.5 The Present Life-Cycle Marginal Cost of a Product and Its Schedule	185
		8.4.6 The Decision Rule for the Level of Software Tools to Rent	185
	8.5	The Software Manager's Short-Run Decision Problem	186
	8.6	The Software Manager's Short-Run Decision Rules	186
	8.7	Special Topics	187
		8.7.1 Advanced Models	187
		8.7.2 Central Management Issues	190
		8.7.3 The Software Cost Function	191
		8.7.4 Software Product Cost Estimating	193
		8.7.5 Computer System Conversion Costs: Estimation and Analysis	194
		8.7.6 Productivity Measurement	198
	8.8	Summary	199
	References		199

Chapter 9   Information Users   200

	9.1	Users and the Information Resource Management System	200
	9.2	User Information Generation Technology	202
		9.2.1 Applications Programs as an Information Resource	203
	9.3	The Information Expenditure Budget	203
		9.3.1 Advanced Budgetary Control Methods	204
	9.4	The Information User's Decision Problem	205
	9.5	The Information User's Decision Rules	206
		9.5.1 The Mix of Specific Information Services and User-Generated Information	206
		9.5.2 The Mix of CPU Time and Memory in the Production of User-Generated Information	208
		9.5.3 The Quantity of CPU Time to Rent	209
		9.5.4 The Quantity to Use of a Specific Information Service	209
	9.6	The Demand for Specific Information Services, Computer Capacity, and Labor	210
		9.6.1 Manpower and Financial Budgets	211
	9.7	Implications for Requirements Determination	213
	9.8	Implications for Cost Performance Analysis	213
	9.9	Implications for Performance Measurement	214
	References		215

Chapter 10 System Planning, Control, and Coordination   **216**
    10.1 The Design Issue   216
    10.2 The Utilization of an Existing System   219
    10.3 Extraorganizational Impacts   221
    Reference   222

Index   **223**

Preface

We now mass-produce information the way we used to mass-produce cars.

John Naisbitt, *Megatrends*

The trend transforming the United States and other developed nations from industrial to knowledge-based societies is the first of 10 major trends identified by Naisbitt. This has led to the creation and rapid adoption of phrases such as *The Information Age* or *The Information Society* to describe the phenomenon of which the symptoms are numerous, most visibly the increasing pervasiveness of electronic computers in all spheres of activity. The practical result for corporate and government decision makers is that they must devote more and more of their attention to choosing the quantity and mix of information needed to adapt their organizations to the new age and to operate in it. Much attention is also required in choosing the best means of supplying that information. One of the basic sets of concepts needed to make effective decisions in this context derives from economic analysis. This book applies economic concepts to designing, implementing, and operating systems for management planning, coordination, and control of computerized information activities. It details the analysis required to determine how much information an organization needs and how it should supply it.

The need for a book of this nature became apparent when we were teaching courses in Computer and Information System Economics to graduate students of information system management. Given the rapidly increasing proportion of organizational and national resources devoted to information processing, there is a striking paucity of books, or even articles, applying the principles and techniques of managerial economics to information production and the demand for information resources in organizations. We hope that this book will prove useful for managers and scholars in providing a consistent and relatively complete view of the creation, collection, and dissemination of information in organizations.

For the Student

It is assumed that this book will be used primarily by students of information systems or by anyone with an interest in and understanding of the use of computer systems in managing information. It has been written so that a single course in microeconomics will suffice as a prerequisite. If you have also studied calculus, operations research, finance, or accounting, they will all be helpful; any knowledge of organizational structuring will also be of benefit. But don't worry—the book is self-contained.

The exercises are provided for your benefit. They are designed to let you check your level of understanding and ability to apply the concepts learned. Thus we strongly recommend you do all the exercises and ask your professor when you feel uncertain about the correctness of your answers. With that, you should enjoy your studies. The problems of information management are real, complex, and perplexing. The material here is designed to aid you in coping with highly uncertain and difficult situations and to facilitate making reasonable, constructive decisions. Our aim is for you to be able to experience the thrill of having difficult material suddenly become obvious when it is finally understood.

Phillip Ein-Dor
Carl R. Jones

Acknowledgments

We owe a debt of gratitude to many of our colleagues and friends who provided suggestions, ideas, and above all encouragement. In particular we thank Norm Lyons, Dan Boger, Kevin Sontheimer, and Rich Burton for their aid and "nagging." We also owe many thanks to the students of information systems and telecommunications at the Naval Postgraduate School and the Faculty of Management, Tel-Aviv University, who continue to serve as guinea pigs for the many drafts of this material.

Last, but infinitely far from least, completion of this book would not have been possible without the loving support and somewhat quizzical tolerance of our wives, Amy E. Jones and Ita Ein-Dor. Ita, in particular, worked with us as a member of the team through multiple frustrations to final completion. To her our special thanks.

Acknowledgments

List of Symbols

$\dfrac{1}{(1+r)^t}$	discount factor—discrete time
Π	profit
a	index of applications software products
APP	average physical productivity
AVGINC	average incremental cost
b	index of system software products
B_{IS}	overall information system life-cycle budget
B_{Iu}	life-cycle information budget of user u
$\tilde{C}$	cost
C	CPU services—generic
C_E	external CPU service
C_k	CPU used in specific service production
C_S	CPU service used in software production
C_v	CPU used in universal service production
E	amount of external information service
e^{-rt}	discount factor—continuous time
H_c	CPU hardware
H_m	memory hardware
H_y	peripheral hardware
H_x	telecommunications hardware
H_{jB}	purchased hardware of type j
H_{jR}	rented hardware of type j

I	amount of information—generic
I_k	amount of specific information service k
I_o	amount of user-developed information service o
I_v	amount of universal information service v
I^*	amount of composite information commodity
INC	incremental cost
IR	information resource
k	index of specific information services
K	capital
KDSI	thousands of delivered program source instructions
L	labor—generic
L_o	operations labor
L_s	systems analyst/programmer labor
L_u	user-supplied information processing labor
m	maintenance
M_E	external storage service
M_k	storage used in specific service production
M_S	external storage service used in software development
M_v	storage used in universal service production
MCNB	marginal contribution
MPIR(I, R)	marginal physical input requirement of a product I, for a resource, R
MPLC	marginal present life-cycle cost
MPLΠ	marginal present life-cycle profit
MPLR	marginal present life-cycle revenue
MPP	marginal physical productivity
MPP(R, I)	marginal physical productivity of a resource, R, in producing information, I
MPSchP	marginal physical schedule productivity
MPT$_B$OPCOST	marginal present value of operating cost at initiation
MPT$_B$REV	marginal present value of revenue at initiation
MRGCOST$_{cp}$	marginal cost (*ceteris paribus*)
MRGINC	marginal incremental cost
MRGREV	marginal revenue
MRGUTIL	marginal utility
MRPS	marginal rate of psychological substitution
MRPT	marginal rate of product transformation
MRTS(R_1, R_2)	marginal rate of technical substitution of resource R_1 for resource R_2

List of Symbols

N_a	quantities of applications programs (in KDSI)
N_b	quantities of systems programs (in KDSI)
N_s	quantities of software development tools
p	price—generic
PAPCOST	present value of acquisition price change opportunity cost
p_c	price change opportunity cost
p_{Hj}	price of hardware of type j
p_{mHj}	maintenance cost of hardware of type j
p_{Nc}	software rental cost
p_k	price of capital
PLCSw	present life-cycle cost of software
PLΠ	present life-cycle profit
p_L	wage rate for labor—generic
PLC	present life-cycle cost
p_{Lo}	wage rate for operations labor
p_{Ls}	wage rate for analyst labor
p_{Lu}	wage rate for user-supplied information processing labor
PLR	present life-cycle revenue
PMRGCOST	present life-cycle marginal cost
POCREVF	present value of acquisition price change opportunity cost
p_{Ri}	price of resource i
q	transfer price—generic
q_{Ii}	value or transfer price of information product i
r	discount rate
RAYAVGCOST	ray average cost—average cost of a composite commodity
RAYMRGCOST	ray marginal cost—marginal cost of a composite commodity
R_i	amount of resource i
s	index of software development tools
SC	index for degree of economies of scope
$SC(\hat{I}_1, \hat{I}_2)$	economies of scope in joint production of $\hat{I}_1, \hat{I}_2$
SN	index for degree of economies of scale
t	time period t
T	number of time periods
T_B	beginning of planning period
T_{Da}	delivery date for applications software product a

T_{Db}	delivery date for systems software product b
T_E	end of planning period
TPP	total physical productivity
u	user u
$\tilde{U}$	user utility
$\tilde{U}_{cm}$	central management utility
v	index of universal information services
V_t	value at time t
X	telecommunications services
Y	peripheral input/output services
Y_E	external peripheral service
Y_k	peripherals used in specific service production
Y_S	external peripheral service used in software development
Y_v	peripherals used in universal service production
$Z_a(t)$	fraction of lines of source instructions needing maintenance at time t

Chapter 1
Information System Management: An Overview

The value of information in managing organizations has been recognized since the dawn of history. Many of the relics found in archeological digs and in museums attest to this. One example from antiquity is the business archives, on clay tablets, of the Sumerian temple at Lagash, dating to the fourth millenium BC. Another is the Domesday Book, made by the order of William the Conqueror in the eleventh century, which was both a data base for tax collection purposes and an accounting of the power and resources of his feudatories. The advent of modern information systems dates to the invention, in the Middle Ages, of double-entry bookkeeping.

The use of computerized information storing and processing technologies has permitted much more intensive use of information. It has heightened the sense of its importance and has led to increasing reliance upon information in managerial decision making. As a result, the level of investment by organizations in information processing systems and the current operating expenditure has risen dramatically in recent years. Less than two decades ago, the total expenditure on information processing was under 1% of the United States gross national product. Currently it is estimated at between 5 and 6%, making it the nation's largest industry. Thus, on the average, organizations devote some 5.5% of their expenditures to information systems. This is the average; in many organizations it is much higher. The above-average expenditures apply especially in large complex business and government organizations.

As increasingly sophisticated means for processing information became available, the importance of information for management also increased until there arose an awareness of the fact that information is an important organizational resource, just as are the manpower, capital, patents, and goodwill that an organization employs. This gave rise to the concept of the *information resource*: the resources and their transformation into useable information. The complete information system includes the information resources and the users of the information.

The increasing investment in and cost of operating information systems led to the need to manage them efficiently and effectively. That is the subject of this book.

1.1 Information Systems and Information Resources

Information resources are all the physical and logical components of the information processing system, such as computers, programs, analysts, programmers, operators, managers, data, operating systems, and communications links. An *information resource management system* consists of the organizational structure for managing information resources, the associated decision rules, and the iterative process among participants for communicating about information resources. The structural components of the organization relevant to information resource management can be typified as (1) the central management of the organization, (2) the computer center, and (3) the software development and maintenance activity.

The *information system* in an organization is defined as the information resource just described plus all the users of information. These users are typically managers or their staffs in all the functional areas of the organization, for example, accounting, manufacturing, or logistics. *Information system management* consists of an organizational incentive structure applied to the system's participants and the iterative process by which the system is planned, coordinated, and controlled.

The increasing allocation of organizational resources to information systems means that decisions concerning such systems are also increasingly significant to the organization's effectiveness. Bad decisions concerning information systems are legion, and the effects of such decisions can be disastrous. On the other hand, good decisions contribute greatly to an organization's ability to adapt to changing circumstances and to work smoothly.

Good decisions concerning information systems have three major attributes:

1. They are technologically sound, that is, they are compatible with the current state of the art, do not require technology that does not yet exist for their implementation, and allow for the rapid change of technology.
2. They are behaviorally sound. This implies that the decisions take into account the relevant psychological, sociological, and political factors in the organization so that the information system is not rejected by potential users.
3. They are economically sound, that is, the costs of systems are balanced against their value to the organization. In profit-maximizing organiza-

1.1 Information Systems and Information Resources

tions, such systems are required to be profitable. Ideally, information system decisions are optimal, that is, they maximize the organizational net benefits from acquiring and operating systems over the planning period.

Until now, much of the literature in the field has dealt with the first two aspects of good information system decisions. To the extent that the economic aspect has been approached, treatment has been piecemeal and informal. The objective of this book is to devise a rigorous formal framework for thinking about the economic aspects of good decision making concerning information systems. The root framework is microeconomics. Microeconomics is the study of firms and consumers in a market-based economic system and of their behavior in that system. The integration of the behavioral and technological aspects of information system decisions with the economic aspect will be addressed here by (1) providing a general model of technology and using its characteristics in studying information system decision making and behavior, and (2) providing the organizational structure and role of management in good information systems. A fuller integration must await further development of many of the concepts.

The remainder of this chapter is devoted to providing an overview of the analytical approach to describing and managing an information system. This overview is the forest of the analysis before the individual trees are considered in detail. Independently of the use of the overview in providing the "big picture" for this book, it also is the first step toward another objective—a managerial view of information systems. The nature of managerial work is typified by the simultaneous consideration of many issues, from the detailed to the aggregate, in a highly charged environment. The typical issue is considered only for a few minutes, then is decided upon, and, finally, implementation actions are taken (Mintzberg, 1973). This wealth of decision opportunities in a highly stressful environment puts additional emphasis on the need for a manager to have a clear vision of goals, as well as existing management systems and their current status. So, independently of the details of specific decisions considered in this book, there is also the opportunity for the reader to develop a vision of the design and operational management of an information system. Such visions are one characteristic of the successful companies noted in the book *In Search of Excellence* (Peters and Waterman, 1982). Such visions need not reflect the details of current practice, the accepted solution in a specific context of the issues addressed. To understand the nature of specific solutions it is necessary to study a representation of an information system designed to highlight the issues and the range of possible solutions at a higher level of abstraction than that of particular practices. The development of that vision for information systems begins with the description of an information system. The specific system that will be discussed is designed to teach the general managerial issues involved in the design and management of information systems.

1.2 Describing an Information System

The elements that constitute an information system are generally divided, both organizationally and conceptually, into three groups. These are the computer center, in which most of the hardware is maintained and operated, the software development and maintenance function, and the users of information products. For the formal analysis of this study, it is assumed that each of the functions of the information system is uniquely associated with one of the three system elements. This is roughly right in terms of how it is done in practice, and is the first example in this book of the use of a model to provide ideas and concepts useful in many specific contexts. It should be stressed that the model is designed to demonstrate the management issues involved and is not necessarily the general solution in all organizations.

The relationships between information system components are of two basic types. One is the provision or supply of resources or information products by one component to another. The other is a demand or requirement for utilization of a resource or for an information product. In Figure 1.1, which exhibits these relationships, resource or information product supplies are represented by solid lines and resource or information product demands by dashed lines.

The computer center. The computer center acquires most of its hardware and personnel resources, and some software, from external markets. In the model, most software is produced internally by the software development and maintenance function and used in the computer center to produce information products and computer services. This is an example of a case in which the model does not fit all organizational design solutions in practice.

Figure 1.1 Demand and supply relationships between information system components.

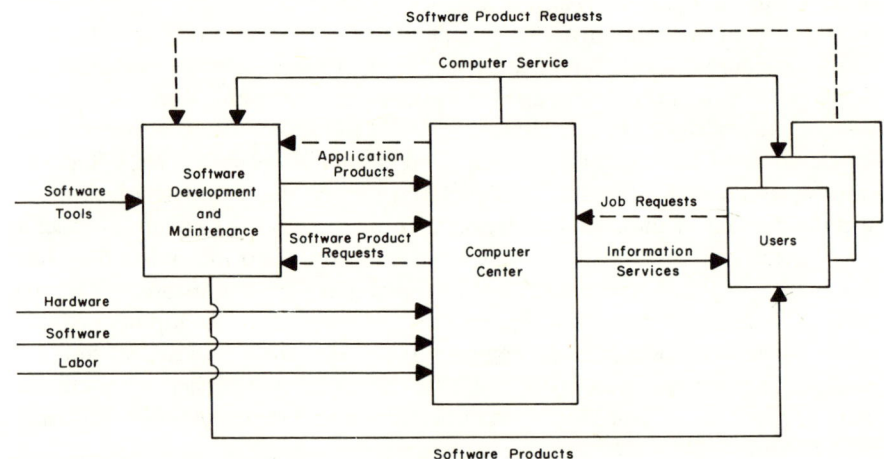

1.2 Describing an Information System

The physical resources, hardware, software, and labor acquired by the computer center generate computer system capacity, which in turn is utilized to produce computer services (i.e., to execute jobs for the users and to assist other components of the system to produce new information products). The trigger for execution of a job of any type is the submission of a job request by users or by the software development and maintenance activity. Job requests are physical flows in that they are accompanied by physical data in one form or another. Information products are routinely produced for the users in synchronization with the general operations of the organization and the information system.

The software activity. The software activity hires personnel from external markets. These personnel utilize computer services in performing their task of producing and maintaining software products. The triggers for these activities are requests for system software from the computer center or for applications programs from the information system's process for initiating new information products.

Users. All managers in the organization, outside the computer center and software activity, are considered to be users, or potential users, of information products. They are, in fact, the rationale for existence of the other two elements.

The demands made by users are either for jobs to be executed (i.e., computer services) or for specific information products. In the first case, this demand takes the form of either a batch job submission or an interactive time-sharing session. The job request is a demand for computer services in the form of central processor time, memory, and input-output services. In the second case, information products are supplied in hard copy (paper) form on a periodic basis, or queries for fixed information are made via a terminal. These queries are for currently available standard information, for example, the names of current employees. New information products are created as part of a capital budgeting system and involve nonroutine decisions. A requirement determination process is invoked to specify new information products.

Four fundamental questions need to be answered for each of the information system components. These recur throughout the book in discussions of various decision problems relating to information system management. The questions are as follows:

1. What should be the scale of operations? At the most general level, the question is, what proportion of an organization's resources should be devoted to information systems vice other uses of those same resources? At the level of the information system components, the question is, how much computer capacity should be provided and how much software production capacity should be provided? At the level of the individual

user, the question is, how much information is enough? That is, which information products should be used, how frequently, and in what quantities.
2. What technology should be employed? In speaking of present-day information systems it is almost inevitable to think of them as being computerized. Indeed, in discussing information systems in this book, the subject is really *computerized* information systems. This assumption, having been made explicit, will not be further belabored. The reader should keep in mind that the analyses presented hold true for any information system, whether manual or computerized. However, even if the discussion is restricted to computerized systems, a vast range of technologies can be considered, from stand-alone microcomputers all the way to interconnected networks of supercomputers; from offline batch processing to online real-time systems, and from transaction-processing systems to decision support and, most recently, knowledge-based systems.
3. What mix should be employed? At a given scale of operation, computer services must be allocated between software product development and maintenance and user-oriented information products. In addition, the mix of information products must be allocated among users. In the computer center and software activity different mixes of resources may be employed. The question is, which mix provides least-cost production at any given time, and how should those mixes be changed, as circumstances dictate?
4. When should production occur? Given that it has been decided to produce a specific information product or to employ a certain resource, the question is, what is the most economic time for this to occur?

The general answers to these problems are presented in Chapters 3 and 4. The elaboration for each element of the information system model and for the total system will occupy most of the book.

1.3 The Structure of Information Systems Management

Given the foregoing schematic of the information system, the question then becomes how to manage it? The answer to this question refers to the organizational structures and procedures implemented. The overall view adopted is that of a central management in the organization, which sets the parameters within which the components of the information system operate.

Note how tightly interrelated are the components of the system depicted in Figure 1.1, and, by implication, how great is the complexity of coordination and control. A small change in one activity ripples throughout the system in a dynamic manner, affecting the scale of operation and mix of resources and products in every component.

1.3 The Structure of Information Systems Management

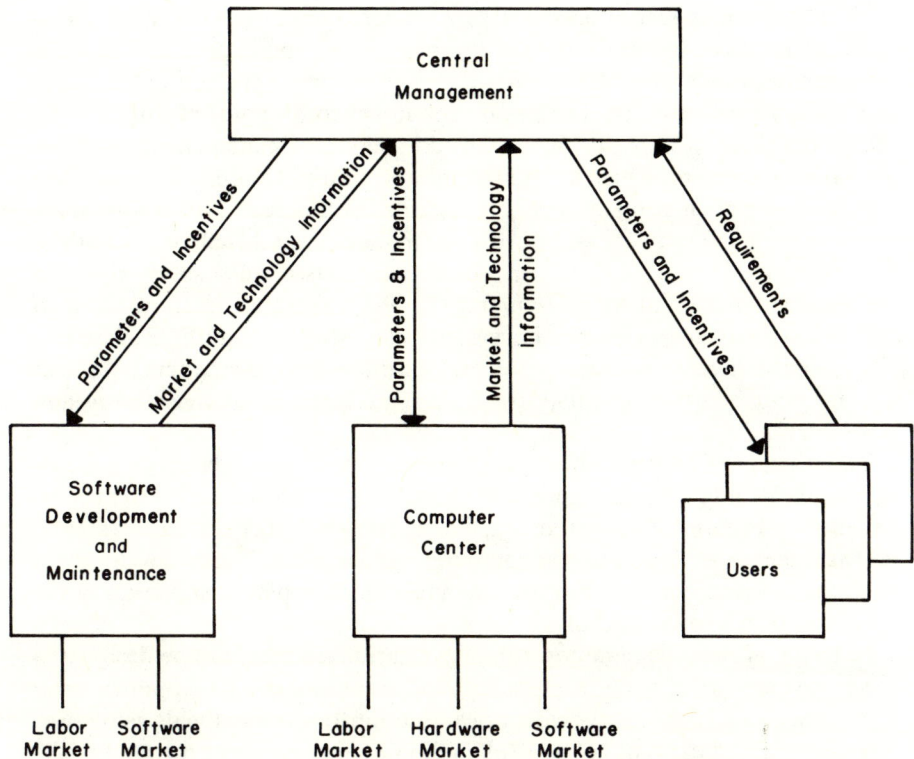

Figure 1.2 Communication between central management and information system components.

The structure of system management is the set of incentives, rewards, and penalties defined for the system components, coupled with communication channels between the components and between them and central management.[1] Two different structures for system management are to be considered. The channels of communication between components are exhibited in Figure 1.1, while Figure 1.2 is a schematic view of the communications between those components and central management. Central management provides lower level management with the parameters within which they are to operate. Lower level managers communicate to central management the information it needs in order to determine the parameters. The nature of the information exchanged is determined by the control structure adopted, as discussed below.

---

[1] For incentives to be effective they must be accompanied by rewards and/or penalties. In order to minimize the need to use the somewhat clumsy phrase "incentives, rewards, and penalties," the terms "incentives" or "incentive structure" will often be used instead.

Note that a manager of information resources per se does not appear specifically in this conception, although it is not uncommon in practice to have a manager responsible for all information resources, both the computer center and the software activity. The reason for not including an information resource manager here is that it would add a layer of management between central management, which is also the information system manager, and the managers of information system components. In this sense, the information resource manager is an emissary of central management. Much of the work of information resource managers in practice consists of reconciling conflicts between hardware and software managers. We forgo this detail in order to emphasize the concepts involved in system management. Figure 1.2 also exhibits the basic incentive structure for each of the system components. Central management uses this incentive structure to guide the behavior of the system components.

The concept of information system management that will be studied focuses on the planning, coordinating, and controlling of interrelated system components. In Figure 1.2, central management, in its role as information system management, was added to the computer center, the software development and maintenance activity, and user-managers to complete the picture of the information system as a whole.

In terms of management control, organizational units may be designated either cost centers or profit centers. Any information system component may be assigned to either of these categories. In order to display the decision processes for both these types of control, different components in the model presented here have been assigned different control mechanisms. The software development and maintenance activity is designated a *cost center*. The decision problem for the software manager is to minimize life-cycle cost constrained by (1) current and future software development and maintenance technology, and (2) the software products required and their delivery and maintenance schedules set by central management. On the other hand, as a *profit center* the manager of the computer center faces a life-cycle profit maximization problem constrained by the computer technology that is, or will be, available over the planning period. Meanwhile, each user subjectively judges the value of information to him or her in managing his or her organizational unit. Users are constrained by office information technology, and an information services financial budget. Last, but not least, central management's decision problem must be discussed. Central management uses it own subjective judgment in seeking to maximize the organization's effectiveness with respect to information systems. It is constrained by an information system budget for the overall organization and its own sense of how the information system operates as a whole.

The process of planning, coordinating, and controlling takes the form of messages sent through the communication channels between central management and each of the system components. The nature of the information

1.3 The Structure of Information Systems Management

transmitted between components and central management and the loci of decisions determines the structure of the information management system.

A Centralized Structure. In a completely centralized structure, central management makes *all* decisions. The other system component managers only provide knowledge of the relevant technologies and market prices. Central management then determines the scale of operations and mix of resources and products to provide. In effect, the system component managers react like puppets rather then decision makers. However unrealistic, due to its impossible requirement that central management know all about everything, it is a procedure worthy of study as the benchmark of *perfect* coordination and control. This is so, since, given complete knowledge and absolute control, central management would achieve maximum efficiency and effectiveness within the bounds of technology and the extraorganizational economic and political environment.

The completely centralized structure emphasizes the organization's (or management's) central decision problem and the associated set of decision rules. The implementation of these decisions assures that the system will be in equilibrium—perfectly planned, coordinated, and controlled.

A Decentralized Structure. In a decentralized structure, central management provides the system components with the structure of their decision problems (e.g., maximize life-cycle profit constrained by technology) and the parameters of the decision problem. The individual system component managers provide detailed knowledge of physical and organizational technology as well as market conditions. In particular, the parameters provided by central management are internal transfer prices of computer services for the software manager, the computer center manager and the users, information services financial budget levels for the users, and what software to produce and when to deliver it for the software manager. The essence of a decentralized procedure is an iterative process in which central management promulgates transfer prices, software specifications and delivery dates, and user budgets to component managers, each of whom solves a component specific capacity and mix decision problem. In turn, each component manager provides central management with the quantities demanded and supplied of every item, the marginal cost of software and its delivery date, and the profit and loss statement for the computer center.

Conceptually, the iterative procedure operates as follows: central management selects an initial set of transfer prices, user budgets, and software products and schedules. These are provided to all. Each manager then formulates and solves the appropriate decision problem (e.g., the computer center manager formulates and solves the technology-constrained profit-maximization problem). Each of the managers and users informs central management of the optimal quantities of software and computer services for them to demand and supply, the marginal cost of software produced by delivery date, and the computer center's profit and loss statement. These are the solutions to the individual component decision problems based on the current parameters supplied by central management.

The next iteration of the procedure begins with central management selecting a new set of transfer prices, budgets, and software specifications and delivery dates based on the rule that if the quantity demanded exceeds the quantity supplied (of any product) then the transfer price should be raised so that less would be demanded and more supplied. In addition, central management can affect users' demands by changing the user information services financial budget level. A higher budget level leads, in general, to a higher level of services demanded. Central management selects a new combination of transfer prices, software products, delivery dates, and user budgets designed to move the information system toward an equality of demand and supply, an equilibrium position. These new transfer prices, budgets and software specifications and delivery dates are provided to the managers and users. They again formulate and solve their respective decision problems and provide central management with their new optimal demands, supplies, marginal cost of software and its delivery, and the computer center's profit and loss statement. The iterative process continues until the equilibrium position is attained.

The crux of the decentralized procedure is that all managers and users need only know about transfer prices and budgets relevant to them and the products they are to provide. They can then manage efficiently and effectively within their sphere of responsibility, guided by the "visible" hand of central management. This leads to an effective operation of the organization as a whole. Correspondingly, central management need not know the technologies employed or anything about the input markets. The knowledge needed to make optimal individual *and* systemwide decisions is carefully decentralized to the appropriate manager, user, or central management. The transaction costs of running the system, relative to alternative systems, are therefore small.

Whether the organizational structure for managing information resources is centralized or decentralized, it is reminiscent of the classic cybernetic model of a feedback control mechanism. As in all such systems, it is essential that balance be maintained between information received and action resulting from that information. When such balance is missing, systems tend to oscillate ever more widely as each new information input leads to ever more disproportionate action. Only if the actions taken are appropriate to the information received will the oscillations be dampened and the system tend to equilibrium. This realization is of great importance in the context of information systems in which decisions frequently require several years for their implementation. Frequent shocks to the system in the course of implementation may prevent decisions from ever fully reaching fruition.

1.4 External Markets

From the preceding discussion and diagrams, it is clear that organizational information systems are dependent on external markets for many of their resources. For the purposes of this book, it is sufficient to assume that all of the input markets operate in such a manner that no participant in the market, demander or supplier, has any perceived individual influence over the market prices and that each participant knows the market prices. Neither of these assumptions is strictly true. For example, prices paid for computers by the Federal Government are not those paid by smaller users. There is also, of course, the effect that a company the size of IBM has on market prices. But for purposes of learning information system management concepts, the assumptions which define pure and perfect markets are a good working approximation and considerably simplify the analysis. It will be adopted with appropriate changes in specific analyses.

1.5 Summary of the Analytical Approach

The management of an information system requires a vision of the system. This vision can be put in terms of an analytical framework. In this framework an information system can be described in terms of

1. the physical flow of resources and products among the technological transformations of resources into products.
2. an organizational structure that groups like tasks into the same organizational unit.
3. a system manager—central management—that plans, coordinates, and controls system balance.
4. a management process that incorporates communications between the system manager and the organizational units which respond according to the incentive structure determined by central management.
5. systemic behavior that is judged effective by central management and is the result of the interactions between it and the organizational units.

1.6 Organization of the Book

The analytical approach described in this chapter is applied throughout the book to the various aspects of information resource management. In addition to the analysis itself, practical techniques based on the analytical approach are described, to the extent that they have been developed. These techniques are usually considered soon after discussion of the analysis on which they are based and the relationship between the analysis and technique is discussed.

The next chapter discusses the costs and benefits of information systems and their measurement; data acquired by the techniques described may be applied in the analyses subsequently developed. Chapters 3 and 4 are devoted to the analytical foundations of information system management as provided by economic theory. Chapter 3 is a brief summary of some basic economics with which the reader of this book is assumed to be familiar; for those who are not, or who would like to refresh their knowledge, some introductory texts are referenced in Chapter 3. Chapter 4 contains a detailed discussion of some more advanced issues relevant to the analysis.

The overall structure of information system management is discussed in Chapter 5, followed by consideration of the theory and techniques of computer center management (Chapters 6 and 7) and of software activity management (Chapter 8). Chapter 9 discusses the role of users in the information generation process, and, finally, Chapter 10 puts the entire process of information resource management in the context of an overall planning and control mechanism.

References

Mintzberg, Henry. (1973) *The Nature of Managerial Work*. New York: Harper & Row.

Peters, Thomas J., and Waterman, Robert H., Jr. (1982) *In Search of Excellence: Lessons from America's Best-Run Companies*. New York: Harper & Row.

Chapter 2
The Cost and Value of Information

Economic analysis is relevant for goods or services that have value. Such analysis generally involves the comparison of values or the consideration of relationships between costs and values. Information products also have costs and values that are amenable to economic analysis; the analyses throughout this book assume that estimates of the relevant costs and values are available. This chapter deals with the estimation of costs and values of information.

2.1 Value of Information

The value of information products is determined by the use of the information these products provide. In most organizational contexts, information has one or both of two major uses. The first major value is the use of information as part of the daily operation of the organization. Orders, shipments, accounts receivable, students' grades, and medical prescriptions, for example, are items of information essential to the operations of organizations that use such information. These examples are raw, detailed items of information known as data. Information systems that acquire, store, process and produce data are called transaction-processing systems because they deal with the simple transaction—an order, a bill, a student's grade, a customer's balance, and so forth. For some organizations, transaction processing is the main order of business. Good examples of the latter are banks and insurance companies, which produce no physical goods but provide extremely useful services simply by processing transactions and managing accounts for their customers. One may think of information processing as the production process of such organizations.

Information of this type is indispensable to the organizations that use it, inasmuch as they could not function without it; in this sense, the information is priceless. The value of the systems that process such information, however, lies not in the information, but in the process; a specific data-processing system has value only if it processes the information more efficiently than alternative systems. In processing transactions, computerized information systems are valuable only if they are cheaper or more effective than manual or other systems performing the identical tasks. If they are not more profitable in some way, there is no point in installing them. Such systems are evaluated in terms of the costs they save in current operations or in terms of more effective operations, for example higher collection rates or smaller inventories.

The second major source of value is in the use of information for making decisions. The assumption here is that when more, better, or different information is available, managers are able to make better decisions. Better decisions, in turn, enhance performance of the organization and lead either to increased profits for corporations or to better service in the case of government or nonprofit organizations. Systems of this type are known as management information systems (MIS) and, more recently, decision support systems (DSS).

From the viewpoint of information system management, a major difference between transaction-processing systems and management information systems is the feasibility of estimating their value as a basis for decision making. It is relatively easy to establish the value of transaction-processing systems in terms of the costs they save or the increased revenue they provide in day-to-day operations. With respect to management information systems, it is much more difficult to establish the value of the information they provide. It is no simple matter to establish the effect of improved decisions because generally, no direct relationship can be identified between a decision and its economic ramifications.

Both of the organizational structures for information system management described in Chapter 1 require that central management determine either the value of information, if it is to make the decisions, or a transfer price for information, if decision making is delegated. Most of the remainder of this chapter is devoted to approaches to determining the value of information. First, two analytical models are presented, then a simulation approach is described, and finally, the value of information is viewed as the outcome of organizational processes.

Two analytical models for determining the value of information in organizational contexts are statistical decision theory and team theory. Both of these theories are built on the assumption that information acquires value when it is used as a basis for decisions, under conditions of uncertainty. When everything is certain, all is known, and information is worthless. How much would you be willing to pay for the information that it will be dark tonight?

Table 2.1 Incomes Associated with Crop Yields

	Crop	
State of nature	Cabbages	Artichokes
low yield	35,000	22,500
high yield	70,000	75,400

PROBABILITY OF ACTION/STATE PAIRS

	Probability of outcome	
Action	Low yield	High yield
cabbages	.4	.6
artichokes	.4	.6

When the future is uncertain, however, the information on events in that future can be very valuable, even when imprecise. Would you be prepared to pay more for prior information on the change in tomorrow's stock exchange index than for the information that tonight will be dark?

2.2 Statistical Decision Theory

Statistical decision theory is a technique for analyzing decision situations when the outcomes of the actions that may be taken are not certain. Thus it relates to decision making under conditions of risk and uncertainty. Instead of stating the theory formally, we shall present it by means of an example.[1]

Think of a California farmer who has to decide whether to plant cabbages or artichokes. He knows that crops sometimes produce high yields and sometimes low yields, depending on a number of factors such as weather and insect infestations. The incomes generated by each crop under the circumstances are established by the farmer, as shown in Table 2.1. From his own past experience and from talking to neighbors, the farmer estimates that the probability of a good year is 0.6 and of a bad year, 0.4. For the sake of simplicity, we will assume that in good years both crops do well and in bad years both do poorly. Note, however, that the relative difference between good and bad years in cabbages is much smaller than in artichokes.

The decision problem facing the farmer may now be exhibited graphically, as in Figure 2.1, in what is known as a decision tree. The purpose of such a tree is to display all elements of the problem in a manner that permits easy

---

[1] For a complete formal discussion of Statistical Decision Theory, see Raiffa (1968).

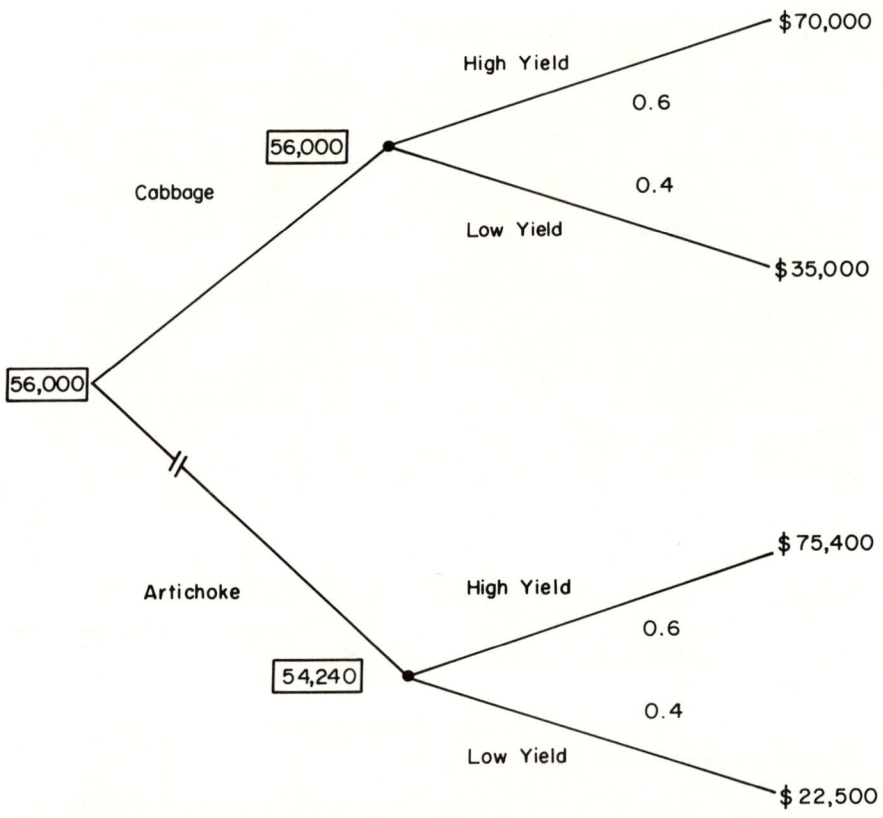

Figure 2.1 Decision tree for farmer's crop problem.

comprehension and evaluation. This particular tree exhibits a decision—cabbages or artichokes—at its first branching, and then a number of events or states that are the possible outcomes of the decisions, namely, a high yield or a low yield for each crop. The probabilities of uncertain outcomes are indicated on the appropriate branches. Note that the probabilities of the outcomes following each decision must add up to 1.0, since all possible outcomes are considered. No probabilities are associated with decisions, since there is no element of uncertainty about them; a choice must be made and only one of the branches can be followed.

Given the tree description of the problem, all that remains to be done is to calculate the expected values of each of the decisions.

$$E(D_i) = \sum_{j=1}^{J} S_{ij} P_{ij},$$

2.2 Statistical Decision Theory

where $E(D_i)$ = expected value of decision i,
S_{ij} = value of the jth outcome of decision i,
P_{ij} = probability of the jth outcome of decision i.[2]

The expected values, $E(D_i)$, appear in boxes at the forks of the tree's branches. Under the situation described in this tree, the expected value of growing cabbages ($56,000) is greater than that of growing artichokes ($54,240). Assuming that our farmer's goal is to maximize income, clearly his decision should be to grow cabbages; the decision not to grow artichokes is symbolized by the bars cutting off that branch of the tree.

We can now see how much information is worth to the farmer. If he could predict accurately in advance whether or not it would be a good year, he would plant artichokes in good years and cabbages in bad years. The expected income would then be

($75,400 × 0.6) + ($35,000 × 0.4) = $59,240.

The expected value of this perfect information to the farmer is equal to his expected income, given the perfect information *less* his expected income in his present state of ignorance, that is;

$59,240 − 56,000 = *$3,240*.

Thus, the farmer should be prepared to pay anything up to $3,240 for a service that would provide him with perfect forecasts. If the service costs more and he subscribes to it, he should expect to be worse off than without it.

Now assume that the farmer has been offered the services of Agricultural Forecasting Consultants, Inc., who provide their clients with forecasts of crop yield. In order to protect themselves against litigation from disappointed customers, AFC advise potential subscribers that their forecasts are not absolutely accurate. They claim that their success rate is bettter than 60% and provide the performance record given in Table 2.2 to anyone interested in their record.

The farmer's problem now is to decide whether he should subscribe to the forecasts. The decision will depend, first, on whether the forecasts, at the level

---

[2] The notation used in this chapter is distinct from that in the rest of the book. Thus, it does not appear in the glossary and, in some cases, the same symbols are used in subsequent chapters to represent other concepts. The glossary for this chapter is as follows:

D_i decision i
$E(\ )$ expected value of term in parentheses
F_i forecast i
M_i team member i
P probability of an outcome
S_k value of a state of nature, or outcome, k
V team decision value.

Table 2.2 Performance of Agricultural Forecasting Consultants

States	Conditional probabilities of forecasts given states		Unconditional probabilities of states
	Low yield	High yield	
low yield	.6	.4	.4
high yield	.35	.65	.6
unconditional probabilities of forecasts	.45	.55	1.0

of accuracy presented, can improve his performance. If not, there is no point in pursuing the matter any further.

Figure 2.2 represents the decision tree with the new information included. The subtree, which follows the decision not to buy the forecast, is exactly that of Figure 2.1, as we would expect; that is if he does not acquire the forecast, the farmer is in exactly the same position as when he was unaware of its existence. The other subtree, which originates with the decision to buy the forecast, represents the sequence of events following that decision. In general, note that the tree cycles between decision and state phases, each decision being followed by the outcome states with their associated probabilities.

The reader may have noticed that the probabilities assigned to the branches of the subtree, which originate with the decision to buy the forecast, are not those of Table 2.2. This is because the table exhibits the probability of a forecast, given the true state. The tree, however, reflects the farmer's problem and the true sequence of events more accurately, and requires establishing the probabilities of the true states, which become known only *after* the forecast is made. What we need is the probability of a true state, given a forecast, rather than the probability of a forecast, given the true state.

The conversion from the conditional probability of a forecast, given a state to the conditional probability of a state, given a forecast is done with the help of Bayes' theorem, which, applied to this case, states:

$$P(S_k|F_n) = \frac{P(F_n|S_k) \cdot P(S_k)}{\sum_{i=1}^{I} P(F_n|S_i) \cdot P(S_i)},$$

where $P(S_k)$ = unconditional probability of a particular state k,

$P(S_k|F_n)$ = conditional probability of a particular state k, given a specific forecast n,

2.2 Statistical Decision Theory

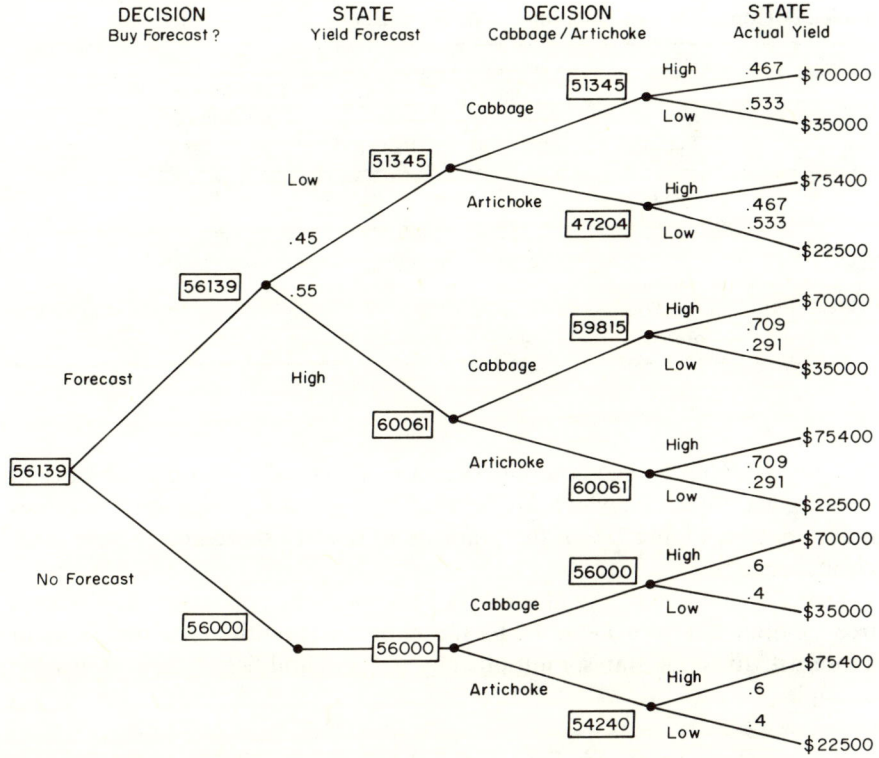

Figure 2.2 Decision tree for farmer's crop problem with forecast available.

$P(F_n|S_k)$ = conditional probability of a particular forecast n, given a specific state k,

i = an index over the possible states.

For example, consider a forecast of a high yield, F_H, and an outcome of a low yield, S_L. Then

$$P(S_H|F_L) = \frac{P(F_H|S_L)P(S_L)}{P(F_H|S_L)P(S_L) + P(F_H|S_H)P(S_H)},$$

where, from Table 2.2,

$$P(F_H|S_L) = .4, \quad P(S_L) = .4,$$
$$P(F_H|S_H) = .65, \quad P(S_H) = .6;$$

thus

$$P(S_L|F_H) = \frac{.4 \times .4}{(.4 \times .4) + (.65 \times .6)} = .291.$$

Table 2.3 Consistency of Outcomes with Forecasts

States	Conditional probabilities of states given forecasts		Unconditional probabilities of states
	Low yield	High yield	
low yield	.533	.291	.4
high yield	.467	.709	.6
unconditional probabilities of forecasts	.45	.55	1.0

In similar fashion we can compute the remaining conditional probabilities of states, given forecasts, which are entered in Table 2.3. These are the values that appear in Figure 2.2 on the branches of the tree representing outcomes, given forecasts.

The probabilities of the alternative forecasts that appear in the decision tree are obtained from Table 2.2 by summing the conditional probabilities of a forecast, given the states, multiplied by the probabilities of those states, for example,

$$P(F_H) = P(F_H|S_H) \cdot P(S_H) + P(F_H|S_L) \cdot P(S_L)$$
$$= (.65 \times .6) + (.4 \times .4)$$
$$= .55.$$

These probabilities appear at the bottom of Table 2.2.

From the revised decision tree we can see that, if the farmer buys the forecast, the decision rule should be to plant cabbages when a low-yield year is forecast and artichokes when a good year is forecast; therefore, he will have an expected income of $56,139, instead of $56,000 if he does not buy the forecast and always grows cabbages. The value of this particular information system is $139 per growing season. Because of the noise in this system in the form of inaccuracies in the forecasting process, it is worth considerably less than the perfect information system which we valued at $3,240.

In conclusion, statistical decision theory provides answers to questions about the economic feasibility of information systems. It permits determination of the maximum amount one should be prepared to pay for a given information system. The nature of the information system is, however, completely obscured. In fact, all we know about the system is its output and its accuracy. Its inputs and processes are invisible.

EXERCISE 2.1 Statistical Decision Theory

Evaluate the decision problem in the text using the following set of data:

Probabilities of Action/State Pairs

	Probability of outcome	
Action	Low yield	High yield
Cabbages	.4	.6
Artichokes	.3	.7

Assume that Agricultural Forecasting now sells separate forecasts for each crop while continuing to maintain the same levels of forecast accuracy for both. (Note that, for artichokes, this will change the probabilities of events given forecasts.)

1. How much is each of the separate forecasts worth?
2. How much should the farmer be prepared to pay for both forecasts?

The interrelationship between information, decision rules, and states of nature is complex enough when information is considered in the abstract. It becomes even more difficult to form a model when one wishes to complete the concept of information by incorporating the structural characteristics of a particular information system that generates the information. For a more detailed look at the interrelationships between the structure of an information system and the decisions to which it is applied, the discussion turns to team theory.

2.3 Team Theory

Team theory deals with decisions and information in organizations, given a set of situations and payoffs. Statistical decision theory deals with the same issues; but in that model, the structure of the organization and the structure of the information system is not explicitly considered. In term theory, both the structure of the organization and the information links between elements of the organization are made explicit. This theory originates with Jakob Marschak (1955) and our discussion will follow his exposition very closely, using a slightly modified version of the example accompanying his trailblazing paper.

A team is defined as a group of persons, each of whom makes decisions about something different, but who receive a common reward as the joint result of all those decisions. A military unit is an obvious example of a team; combat, supply, transport, and medical commanders all make decisions about different problems in their areas of competence and receive a common reward in the form of victory or defeat. Similarly, business organizations are teams in which a number of managers are responsible for decision making in different fields such as production, marketing, finance, and personnel. Their common reward is in the economic well-being of the firm from which they derive their livelihood.

The team's problem is to find the best communication system and the best decision rules, given the payoffs, the probabilities of various situations, and the cost of communication, that is, the cost of processing information. What makes the problem so complex is that all the decision variables are mutually dependent and also dependent on the situational variables. Thus an optimal solution can be found only by solving the information and decision rule problems simultaneously for a given situation, that is, outcome probabilities and information costs.

Because of the complexity of the problem, it is virtually impossible to discuss problems of realistic size and we are constrained to use highly abstract approximations of the real world. Even these, however, are sufficient to provide significant insights into the information problem of organizations.

Our example concerns the simplest possible team organization consisting of two members denoted as M_1 and M_2. The team members are faced by a simple binary decision—to act or not to act—in view of what is known to them about two state variables, each of which can take on one of three values. The state variables are labeled S_1 and S_2 and their values are labeled $+$, 0, and $-$, denoting positive, neutral, and negative values of the states.

Assume now that the gross payoffs to the team's decisions are given by the formula

$$(D_1 + D_2) \cdot (S_1 + S_2),$$

where D_i is the decision of team member i and takes on values of 0 (no action) or 1 (action); and S_j is the value of state variable j and takes on values -5 (negative outcome, "$-$"), -1 (neutral outcome, "0"), or $+10$ (positive outcome, "$+$"). As an example, assume that

team member 1 takes no action,	$D_1 =$	0;
team member 2 does act,	$D_2 =$	1;
state variable 1 is negative,	$S_1 =$	-5;
state variable 2 is positive,	$S_2 =$	$+10$.

Thus the payoff to the team's decisions, given the actual state of nature, is

$$(0 + 1) \cdot (-5 + 10) = +5.$$

2.3 Team Theory

Table 2.4 Gross Scores Without Interaction

		S_2					
	State variable S_1	M_2 doesn't act ($D_2 = 0$)			M_2 acts ($D_2 = 1$)		
		−	0	+	−	0	+
M_1, doesn't act	−	0	0	0	−10	−6	5
$D_1 = 0$	0	0	0	0	−6	−2	9
	+	0	0	0	5	9	20
M_1, acts	−	−10	−6	5	−20	−12	10
$D_1 = 1$	0	−6	−2	9	−12	−4	18
	+	5	9	20	10	18	40

By evaluating the effects of all four possible decision combinations (0,0; 0,1; 1,0; 1,1) in all nine states of the world (−,−; −,0; −,+; 0,−; 0,0; 0,+; +,−; +,0; +,+), a gross payoff table can be constructed and is exhibited as Table 2.4. The result of the preceding example is located in the upper right-hand corner of this table. The formula on which the table is based assumes no interaction between decisions—each decision brings its payoff irrespective of the other decision, and the results are additive.

Some of the outcomes in the gross score table are positive, some are negative, and some are zero. What decision rule should the team members adopt in order to achieve the best outcome? The answer depends on the probabilities of the outcomes and on the information available to them concerning the outcomes following their decisions.

First, assume that the probabilities of outcomes are as in Table 2.5 where an outcome is defined by the joint condition of the two state variables. Multiplying the gross payoffs to the outcomes under each action regime of Table 2.4 by the probability of that outcome from Table 2.5, the expected payoffs are generated and are exhibited as Table 2.6.

Table 2.5 Probabilities of Outcomes

	S_2		
S_1	−	0	+
−	.05	.1	.05
0	.1	.05	.1
+	.05	.2	.3

Table 2.6 Expected Values of Gross Scores

		State variable S_2					
	State variable S_1	M_2 doesn't act ($D_2 = 0$)			M_2 acts ($D_2 = 1$)		
		−	0	+	−	0	+
M_1, doesn't act $D_1 = 0$	−	0	0	0	−.5	−.6	.25
	0	0	0	0	−.6	−.1	.9
	+	0	0	0	.25	1.8	6.0
M_1, acts $D_1 = 1$	−	−.5	−.5	.25	−1.0	−1.2	.5
	0	−.6	−.1	.9	−1.2	−.2	1.8
	+	.25	1.8	6.0	.5	3.6	12.0

If the team members have no information about the current outcome but do know the probabilities, the expected values of the decision rules feasible for them are as follows;

1. Neither member should ever act ($D_1 = 0$, $D_2 = 0$). The expected value of this decision is

$$V = \sum_{S_1}\sum_{S_2} (D_1 + D_2) \cdot (S_1 + S_2)$$
$$= 0,$$

the sum of the scores in the top left quadrant of Table 2.6.

2. M_1 always acts, M_2 never acts ($D_1 = 1$, $D_2 = 0$);

$$V = \sum_{S_1}\sum_{S_2} (D_1 + D_2) \cdot (S_1 + S_2)$$
$$= 7.4,$$

the sum of scores in the bottom left quadrant.

3. M_1 never acts, M_2 always acts ($D_1 = 0$, $D_2 = 1$); $V = 7.4$.
4. M_1 and M_2 always act ($D_1 = 1$, $D_2 = 1$);

$$V = 14.8.$$

Let us now consider a perfect information system in which both team members know the current value of both state variables. With this amount of information they can be more discriminating in their actions, choosing to act at some times and not at others. Since both team members know everything, they can determine an appropriate course of action for every possible outcome; the payoffs to all action/state combinations are listed in Table 2.7.

2.3 Team Theory

Table 2.7 Payoffs to Action/State Combinations (Perfect Information)

State		Neither acts	M_1 acts, M_2 doesn't[a]	Both act
S_1	S_2			
+	+	0	6.0	12.0*
+	−	0	0.25	0.5*
−	+	0	0.25	0.5*
+	0	0	1.8	3.6*
0	+	0	0.9	1.8*
−	−	0*	−0.5	−1.0
0	0	0*	−0.1	−0.2
0	−	0*	−0.6	−1.2
−	0	0*	−0.6	−1.2

[a] Since the payoffs tables are identical for $D_1 = 0, D_2 = 1$, and $D_1 = 1, D_2 = 0$, the payoffs are symmetrical.

From this table, the optimal action for each state can be identified. The outcomes of these actions are emphasized in the table by asterisks. The best decision rule is that both team members should act if either state is positive, otherwise neither should act. In no case is it optimal for one team member to act and the other not to act. The expected score for the best decision rule, given perfect information, is *18.4*. Recall that with no information the expected score is *14.8*. Thus, an information system that provides perfect information is worth no more than *3.6*.

Now consider a case intermediate between the null and the perfect information systems. Say team member M_1 knows the value of state variables S_1 and team member M_2 knows nothing. While M_1 can still adjust his behavior somewhat on the basis of his knowledge of the state variable, M_2 must adopt a consistent "always act" or "never act" decision rule. Table 2.8 exhibits the possible outcomes. M_1's actions are based on choosing the highest payoff from Table 2.8, given his knowledge of S_1 and M_2's decision rule, Note that

Table 2.8 Payoffs to Action/State Combinations (M_1 knows S_1)

State		M_2 always acts			M_2 never acts		
S_1	S_2	M_1 should	Payoff	Alternative	M_1 should	Payoff	Alternative
+	?	act	16.1	8.05	act	8.05	0
0	?	act	0.4	0.2	act	0.2	0
−	?	not act	−0.85	−1.7	not act	0	−0.85
Total			15.65			8.25	

M_1 cannot condition his decision on S_2 because he does not know it—he must always act or always not act on each of the values of S_1; the payoff then is the sum of the expected values in the row corresponding to S_1 of the quadrant in which M_2 places the team by acting or not acting (see Table 2.8). The optimal decision rule is for M_1 to act when S_1 is + or 0 and not to act when S_1 is −. The expected payoff is then 15.65, in contrast to 14.8 in the null information situation. Thus information to one of the team members on one variable is worth up to 0.85 each decision period.

Nothing has been said yet about the way information is obtained by team members. The two basic possibilities are direct observation or reports communicated to those who do not observe directly. This implies that an information system is a communications network with observation capabilities at some of the nodes; the configuration of the network and location of observation nodes determine the information available to any team member. Following Marschak, denote an observation node by X, a node with no observation capability by □, and a communication link between two nodes by → or ←. Assuming that team member M_1 can, in principle, observe state variable S_1, and M_2 can observe S_2, then a number of information system structures for the two-member team can be evaluated as shown in Table 2.9.

The information networks specified in Table 2.9 are listed in order of increasing value. This permits evaluation of marginal additions to the network, as demonstrated in Table 2.10. The first entry in Table 2.10 is the expected score for the team with null information. The last entry is the expected value of a perfect information system; the intervening entries are for increasingly more valuable systems. Conceptually, team theory provides a basis for making the decisions necessary for structuring cost-effective information systems.

Although team theory is conceptually appealing, there are two real problems in its practical application. The first is its complexity. With only two

Table 2.9 Some Information Structures for a Two-Member Team

	Information network nodes		Information structure		Expected gross score
	M_1	M_2	M_1 knows	M_2 knows	
a.	□	□	nothing	nothing	14.8
b.	X	□	S_1	nothing	15.65
c.	X	X	S_1	S_2	16.5
d.	X →	□	S_1	S_1	16.5
e.	X →	X	S_1	S_1 and S_2	17.45
f.	X ↔	X	S_1 and S_2	S_1 and S_2	18.4

2.3 Team Theory

Table 2.10 Value of Marginal Additions to Network

Addition to network	Derivation[a]	Value
none	a	14.8
first observation	b − a	0.85
second observation	c − b	0.85
one-way communication given one observation	d − b	0.85
one-way communication given two observations	e − c	0.95
second-way communications given two observations	f − e	0.95

[a] From Table 2.9.

EXERCISE 2.2 Team Theory

For the example given in the text, assume one change in the function which generates gross payoffs so that it is now

$$(2D_1 + D_2)(S_1 + S_2).$$

What are the expected gross scores, optimal decision rules, and value of information system for the following information networks?

M_1	M_2
□	□
X ⟶	□
X ⟵	X
X ⟵⟶	X

Show how you derived your answers.

---

members in the team, who can each take one of two actions, there are four possible action combinations, each of which can be applied to one of the situations faced by the team; with state variables assuming three values each, there are nine possible situations. Four team actions for nine situations give rise to 36 action/state combinations. Now think of a somewhat more realistic situation with, say, 20 team members, each of whom can take 5 different actions with respect to a situation composed of 10 variables assuming 6 values each; this problem then gives rise to 5^{20} actions and 10^6 situations, or 9.5×10^{19} action/state combinations. Such problems simply expand explosively when applied to anything approaching reality.

The second problem in applying team theory is the assumption that, given all the necessary data, managers will be able to design optimal information systems. This assumption has been the subject of an empirical study by Mac-Crimmon (1974). In his experiment, MacCrimmon required his subjects, 60 experienced executives, to devise an information system and decision rules for a three-member team in a situation with four possible outcomes and some constraints. Costs were associated with observation and communication. Some of the parameters of the problem, such as outcome probabilities and the types of events, had to be derived by the executives from historical data. Of the 60 subjects, only six subjects found one of the several optimal solutions; another 32 subjects devised feasible, but suboptimal systems; finally, 22 subjects designed infeasible solutions which required, for example, that action be taken on the basis of information not observed, or observed but not communicated to the team member who was to take action. Given this difficulty on the part of managers to devise optimal systems in a team-theoretic environment, we can conclude that team theory may describe a desirable method of system design, but probably does not describe actual behavior.

Both statistical decision theory and team theory provide valuable insights on the role of information systems in organization decision processes and on the value of such systems. Because of the complexity of real organizations, however, it does not seem practical to use either of these theories in actually designing any but the most elementary systems. The most successful practical approach to modeling information systems has been simulation, the next approach discussed.

2.4 Simulation: Industrial Dynamics

A simulation model and language constructed specifically for modeling information and decision systems are Jay Forrester's (1961) Industrial Dynamics model and its computer language counterpart, DYNAMO. The model describes the state of the organization by information on the *levels* of various activities and entities in it. The number of employees, the rate of production, average sales, and raw materials inventory are all examples of the levels that together form a representation of the organization.

Activity in the organization takes the form of *flows* of physical values between the levels (see Figure 2.3). Thus, the production level receives a flow of employees and a flow of raw material from the raw material inventory level. The production level in turn releases a flow of finished goods to the appropriate inventory level.

In addition to physical values, each level produces information *representing* those values. This information flows into decision points that use it to regulate the rates of flow. These double flows of information and physical entities are shown in Figure 2.4. As a result, a network of information flows is

2.4 Simulation: Industrial Dynamics

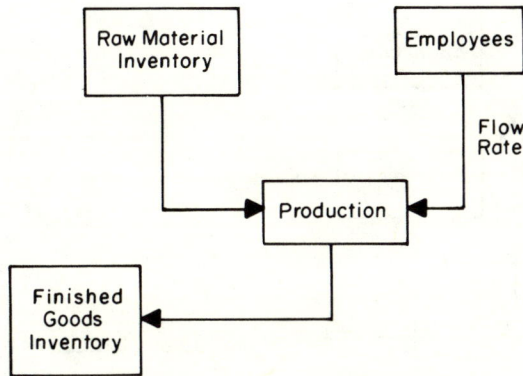

Figure 2.3 Flows and levels description of organization. [Adapted from Forrester, Jay W. "Managerial Decision Making," In Greenberger, Martin (ed.) *Computers and the World of the Future.* Cambridge, MA: M.I.T. Press (1962), by permission of the M.I.T. Press.]

superimposed on the physical network and controls it. According to Forrester (1962),

> An industrial organization is a complex, interlocking network of information channels. These channels emerge at various points to control physical processes such as hiring employees, building factories, and producing goods.

The composition and functioning of the decision points posited by Forrester are also of some interest. In the decision points, the *apparent* state of actual conditions is considered because the information available at the decision point is an incomplete and only partly accurate reflection of the physical facts it represents. An important aspect of any information system is how accurate and up-to-date are its descriptions of the physical world it represents.

Forrester's model illuminates three important aspects of information systems: (1) information is an explicit and integral part of organizational decision making (it has already been pointed out that information derives its value from its utilization in the decision process); (2) information's function is to represent the physical values of which the organization is composed; and (3) the information is only a partial and less than perfectly accurate representation of the true state of the organization.

Once an organization has been structured in terms of the Industrial Dynamics model, it is readily translated into a computer simulation model by means of the DYNAMO language. With the help of the simulation, the benefits of changes in information flows and decision rules can be evaluated and

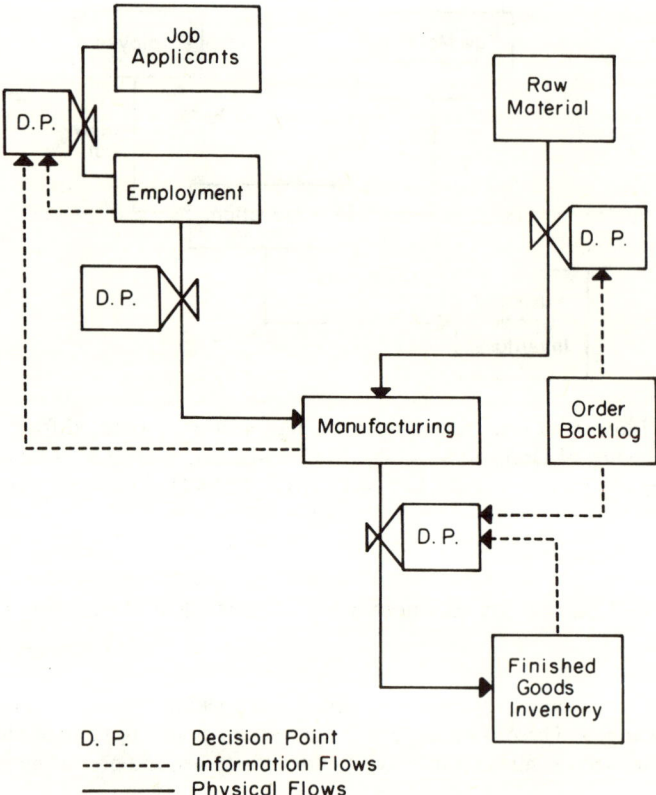

Figure 2.1 Physical and information flows in a production organization. [Adapted from Forrester, Jay W. "Managerial Decision Making." In Greenberger, Martin (ed.) *Computers and the World of the Future.* Cambridge, MA: M.I.T. Press (1962), by permission of the M.I.T. Press.]

the value of information systems derived. The great advantage of the simulation approach, as compared with the two analytical approaches presented earlier, is that it permits evaluation of information systems for realistically complex situations.

2.5 Subjective Evaluation of Information

Given the difficulty in applying all of the formal methods of valuing information, managers are in most cases left no alternative but to rely on subjective evaluation. Managers must use their experience, intuition, and gut feeling to determine the value of information resources within the context of a specific information system. In most cases, managers need not actually provide a

2.5 Subjective Evaluation of Information

precise numerical value—it is sufficient for them to state whether a proposed system is worth more or less than its cost. For incremental decisions, this implicit valuation is sufficient.

However, the formal analysis presented in this book is predicated on managements being able to establish the value of information explicitly, by a process of communication between the system components. Where the analytical methods are inappropriate, this may still be done subjectively. However, it is extremely desirable to introduce some structure into the subjective evaluation process rather than having managers "pull numbers off the tops of their heads."

Several methods are available to the analyst attempting to elicit information values from top management. The first method is an elaboration of the implicit evaluation method mentioned above. Rather than asking whether a certain information product is worth more or less than its cost, the analyst can pose a series of questions of the form "Is this product worth more or less than \$$x$?" where x varies over a range above and below the value of the product. Such a series of questions should provide a reasonably accurate estimate of the value of the product to the manager questioned. Furthermore, it permits testing for consistency of responses in order to determine how confident the manager really is about the product's value.

A second method of establishing the value of an information product is by analogy: is product B worth more or less than product A? A series of questions of this type establishes the *relative* values of a number of products. For purposes such as prioritization, this may be sufficient. For the analytical methods of this book, relative value may be used to calibrate values derived by the first method.

A technique for further enhancing the validity of subjective methods of information valuation is the Delphi method. This involves applying methods such as those described above to a panel of managers. The subjective evaluations of each of the managers, together with the rationales for their replies, are communicated to all the other panelists. The managers are then requested to revise their previous estimates after seeing their colleagues' evaluations, and the revised values and rationales are distributed among the panel. This process continues until a consensus of the panel is achieved. The consensus may then be regarded as the considered subjective organizational evaluation of the product in question.

In the decentralized management structure described in Chapter 1, central management must not only determine the value of information, but it must set transfer prices for information products in such a way that organizational information resources are managed and utilized in an effective manner. The establishment of transfer prices is discussed in detail in Chapter 4. At this point it is sufficient to keep in mind that such prices should be established to lead subordinate managers to behave in such a manner that the information system's systemic balance will move toward equilibrium. That is, prices are used to explicitly relate the subjective valuations of the users in a systemic manner. The result is a system equilibrium that sets the value of information, however subjectively derived, in balance with its cost of production. The interaction among participants using their specific decision rules, central management, and the available technology, all set in an environment of risk, determines the value of information in the organization.

2.6 Costs of Information

The cost of information is essentially the cost of the resources—computers, software, and labor—used to produce it. Unlike the value of information, which is a somewhat abstract construct, the cost side is concrete and therefore much easier to estimate. In spite of this relative ease, the achievement of accurate estimates in advance of project execution is by no means a trivial task, especially in the context of software production. As a result, considerable effort has been expended on devising models for software cost engineering; some of these models are discussed in Chapter 8.

The degree of accuracy required in estimating costs associated with information systems is dependent to a considerable extent on the purposes of the estimate. There are a number of cost estimation methods, requiring more or less effort and providing more or less accurate estimates. The principal cost estimation methods are industrial engineering, parametric cost estimation, analogy, and the Delphi technique. Each of these will be briefly described and discussed.

Industrial engineering. The industrial engineering method of cost estimation is the most detailed and, on the face of it, the most precise. Sometimes referred to as "bottom up" cost estimation, it proceeds by breaking a system down into its elements, establishing the cost of each element, and then totaling these costs to arrive at the cost for the system as a whole.

In the context of computer systems, this requires the establishment of costs for the CPU, memory, disk drives, tape drives, printers, and so on. Clearly, such an approach is feasible only if considerable planning has been done so that requirements are available for each of the system elements. If detailed requirement specifications are available, this is quite an accurate method of cost determination. Because of the need for detailed requirement analysis, this approach is applicable in the later stages of a system acquisition process. In the earlier stages—an initial feasibility study, for example—when detailed specifications have not yet been established, some more global or "top down" approach is called for, such as those discussed in the remainder of this section.

In the software development context, the industrial engineering approach to cost estimation is based on the reduction of programs to modules, and then to lines of code. The number of lines of code then serves as the basis for estimation programming costs. In practice, this method has proved to be extremely unreliable, apparently because human factors play a very large role, and the totality of the software production process is much more than the sum of its parts. Consequently, as mentioned earlier, considerable effort has been spent in devising alternative methods for software cost estimation.

Parametric cost estimation. Parametric cost estimating methods, assume a fixed relationship between design attributes of systems and the cost of their realization. Given the design attributes, the cost estimate is then given by a formula which integrates all the data. This may be a simple summation of the costs of each of the features desired, or it may be more complex, taking into consideration interrelationships between the features in determining the cost of the total system. In the computer context, this implies a knowledge of the relationships between storage requirements, input requirements, output requirements, and their costs. In the software context, relationships are established between program size, program complexity, availability of software tools, and program cost.

The major problem with the parametric method is in establishing the relationships between design parameters and costs. Given a mature technology and a database of previous cases, the parameters and their relationships may be established with considerable accuracy. On the other hand, if the technology is changing rapidly or if the system is the first of its kind, it may be quite difficult to establish sufficiently accurate relationships; at least one of these caveats always applies to computer and software systems, and often both.

Analogy. Where it is yet too early in the design process to apply the industrial engineering method and where historical data are not available for establishing cost parameters, it may yet be possible to apply analogies from previous experience. If one has experience with developing, say, a number of accounting systems, it may be possible to use that experience to estimate the cost for a new accounting system, based on minimal data concerning the type of system and the volumes involved. The same would apply to any other category of system with which the estimator is intimately acquainted. In fact, it has been suggested that the best way to get good forecasts of system costs is to ask those managers whose forecasts have proved to be most accurate. This method is, of course, highly judgmental; before accepting a judgment of this type it is useful to know the expert's track record, if any, on this type of estimate. This brings us to the Delphi technique, which employs a panel of experts rather than a single estimator.

The Delphi technique. The Delphi technique, as described above in the context of evaluating information, is applied primarily in cases where little information is available. It is a method for eliciting a consensus judgment from a number of experts who, individually, would probably produce wildly varying opinions. Each member of the panel is asked for his or her opinion on the topic under consideration, say the relative power of different computers or the projected cost of a software project. The estimates, with justifications, of all members of the panel are then made known, anonymously, to all other members. On the basis of their colleagues' reasoning and their own reevaluation, the panelists are requested to submit revised estimates. This process is continued until a consensus is reached among all the panelists. The main advantage of this technique is that it permits incorporation of the accumulated knowledge and experience of a number of experts, in a structured fashion, to produce one best estimate in cases where little objectively verifiable information is available.

2.7 Summary

Statistical decision theory makes explicit the interaction between *information*, *decision problems*, and *decision rules* and provides insight into the value of information in risky circumstances. In this theory, however, neither the *information system* nor the *organization* is considered explicitly—information is somehow factored into decisions, but the mechanisms for collecting and transferring it, as well as the decision makers and the physical organization, are not explicit.

Team theory elucidates the *structure of the organization* and *the structure of the information system* and shows their importance in valuing information. This results, however, in a model of great complexity, which is not applicable in practical situations, nor does it seem to describe observed organizational behavior in many cases. Furthermore, the physical organization is still not explicitly considered in this model.

Simulation permits inclusion of *information structures* and *decision rules* as well as the *physical organization* in one model and so makes possible the evaluation of information systems in a dynamic way. But again it is exceedingly complex and does not provide for users' subjective judgment about the value of information to them.

In actual practice, managers must frequently determine the value of information subjectively. A number of techniques such as iteration, analogy, and Delphi are available to enhance the accuracy and consistency of such subjective evaluations, but they are still subjective.

As with the value of information, there exist both objective methods—the industrial engineering and parametric techniques—and subjective methods—analogy and Delphi panels—for evaluating the cost of information resources.

The analytical approach to information systems used in this book is designed to synthesize these approaches. By incorporating physical flows, technology, organizational structure and incentives, and an iterative dialogue between the system manager and the organizational units, the outcome is a context-specific evaluation of information and its balance with cost. All the information valuation methods described in this chapter can be applied where practical. But the information system can operate without them and even without there being a universal method of evaluating information. The remainder of the book develops this idea.

References

Forrester, Jay W. (1961) *Industrial Dynamics.* Cambridge, MA: M.I.T. Press.

Forrester, Jay W. (1962) "Managerial Decision Making." In Martin Greenberger (ed.) *Computers and the World of the Future.* Cambridge, MA: M.I.T. Press, pp. 36–68.

MacCrimmon, Kenneth, R. (1974) "Descriptive Aspects of Team Theory: Observation, Communication and Decision Heuristics in Information Systems." *Management Science* 20, 10 (June): 1323–1334.

Marschak, Jakob. (1955) "Elements of A Theory of Teams." *Management Science*: 127–137.

Raiffa, Howard. (1968) *Decision Analysis.* Reading, MA: Addison-Wesley.

Chapter 3
Economic Foundations for Information System Management:
PART 1

The economic analysis of information systems requires a relatively small number of general decision rules, which are applied in a large number of specific settings. When the rules are applied and implemented in all the relevant settings, the organization achieves an efficient and effective use of its information resources.[1] The objective of this chapter and the next is to present the general forms of these rules and to introduce the symbols by which they will be represented. In later chapters, the rules will be applied to specific problems.

It is assumed that the reader is conversant with basic microeconomic concepts. Where appropriate, the economic theory is stated as the starting point for incorporating it in the information resource management decision rules. For those students who desire to refresh their knowledge of economics, or who perhaps have not been exposed to this material before, there are many excellent textbooks containing introductory expositions of the microeconomic concepts necessary for reading this book; the well-known texts by Coyne (1984), Seo (1984), and Truett and Truett (1984) are recommended.

The general rules, identified in Chapter 1, relate to the scale of operations, the technology to employ, mixes of resources and products, and to the timing

---

[1] Economists typically refer to a resource as "input" and to a product as "output." Unfortunately, computer and information processing people have adopted the same words for much more specific entities, namely, data input and report output. Given the context of this book, using the same words for both meanings could become highly confusing, as it did to the authors. We have therefore tried to consistently use "resource" rather than input for labor, hardware, and software, and "product" rather than output for the generic output of information processing systems, although the latter distinction is less important, since outputs, in the information processing sense, are the product of information systems.

of execution of the previous three. As the rules for the first three areas also incorporate the timing decisions, it is necessary to address this issue first in the context of the information system life cycle.

3.1 The Information System Life Cycle

Time is an important element in all economic decisions. This is because a given amount of income or expense may be valued differently, depending on the way in which it is structured over time; different time patterns have different values. In information systems, indeed for all systems, the basic period for temporal analysis is the *system life cycle*.

The concept of an information system life cycle came into being when it was realized that information systems follow a pattern, analogous to a biological life span, in which they are created, provide useful services over a period of time, decline, finally become ineffective, and are then usually replaced by another system. In the information resource environment, this phenomenon is observed in computer hardware, software, and systems.

With respect to hardware, it is generally the advance of technology that leads to the replacement of existing computers. Very few computers are operated until the end of their physical lives; they are generally replaced because new, cheaper, and more powerful computers become available. The old ones are rendered uneconomical, and so they are replaced while still functioning perfectly. The life cycle of computer hardware is generally 5 to 8 years, but many such machines function well, from the physical point of view, for 20 years or more.

Computer software is generally replaced because, in a sense, it reaches the end of its "physical life." This occurs when software has been functioning for a number of years, has been constantly fixed and upgraded, and finally has reached a point where maintenance is so difficult and costly that it is deemed preferable to replace it with new programs, which incorporate from the beginning the many changes introduced piecemeal in the old. The life cycle for software around 8 to 12 years—is somewhat longer than that for hardware. It is the relatively longer life of software that makes compatibility across hardware systems so important. If longer-lived software is to survive the passing of shorter-lived hardware, it must be easily transported to the new hardware.

Information systems, as collections of hardware and software, also have finite life cycles. Entire systems are replaced when organizations or their requirements change to such an extent that the old systems are no longer adaptable and must be replaced *in toto*. A good example of this is when organizations decide to move from batch processing to online real-time operations. This almost always calls for a complete renewal of hardware, software, and organizational procedures.

The phenomenon of the system life cycle implies that economic decisions should be made not with respect to a point in time, or even to a budgetary period, but that costs and benefits of alternatives should be considered over the entire life cycle. This is what renders the issue of the economic dimension of time so important in the context of this book.

3.2 The Role of Time in Economic Decisions

The basic economic property of time is that the value *now* of economic entities to be received or spent in the future is lower, the further in the future the exchange occurs. Looking at it the other way, the future value of economic transactions must be discounted in order to obtain their present value. Thus, the present value of some future transaction is its current value adjusted to account for the discount rate and the amount of time that will elapse until it is realized. The formula for computing the present value of a future amount is

$$V_0 = \frac{V_T}{(1+r)^T}, \quad (3.1)$$

where T is the number of periods in the future when the amount will be realized,

V_0 is the present value (at time 0),

V_T is the value t periods in the future,

$\frac{1}{(1+r)^T}$ is the discount factor for a single period.

It should be stressed that T must relate to the same time period as r. If T refers to years, then r is the annual discount rate. If T is in months, then r is the monthly rate.

If a series of transactions is to be considered that will recur over a number of periods, then the present value of the entire series is

$$V_0 = \sum_{t=0}^{T} \frac{V_t}{(1+r)^t}, \quad (3.2)$$

where T is the number of periods under consideration and t varies over that number of periods. When considering decisions relating to the information system life cycle, T will generally represent the length of that cycle. More generally, it represents the end of the planning period, which may not exactly coincide with the life cycle of a specific piece of hardware or software.

The formulation of equation (3.2) is for discrete time periods, that is, where recognizable periods of time such as days, months, or years are considered. In some cases, and frequently in this book, it is convenient to consider time as a continuum rather than as a series of discrete periods. Summation over infinitely small time periods is called integration and is the appropriate mathematical technique. It can be shown that, for the continuous case,

$$V(0) = \int_0^T V(t) e^{-rt} \, dt, \quad (3.3)$$

3.2 The Role of Time in Economic Decisions

where t and T are as defined above,

$V(t)$ is the value at a specific time t,

e^{-rt} is the discount factor for any instant of time: as the length of period t becomes shorter and shorter, this is the limiting value of the discount factor (Massé, 1962):

$$\lim_{t \to 0} \frac{1}{(1+r)^t} \to e^{-rt}.$$

The discount rate r, actually adopted, may (and usually does) vary from organization to organization. This is partly a result of differing interpretations of the discount rate, but mostly it is a result of different realities faced by different organizations.

One interpretation of the discount rate is as the cost of capital to the organization, that is, how much does the organization pay in the form of interest rates, dividends, and so on for any additional capital it raises, or how much will it save if it requires less capital. This determines the value to it of future incomes and expenses. Another interpretation of the discount rate is as the opportunity cost of capital, that is, what would be the organization's rate of profit from its best, as yet unexploited, use of capital. The assumption is that the organization first uses capital where it is most profitable, then in its next most profitable use, and so on; the opportunity cost at any time is the rate of profit from the best project not yet undertaken. Each of these interpretations leads to the same numerical value for the discount rate if the overall economic system operates efficiently. Reality is not usually that benign, however, so the alternative interpretations can lead to the adoption of different discount rates within an organization. Furthermore, it is clear that, under each of these interpretations, different organizations face different realities generating different discount rates.

Yet another possible interpretation of the discount rate is some standard rate accepted throughout the economy. The prime rate is a good example of a rate of this type. Other examples are the rate on Treasury bills or on Grade A municipal bonds. A particularly relevant standard of this type is the discount rate mandated by the federal government for computing the present value of future outlays internal to the federal government; currently (1984) it is 10%. This rate is supposed to represent the real opportunity cost of capital between the public and private sectors in the United States economy. Conceptually, it is the real profit rate that would accrue to the expenditure if it were made by the private sector rather than having the government collect it as a tax or loan and spend it.

No matter which interpretation of the discount rate is adopted, its computation in any given situation is a complex problem. This need not occupy us here, since in most organizations it is top management's function to decide on the rate, and for information system decisions it can be regarded as a given. The concept and its use, however, are extremely important.

3.3 Production Plans

With the mechanism for accounting for time in hand, it is now possible to address the scale, mix, and technology decisions. In order to maximize the benefits to the organization from the information resource, the three decisions must be made simultaneously. In some way the organization must choose the optimal mix of resources to apply via the optimal technology at the optimal scale and to produce the optimal mix of products.

To start the analysis, assume that there are only one resource (a basket of hardware, software, and labor inputs) and one product ("information"). For any given technology, the production function then describes the relationship between the amount of the resource and the amount of the product (Massé, 1962), that is,

$$I = f^I(R), \tag{3.4}$$

where R is the amount of the resource used,

  I is the amount of the information produced,

  f^I is the functional relationship for a given technology.

We may then define a *production plan* as a technologically feasible combination of specific values of I and R (say I', R'), that is, one for which there exists a technology that permits the production of I' with R'.

A production plan is *technically efficient* when no other plan will produce more product with the same amount of resource. It must represent the most efficient technology then available. It is clearly optimal to utilize a technically efficient production plan to produce any given level of product I', and other plans will generally be avoided wherever possible.

EXERCISE 3.1

List cases when it might not be possible to utilize a technically efficient production plan.

The relationship between R and I may be one of constant, increasing, or diminishing returns, depending on whether the increase in amount of product is proportional to, relatively greater than, or relatively less than a change in amount of resource. These three cases are exhibited graphically in Figure 3.1. The curves represent total, average, and marginal physical productivity for each of the cases. The total physical productivity curve (TPP) in the one-input–one-output case represents the production function f^I. The average physical productivity of R in producing I, APP(R, I), is defined for each pro-

3.3 Production Plans

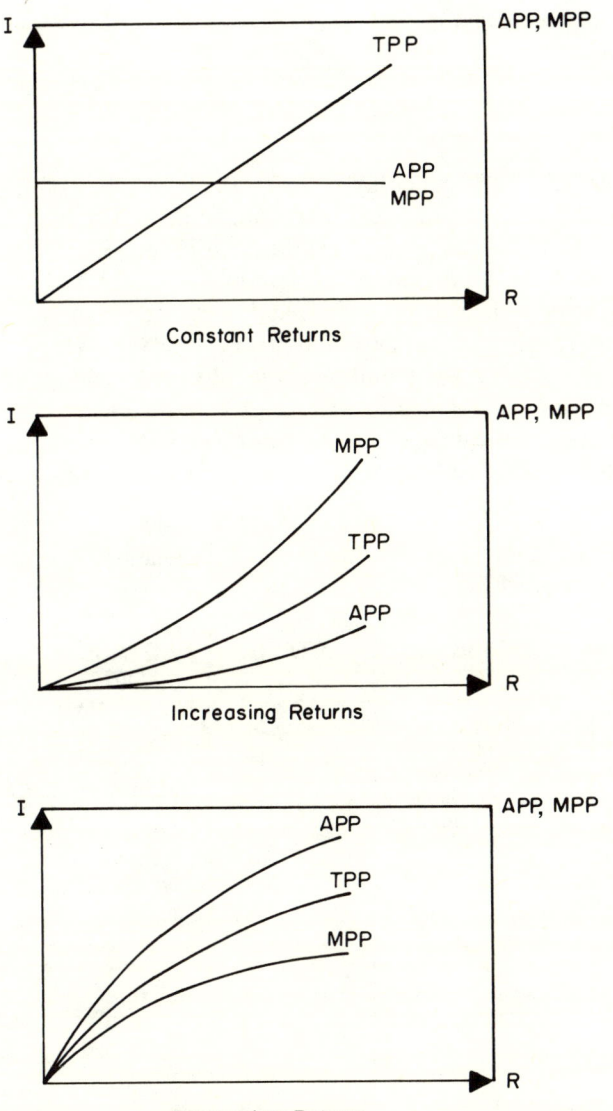

Figure 3.1 Relationships between resources used (R) and information produced (I).

duction plan (R', I');

$$\text{APP}(R, I) = \frac{R'}{I'}$$

for all production plans (R, I). Finally, the marginal physical productivity of R in producing I, $\text{MPP}(R, I)$, is the change in amount of product (dI) caused by an infinitely small change in amount of resource (dR) at a specific production plan (R', I'),

$$\text{MPP}(R', I') = \frac{dI}{dR}.$$

Production functions generally contain all three types of situations and hence a combination of, first, an increasing phase, and then a decreasing phase. A representative example is exhibited in Figure 3.2. There is an initial phase in which only small amounts of resource are employed and each additional amount permits a disproportionately large increase in product. Thus increasing marginal physical productivity is observed, which is also associated with increasing total and average physical productivities. As the amount of resource employed increases, a transition eventually occurs after which marginal physical productivity begins to fall, but average and total physical productivities still increase. In the course of this transition there may

Figure 3.2 Stages of the production function and the relationship of total, marginal, and average productivity.

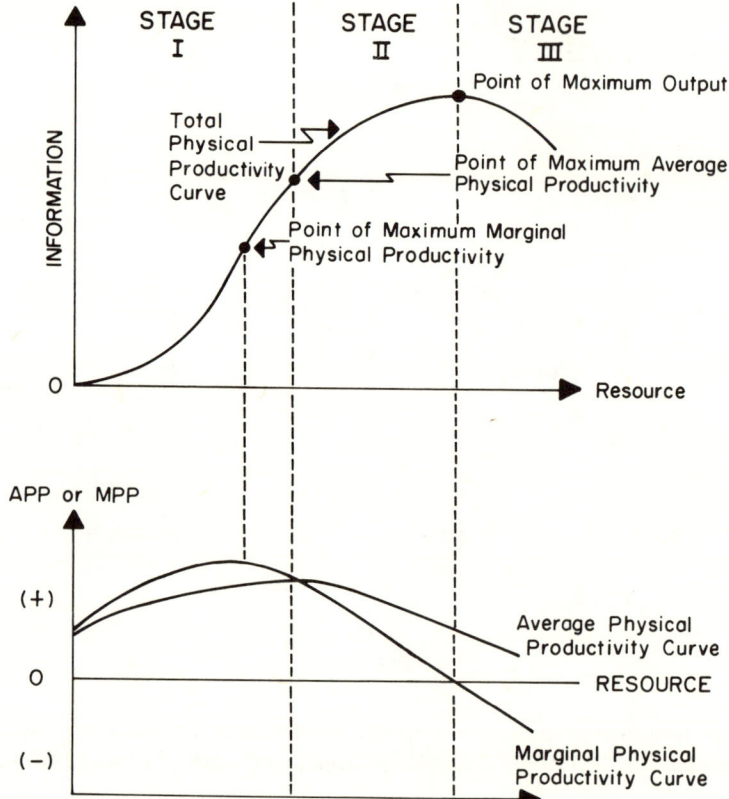

3.3 Production Plans

be a segment in which there are constant returns, additional units of resources producing the same amounts of product. Eventually, as marginal returns diminish to the point where they become negative, there is a range of production plans that are technically feasible, with both total and average physical productivity decreasing. This last stage is technically inefficient and is rarely seen in practice (although some real examples will appear later in the book), so that only the stages that exhibit positive marginal productivity are of practical interest.

Given the description of a production function, technological change can be described as a shift in the production function. If the new technology is more efficient than the old, it will result in new production plans in which a given product may be produced with less resource, as, for example, the product $\hat{I}$ in Figure 3.3. As the example in Figure 3.3 also indicates, however, the new technology need not be more efficient over the entire range—it may be more efficient for some levels of resource use and not for others. The new technology will tend to replace the old where the scale of operations falls within its range of greater efficiency.

Figure 3.3 Technological changes as a shift in the production function.

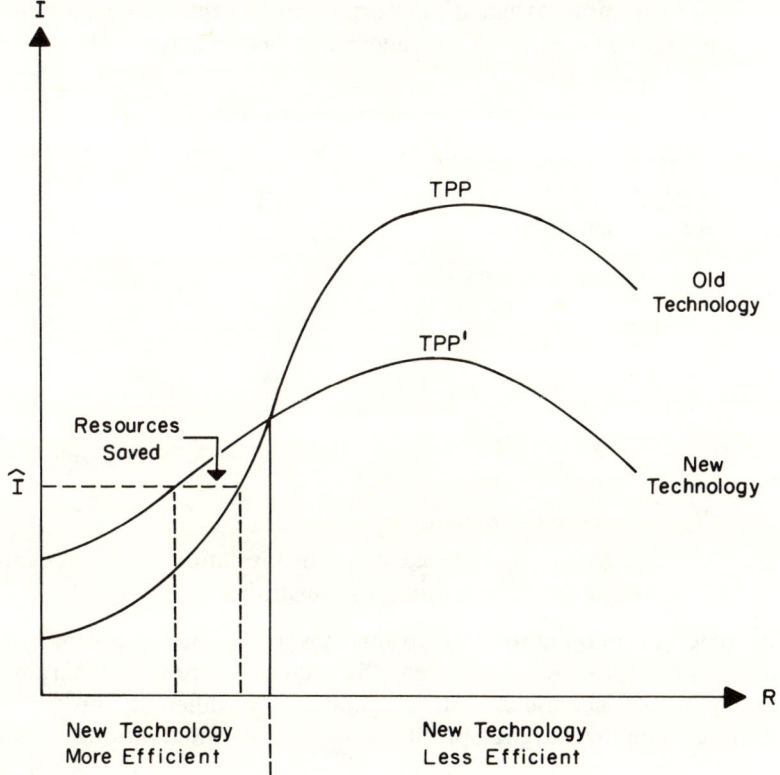

3.4 Scale of Operations: The Decision Problem and Decision Rules

3.4.1 The Production Function Approach

The organization's general decision problem with respect to the information resource is to maximize its net benefits from information systems, over their life cycles, subject to the constraints imposed by the current state of technology. For simplicity, it will be assumed that the value of information and prices of resources remain constant throughout the life cycle. In this first approximation of one generalized resource and one generalized product, the present value of the life-cycle profit (PLΠ), is given by

$$\text{PL}\Pi = \sum_{t=0}^{T} \frac{(q_I I - p_R R)}{(1 + r)^t}, \quad (3.5)$$

where I is the amount of information produced,
R is the amount of resource utilized,
p_R is the market price of the resource,
q_I may be interpreted as the value of information to central management in the case of a centralized decision structure, or as the transfer price assigned to information by central management and communicated to IR management when decision-making authority is delegated.
T is the planning horizon in discrete time periods,
r is the discount rate, and $(1 + r)^t$ is the discount factor for a given period t.

The decision problem then is

max PLΠ,

by choice of (I, R),

subject to

$I = f^I(R)$,

$I, R \geq 0$, (3.6)

where PLΠ is as defined above,
(I, R) is a production plan,
f^I is a technologically feasible transformation of resource into information—the technology constraint.

The general economic solution to this type of business problem is to expand production to the point where the increase in revenue, marginal revenue, equals the increase in cost, marginal cost. In different words, profit is maximized when the marginal profit is zero, and marginal profit is zero when

3.4 The Decision Problem and Decision Rules

marginal revenue equals marginal cost. The present life-cycle marginal cost of using one more unit of resource is the market price of the resource, p_R, appropriately discounted. The use of one more unit of resource will produce more product and the marginal physical productivity measures the quantity of the additional product. The revenue generated by this additional product is the transfer price of information, appropriately discounted. The production plan that maximizes profit can be identified by the decision rule:

$$\sum_{t=0}^{T} \frac{q_I}{(1+r)^t} \text{MPP}(R, I) = \sum_{t=0}^{T} \frac{p_R}{(1+r)^t}. \quad (3.7)$$

This could be looked at in terms of the same requirement that marginal profit equals zero, but the initiating change is in terms of the product, information. The marginal revenue from selling one more unit of information is, again, the transfer price of information appropriately discounted. The production of an additional unit of information requires the use of an additional amount of the resource. The increase in resource needed is the marginal physical input requirement, which is the inverse of the marginal physical productivity. From this perspective, the maximum profit production phase is identifed by the decision rule:

$$\sum_{t=0}^{T} \frac{q_I}{(1+r)^t} = \text{MPIR}(I, R) \sum_{t=0}^{T} \frac{p_R}{(1+r)^t}. \quad (3.8)$$

Finally, the perspective can be from the point of view of profit maximization, which requires matching the internal technological tradeoffs with the external economic tradeoffs. The internal technological tradeoff is measured by the marginal physical productivity. The external economic tradeoff is measured by the ratio of prices for resources and information. The resulting decision rule for the maximum profit production plan is

$$\text{MPP}(R, I) = \frac{\sum_{t=0}^{T}[q_I/(1+r)^t]}{\sum_{t=0}^{T}[p_R/(1+r)^t]} = \frac{q_I}{p_R}. \quad (3.9)$$

All these decision rules lead to the same result; only the managerial perspective is different. The orientation may be toward resources, products, or economic-technical tradeoffs.

3.4.2 The Cost Function Approach

Instead of beginning the analysis as above, with the production function for information,

$$I = f^I(R),$$

one can begin with the resource or input requirement function

$$R = f''(I), \quad (3.10)$$

where f'^I relates levels of production, I, to the amount of resource required to produce them and is the mathematical inverse of the production function. Thus, the present life-cycle cost of information [PLC(I)] is given by the product of the required resource and its price, appropriately discounted:

$$\text{PLC}(I) = \sum_{t=0}^{T} \frac{1}{(1+r)^t} [p_R \cdot f'^I(I)], \tag{3.11}$$

where all the terms are as previously defined. Present life-cycle profit, PLΠ, is now defined as present life-cycle revenue minus present life-cycle cost, that is,

$$\text{PLΠ} = \text{PLR}(I) - \text{PLC}(I) = \sum_{t=0}^{T} \frac{q_I I}{(1+r)^t} - \sum_{t=0}^{T} \frac{p_R f'^I(I)}{(1+r)^t}.$$

The decision problem, the maximization of returns from the information resource, remains unchanged, but its formulation is now

$$\max \sum_{t=0}^{T} \frac{q_I I}{(1+r)^t} - \sum_{t=0}^{T} \frac{p_R f'^I(I)}{(1+r)^t},$$

by choice of I,

subject to

$$I \geq 0. \tag{3.12}$$

The decision rule in this formulation assumes a bell-shaped total profit curve. Profit is then maximized at that scale of operations at which the marginal present life-cycle profit is zero. This occurs when the marginal present life-cycle revenue from information, MPLR(I), equals the marginal present life-cycle cost, MPLC(I). The decision rule, then, is to produce information until

$$\text{MPLΠ} = \text{MPLR}(I) - \text{MPLC}(I) = 0. \tag{3.13}$$

The marginal revenue from information is the revenue from producing one additional unit, as before:

$$\text{MPLR}(I) = \sum_{t=0}^{T} \frac{q_I}{(1+r)^t}. \tag{3.14}$$

Similarly, the marginal cost of information is the cost of producing the marginal unit. This is the slope, the rate of change, of the cost function. Using the production function data, the marginal cost is a function of the marginal physical requirement of I for R, MPIR(I, R), and of the price of R. Thus,

$$\text{MPLC}(I) = \sum_{t=0}^{T} \frac{p_R}{(1+r)^t} \text{MPIR}(I, R). \tag{3.15}$$

3.5 Scale of Operation and Resource Mix

Substituting in equation (3.13) and rearranging, the decision is to produce information until

$$\sum_{t=0}^{T} \frac{q_I}{(1+r)^t} = \sum_{t=0}^{T} \frac{p_R}{(1+r)^t} \text{MPIR}(I, R), \tag{3.16}$$

that is, until marginal present life-cycle revenue equals marginal present life-cycle cost.

3.5 Scale of Operation and Resource Mix

The first extension of the one-resource one-product case considered until now is to generalize to two resources. This requires a solution to the resource mix problem in addition to a decision on the scale of operations.

If the two resources employed are defined as capital, K, and labor, L, then the production function for information is

$$I = f^I(K, L), \tag{3.17}$$

which defines all technologically feasible production plans. A mapping of the combinations of K and L that produce a fixed level of I, say I_o, is an *isoquant* (see Figure 3.4). For any level of one of the resources, an isoquant indicates how much of the other resource is required in order to produce a specified amount of information. A movement along an isoquant indicates how much of one resource must be substituted for the other in order to maintain a given level of production.

If at any point on an isoquant one of the resources is increased by a very small amount, this will raise the quantity produced to a new isoquant, representing a higher level of production. The additional information produced is the marginal physical productivity of the resource at the point in question. Thus, for labor,

$$dI = dL \cdot \text{MPP}(L, I), \tag{3.18}$$

and for capital,

$$dI = dK \cdot \text{MPP}(K, I). \tag{3.19}$$

If instead of simply adding to one of the resources, it is exactly substituted for by the other, so that the product remains unchanged, this implies that

$$dL \cdot \text{MPP}(L, I) = (-dK) \cdot \text{MPP}(K, I). \tag{3.20}$$

Rearranging,

$$\frac{dK}{dL} = \frac{\text{MPP}(L, I)}{\text{MPP}(K, I)}. \tag{3.21}$$

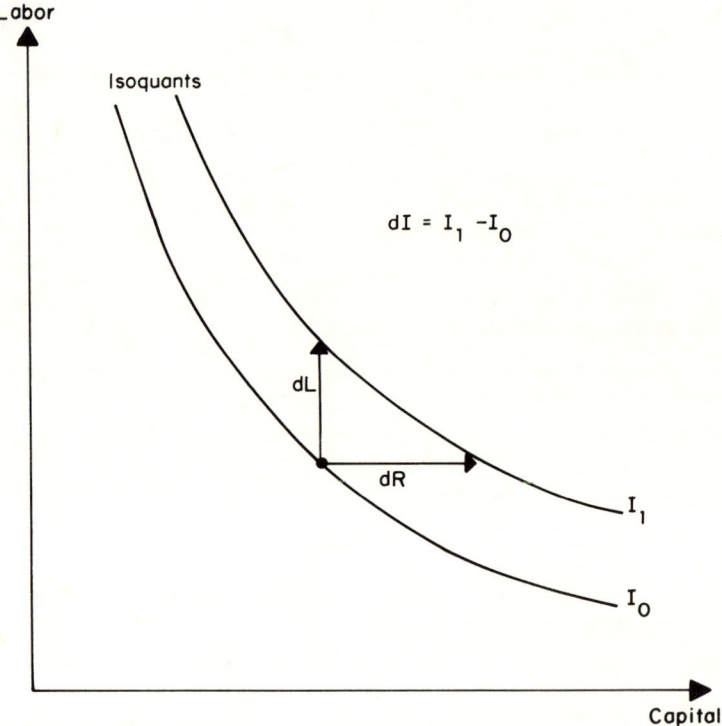

Figure 3.4 Isoquants representing resource substitution for a fixed level of production.

In the limit, the relative changes in resource levels on the left-hand side, and the ratio of marginal physical productivities on the right-hand side, both measure the slope of the isoquant at the point at which they are derived; this slope is known as the *marginal rate of technical substitution* of capital for labor, MRTS(K, L). Inverting equation (3.21) would give the marginal rate of substitution of labor for capital, MRTS(L, K).

An issue relating to the multiple-resource production function is that of *returns to scale*. This refers to the effect of an equal and simultaneous increase in *all* resources utilized. Assume a specific production plan denoted by

$$f^I(K_0, L_0) = I_0. \tag{3.22}$$

Now increase all resources by the same proportion n. If the amount of information now produced is labeled I_1, and if

$$I_1 = nI_0, \tag{3.23}$$

then there are constant returns to scale.

3.6 The Two-Resource Decision Problems and Decision Rules

If
$$I_1 < nI_0,$$
then there are decreasing returns to scale. Finally, if
$$I_1 > nI_0,$$
there are increasing returns to scale. Returns to scale in computers have been often discussed in the literature and are also addressed later in Chapter 7. Care should be taken to differentiate returns to scale when *all* resources are varied proportionately, from marginal physical productivity when *one* resource is varied, the others remaining constant.

3.6 The Two-Resource Decision Problems and Decision Rules

3.6.1 *The Production Function Approach*

As in the one-resource case, the organization's objective is to maximize benefits from the information resource. Still assuming constant prices and values throughout the life cycle, present life-cycle profit is now given by

$$\text{PL}\Pi = \sum_{t=0}^{T} \frac{1}{(1+r)^t} \cdot (q_I I - p_L L - q_K K), \quad (3.24)$$

where q_I is, as before, the value or transfer price of information, depending on the organizational structure,

p_L is the price of labor services,

q_K is the price of capital services.

The decision problem is now formally stated as

$$\max \sum_{t=0}^{T} \frac{1}{(1+r)^t} \cdot (q_I I - p_L L - q_k K),$$

by choice of I, L, K,

subject to

$I = f^I(L, K)$

$I, K, L \geq 0. \quad (3.25)$

It is now necessary to solve simultaneously for the amount of information to produce and the amounts of each of the resources to employ, as well as to solve the resource mix problem. In the simpler case, studied earlier, the decision rule was to produce information until the present life-cycle marginal cost of the resource equaled the present life-cycle marginal revenue from information, that is, until the present life-cycle marginal profit equaled zero. In the present case, this equality must be achieved for *each* of the resources. In order to do so on a step-by-step basis, conceptually it is assumed that the level of product and of all resources but one have already been chosen to maximize profit. One can then solve for the remaining resource, assuring a maximum profit outcome.

Consider the case of labor. As for a single resource, the present life-cycle marginal cost of labor is given by

$$\text{MPLC}(L) = \sum_{t=0}^{T} \frac{p_L}{(1+r)^t}. \tag{3.26}$$

Also as before, the marginal revenue from information is given by

$$\text{MPLR}(I) = \sum_{t=0}^{T} \frac{q_I}{(1+r)^t}. \tag{3.27}$$

The present life-cycle marginal revenue due to labor is then the product of the marginal physical productivity of labor in producing information and the revenue from the information produced:

$$\text{PLMR}(L) = \text{MPP}(L, I) \cdot \sum_{t=0}^{T} \frac{q_I}{(1+r)^t}. \tag{3.28}$$

As the optimal amount of labor to employ is where the present life-cycle marginal profit of labor is zero, the decision rule is to employ labor until its marginal cost equals the marginal revenue created by it:

$$\sum_{t=0}^{T} \frac{p_L}{(1+r)^t} = \text{MPP}(L, I) \cdot \sum_{t=0}^{T} \frac{q_I}{(1+r)^t}. \tag{3.29}$$

The discount factors cancel out when prices and values are constant over the planning period, so the correct decision reduces to

$$p_L = \text{MPP}(L, I) \cdot q_I. \tag{3.30}$$

Similarly for capital, the profit-maximizing decision is to employ capital until

$$q_K = \text{MPP}(K, I) \cdot q_I. \tag{3.31}$$

The decision rule must specify not only the amounts of each resource to use at the optimum, but also their optimal mix. The mix decision is implicitly also a choice of technology, as each such mix defines a specific technology. The general economic solution to problems of this type is to employ both resources to the point where the marginal profits for both are equal. In this case,

$$q_I \cdot \text{MPP}(K_I) - q_K = q_I \cdot \text{MPP}(L, I) - p_L. \tag{3.32}$$

3.6 The Two-Resource Decision Problems

Algebraically, it can be shown that this rule is equivalent to an alternative statement that resources should be employed until the ratio of the marginal physical productivities (the marginal rate of technical substitution) equals the price ratio, namely,

$$\text{MRTS}(L, K) = \frac{\text{MPP}(K, I)}{\text{MPP}(K, L)} = \frac{q_K}{p_L}. \tag{3.33}$$

Finally, the amount of information to produce (the scale of operations) must be determined. The correct decision in this case is to equate the marginal present life-cycle revenue from information to the marginal present life-cycle cost, that is, marginal present life-cycle profit should be zero. In this context, note that equation (3.33) can be rewritten as

$$\frac{\text{MPIR}(I, L)}{\text{MPIR}(I, K)} = \frac{q_K}{p_L}, \tag{3.34}$$

so that

$$p_L \cdot \text{MPIR}(I, L) = q_K \cdot \text{MPIR}(I, K). \tag{3.35}$$

Thus, the marginal present life-cycle cost can be expressed in terms of capital or labor—the choice is not important given an optimal mix. Hence, at the optimum, the amount of information to produce is given by

$$\sum_{t=0}^{T} \frac{1}{(1+r)^t} \cdot q_I = \sum_{t=0}^{T} \frac{1}{(1+r)^t} \cdot q_K \cdot \text{MPIR}(I, K), \tag{3.36}$$

that is,

$$q_I = q_k \text{MPIR}(I, K) \tag{3.37}$$

or

$$q_I = p_L \text{MPIR}(I, L). \tag{3.38}$$

It is now important to note that the three decision rules developed above are consistent. The last rule, for *quantity of information*, requires that the marginal life-cycle profit from information reach zero [equations (3.37) and (3.38)]. The rule for *mix of resources* requires that the marginal life-cycle profits for both resources be equal [equation (3.32)], that is, marginal life-cycle profits must therefore be equal at the zero level. This is consistent with the rule for amount of each resource to employ, which requires that the marginal profit due to each resource reach zero [equations (3.30) and (3.31)].

3.6.2 The Two-Resource Problem. Cost Function Approach

Given two resources, the optimal mix to employ in any production plan is given by equation (3.33). Each such specific plan (I^*, L^*, K^*) has a minimum cost, say $\tilde{C}^*$, associated with it.[2] Tracing out the least cost mixes for each level of output, I, yields the cost function

$$\tilde{C}_I = g^I(I). \tag{3.39}$$

The decision problem now becomes

$$\max \sum_{t=0}^{T} \frac{1}{(1+r)^t} \cdot (q_I I - \tilde{C}_I),$$

by choice of I,

subject to $I \geq 0$. \hfill (3.40)

This is essentially the problem of equation (3.26) with the mix decision, posed there as $-p_L L - q_K K$, subsumed by the cost function, which assumes optimal mixes for every value of I.

The decision rule that solves this problem is to equate the marginal present life-cycle value of information, q_I, to its marginal present life-cycle cost, MPLC(I), as in the production perspective through equations (3.37) and (3.38). The rate of change of the cost function, its slope, also measures the marginal present life-cycle value of information, since in order to maximize profit, the marginal present life-cycle cost must equal marginal present life-cycle value.

References

Coyne, Thomas J. (1984) *Managerial Economics: Analysis and Cases* (5th edition). Plano, TX: Business Publications.

Massé, Pierre. (1962) *Optimal Investment Decisions.* Englewood Cliffs, NJ: Prentice-Hall, pp. 15–17.

Seo, K. K. (1984) *Managerial Economics* (6th edition). Homewood, IL: Richard D. Irwin.

Truett, Lila J., and Truett, Dale B. (1984) *Managerial Economics* (2nd edition). Cincinnati, OH: South Western.

---

[2] In order to differentiate between CPU services and cost, for both of which the letter "C" is the most natural symbol, the plain C has been adopted for CPU-related variables, while cost is denoted $\tilde{C}$.

Chapter 4
Economic Foundations for Information System Management: PART 2

The last two sections of Chapter 3 dealt with the case of two resources and one product, which involved the resource mix problem. This chapter considers the case of one resource and two products, so that the emphasis here is on product mix rather than resource mix. The material in Chapter 3 and at the beginning of this chapter is presented in summary form, since it is readily available in standard microeconomics textbooks. The material on the two-product cost function is not generally treated, and it is probably not familiar to the reader; for that reason, this subject is included here in detail.

4.1 The Production Function Formulation

Just as one can visualize isoquants that represent the tradeoffs between resources for a given level of product, one can also think of a different family of isoquantlike curves called product transformation curves. These represent the tradeoffs between products for a given level of resource utilization. Thus, a resource requirement function can be defined, analogous to the production function, which relates product combinations to the minimum levels of resource required for their production, that is,

$$R = f^R(I_1, I_2), \qquad (4.1)$$

where R is the amount of resource required,

I_1, I_2 are the amounts of information products 1 and 2, respectively,
f^R is the resource requirement function that maps product combinations into resource requirements.

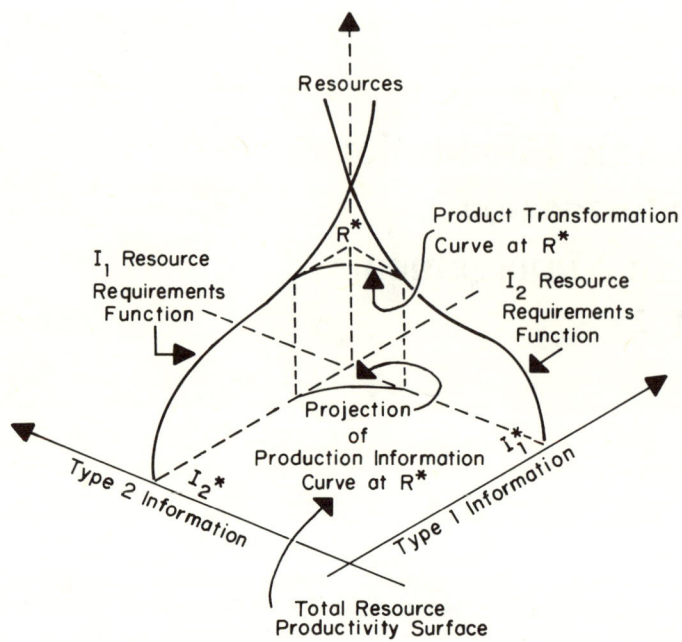

Figure 4.1 Resource requirements functions.

Figure 4.1 is a three-dimensional diagram of this function with the product transformation curves and the total resource productivity surface-labeled. The total resource productivity surface is the resource view of the total productivity curve discussed earlier from the product point of view. The slope of this surface is the marginal physical input requirement [$\text{MPIR}(I_1, R)$ or $\text{MPIR}(I_2, R)$] for resource due to a small change in the information produced.

As in the analysis of isoquants in Chapter 3, the slope of the product transformation curve has analytical value; it measures the marginal technical tradeoff between the products and is called the marginal rate of product transformation, $\text{MRPT}(I_1, I_2)$. The following exercise is designed to apply the logic of the marginal rate of technical substitution to the development of the marginal rate of product transformation.

EXERCISE 4.1 Development of Marginal Rate of Product Transformation

Show that

$$\text{MRPT}(I_1, I_2) = -\frac{dI_2}{dI_1} = \frac{\text{MPIR}(I_1, R)}{\text{MPIR}(I_2, R)}. \tag{4.2}$$

4.1 The Production Function Formulation

4.1.1 The Product Mix Decision Problem

The product mix decision problem again uses the criterion of profit maximization. The decision variables are the levels for both types of information, the mix of types of information to produce, and the level of the resource to employ. The constraints on the manager are the technology represented by the input requirements function and the logical necessity that the decision variables not take on negative values.

The present life-cycle profit is composed of the present life-cycle revenue and present life-cycle cost. The following exercise permits you the opportunity to provide the step-by-step development of the present life-cycle profit function.

EXERCISE 4.2 Present Life-Cycle Profit

Provide a logical development for the present life-cycle profit function:

$$\text{PL}\Pi = \sum_{t=0}^{T} \frac{1}{(1+r)^t} (q_{I_1} I_1 + q_{I_2} I_2) - \sum_{t=0}^{T} \frac{1}{(1+r)^t} p_R R.$$

The formal statement of the manager's decision problem is

$$\max \sum_{t=0}^{T} \frac{1}{(1+r)^t} (q_{I_1} I_1 + q_{I_2} I_2 - p_R R),$$

by choice of I_1, I_2, R,
constrained by

$$R = f^R(I_1, I_2),$$
$$R, I_1, I_2 \geq 0. \tag{4.3}$$

4.1.2 The Decision Rules

There are four decision rules in this case: the levels of each of the two types of information to provide, the mix of the two types of information to provide, and, lastly, the quantity of the resource to employ. These decision rules will be studied in turn.

The decision rule concerning the level of each type of information to provide should by now be familiar. Exercise 4.3 asks for its development.

EXERCISE 4.3 The Levels of Information to Provide

Develop the two decision rules for the quantity to provide of each information product.

The decision rule for the product mix is developed using logic analogous to that used in developing the decision rule for the mix of resources. That is, the marginal profits from both types of information provided must be equal for the production plan to maximize profits. If this is not the case, the manager can increase the level of profit by increasing the supply of one product relative to the other. Any such action then reduces the magnitude of the marginal profit of the product increased, and increases the magnitude of the marginal profit of the product decreased. [Remember that, ultimately, the marginal physical input requirement rises (falls) as the quantity of the product increases (decreases).]

Alternatively, the mix decision rule can be developed by thinking in terms of the marginal revenue obtained per dollar of marginal cost expended. For type 1 information, the marginal revenue is

$$\sum_{t=0}^{T} \frac{1}{(1+r)^t} q_{I1}.$$

The associated marginal cost is

$$\sum_{t=0}^{T} \frac{1}{(1+r)^t} p_R \cdot \text{MPIR}(I_1, R).$$

So the marginal revenue per dollar of marginal cost expended is

$$\frac{q_{I1}}{p_R \text{MPIR}(I_1, R)}.$$

Correspondingly, for the type 2 information, it is

$$\frac{q_{I2}}{p_R \text{MPIR}(I_2, R)}.$$

In the profit-maximizing production plan, these must be equal. If they are not, it is advantageous for the manager to increase the quantity of product that yields a higher marginal revenue per dollar of marginal cost expended. At the same time this profit-maximizing move reduces the quantity of the other product. With the new mix, the increased (decreased) product's marginal revenue per dollar of marginal cost expended is smaller (larger) than with the old mix. (Remember what happens to marginal physical input requirements.) So at a profit-maximizing production plan,

$$\frac{q_{I1}}{p_R \text{MPIR}(I_1, R)} = \frac{q_{I2}}{p_R \text{MPIR}(I_2, R)}. \tag{4.4}$$

Algebraic rearrangement yields

$$\frac{\text{MPIR}(I_2, R)}{\text{MPIR}(I_1, R)} = \frac{q_{I2}}{q_{I1}}. \tag{4.5}$$

4.1 The Production Function Formulation

From Exercise 4.2, the left-hand side of equation (4.5) can be identified as the marginal rate of product transformation. Thus the decision rule is

> At a profit-maximizing production plan, *ceteris paribus*, the manager equates the marginal rate of product transformation of the two types of information to the relative price of the two types of information.

The last decision rule is concerned with which profit-maximizing level of resource to employ. This type of analysis has been studied, so the decision rule development is stated as an exercise.

EXERCISE 4.4 The Quantity of Resource to Employ

Develop the decision rule for the profit-maximizing level of the resource to employ. *Reminder*: Do not forget the relationship between MPIR and MPP.

While the profit-maximizing approach clearly contains the product mix decision, it is useful to study the mix as a resource-constrained revenue-maximization problem. Its development is analogous to the least-cost input mix problem. Exercise 4.5 asks for this development.

EXERCISE 4.5 The Resource-Constrained Revenue-Maximization Problem

Formulate the manager's decision problem when required to maximize revenue, given that the resource is constrained. Let the level of the resource be designated $\bar{R}$.

The production decision rule associated with this decision problem is the same as that developed for the profit-maximization problem. The following exercise is provided to develop this decision rule.

EXERCISE 4.6 Decision Rules for Resource-Constrained Revenue Maximization

Develop the decision rule for the mix of information to provide for the resource-constrained revenue-maximization decision problem.

The resource-constrained revenue-maximization problem also contains an analogy to the minimum cost expansion path. It is called the revenue-maximizing expansion path. Figure 4.2 exhibits a graphic representation of the

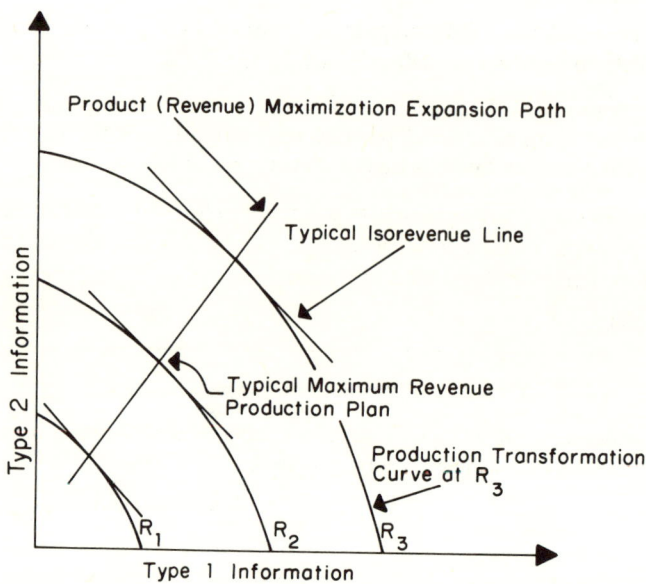

Figure 4.2 Revenue-maximization expansion path.

expansion path. As can be seen, the curve connecting the resource-constrained revenue-maximization points is the revenue-maximizing expansion path. That is, it is the locus of revenue-maximizing production plans that a manager should adopt as more resource is made available. This together with the cost-minimizing expansion path are analytical tools indicating the best way to expand or contract an activity when the flow of resources and products is completely flexible.

4.2 The Multiple-Product Cost Function

In the multiple-product case, as in the single-product situation, the cost function is a useful managerial tool. However, the existence of multiple products does add considerable complexity. In contrast to the single-product case, in which the cost function can easily be seen graphically to represent the least-cost combination of resources needed to produce an output level, the requirement for a least-cost resource mix remains in the multiple-product case, but it is no longer easy to show this graphically because of the multiple resources and products. The only recourse is to formulate this case analytically without seeing it pictorially. The next exercise is to formulate the minimum-cost product mix decision problem for the simple one-resource case. Intuitively the solution to this least-cost decision problem for every conceivable product mix (I_1, I_2) leads to a multiple-product cost function.

4.2 The Multiple-Product Cost Function

EXERCISE 4.7 Multiple-Product Minimum-Cost Decision Problem

Formulate the minimum-cost decision problem for the case of one resource and two types of information.

The most interesting characteristic of multiple-product production is seen when the interaction of the products' production processes causes the cost of joint production to be lower than the sum of costs for each of the products when produced separately. This characteristic of joint production is called *economies of scope*. The formula for this is written for the case of two types of information as

$$\tilde{C}(I_1) + \tilde{C}(I_2) \geq \tilde{C}(I_1, I_2). \tag{4.6}$$

An easily visualized picture of this is seen in the three-dimensional representation in Figure 4.3. Overall, the cost function is a funnel-shaped object that

Figure 4.3 A multiple-product cost function.

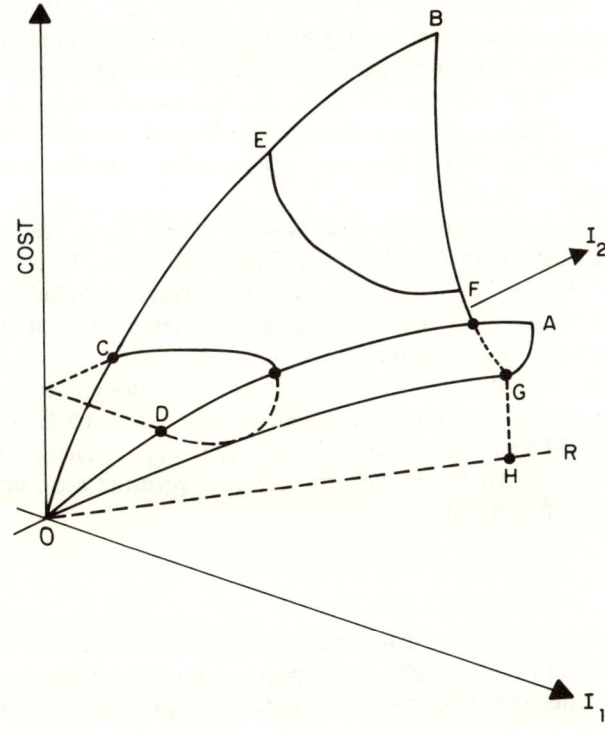

has its spout at the origin and that opens up as the output levels are further from the origin. Thus a "cut" across the funnel looks like the curve *AGFB*. Since the "middle" of the "cut" is lower than the "ends," it costs less to produce the two outputs jointly than separately. That is, this is a multiple-product cost function that exhibits economies of scope. For now we will continue to work with this particular picture of the cost function, but the reader will soon notice that it exhibits rather extreme cost behavior in the sense that economies of scope are so strong that intuition suggests that the example is unrealistic. That intuition is most likely correct, but the necessary concepts are more easily understood in the extreme case. A more realistic picture will be drawn later.

Now consider the curve *CD*. At a constant level of cost, the cost function curves away from the cost axis. Thus, the isocost curve resembles the product transformation curve studied earlier in this chapter. This shape is not a surprise, given that there is only one resource and that the cost function is determined by the underlying technology and resource market behavior. It is also the case that, if multiple-product production is economical, the shape remains when multiple resources are considered.

Another characteristic relates to the shape of the cost function when the quantity of one of the products is held constant. This curve represents the incremental cost of the product not held constant. For example, at a zero level of I_2, the incremental cost of product I_1 is the curve *ODA*. At level $\hat{I}_2$ of type 2 information, the incremental product cost curve for I_1 is *EF*. The great change in the shape of the cost curve, from always rising to at first falling then rising, is the result of economies of scope due to multiple-product production. Notice that, for the initial range, the more produced the lower the total cost. This is unlikely to occur in reality, but remember that this picture is designed to demonstrate the concepts.

Finally, there is the shape characteristic of the cost curves corresponding to rays from the origin in the (I_1, I_2) plane. The straight line *OR* is one such ray; the resulting ray cost behavior is the curve *OG*, which is the projection of the ray on the cost surface. Each possible ray has its own individual cost curve, so in general there is no universal ray cost behavior.

For each of the characteristics, a more detailed analysis follows. In each case, the concepts of average cost, marginal cost, cost subadditivity, and returns to scale will be discussed, as will their use in decision making. The order of discussion is ray cost behavior, incremental product cost, economies of scope, and isocost contours.

4.2.1 *Ray Cost Behavior*

The study of ray average cost refers to the ray *OR* in Figure 4.3. For ease of visualization, the ray cost behavior aspects of Figure 4.3 are reproduced as Figure 4.4. Notice that total ray cost increases as product levels move along

4.2 The Multiple-Product Cost Function

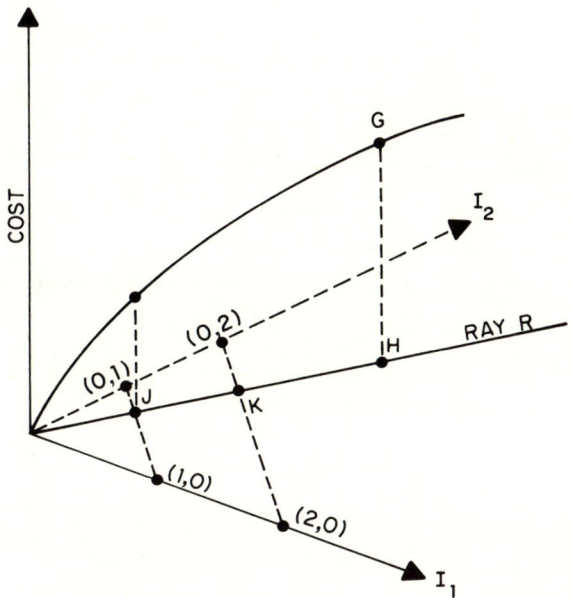

Figure 4.4 Ray cost behavior.

the ray away from the origin. In order to facilitate discussion of ray behavior it is necessary to devise an index for locating a ray. Note that any ray, OR, represents a fixed proportion between the products. This can be seen by considering the line from (1,0) to (0,1) in Figure 4.4. The fixed proportion between the outputs is represented by the ratio of the length of the segment of the line from (1,0) to J divided by the length of the line segment from (0,1) to point J. This is the same as the proportion of the segments from (0,2) to K and from K to (2,0). This proportion uniquely defines a ray, as any shift in the ray will change it. This fixed proportion, and the ray it identifies, also define a composite information commodity that contains both information products. Thus, a composite commodity is formed by appropriate weighting of each of the two types of information. To define the unit level of the composite commodity, consider point J to be exactly in the middle of the line from (1,0) to (0,1). Then the composite commodity (symbolized as I^*) would be formed by the equation

$$I^* = 0.5I_1 + 0.5I_2. \tag{4.7}$$

Since I_1 and I_2 are at the unit level, the quantity of the composite commodity is 1. That is, the line from (1,0) to (0,1) is a unit level isoproduct line for a composite commodity. What this does, then, is (1) to form a fixed proportion composite commodity for a specific ray (such as OR), and (2) to relate the

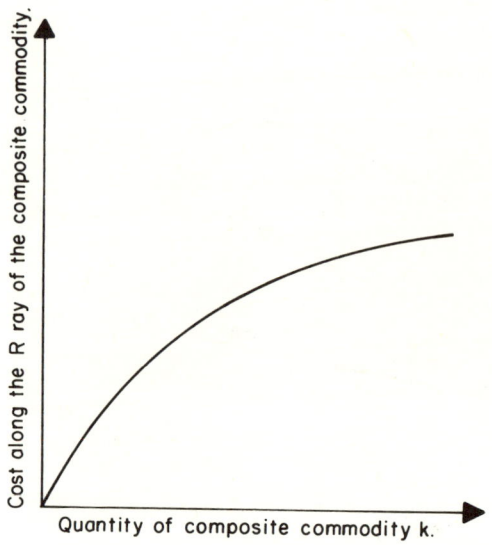

Figure 4.5 Ray cost behavior of a composite commodity.

composite commodity to the ray cost. Hence the three-dimensional diagram in Figure 4.4 can be reduced to a series of two-dimensional diagrams, as in Figure 4.5.

The seemingly complicated ray cost behavior has now been reduced to a single-product cost function, that of the composite commodity. Thus all the concepts appropriate to the single-output cost function can be applied. Figure 4.6 shows the composite commodity version of the already familiar cost function. (Note that this ray cost function is not that seen in Figure 4.4 but a generalization.) Following are definitions and formalizations of these concepts in the context of composite commodities.

Definition 4.1 Ray (Composite Commodity) Average Cost

Ray average cost is the cost at a given level of the composite commodity divided by the quantity of the composite commodity:

$$\text{RAYAVGCOST}(I^*) = \frac{\tilde{C}(I^*)}{I^*}, \tag{4.8}$$

where I^* is the quantity of composite commodity,
$\tilde{C}(I^*)$ is the cost function for the composite commodity.

Definition 4.2 Ray (Composite Commodity) Marginal Cost

Ray marginal cost is the additional cost incurred by the production of an additional unit of composite commodity as measured from a specific point

4.2 The Multiple-Product Cost Function

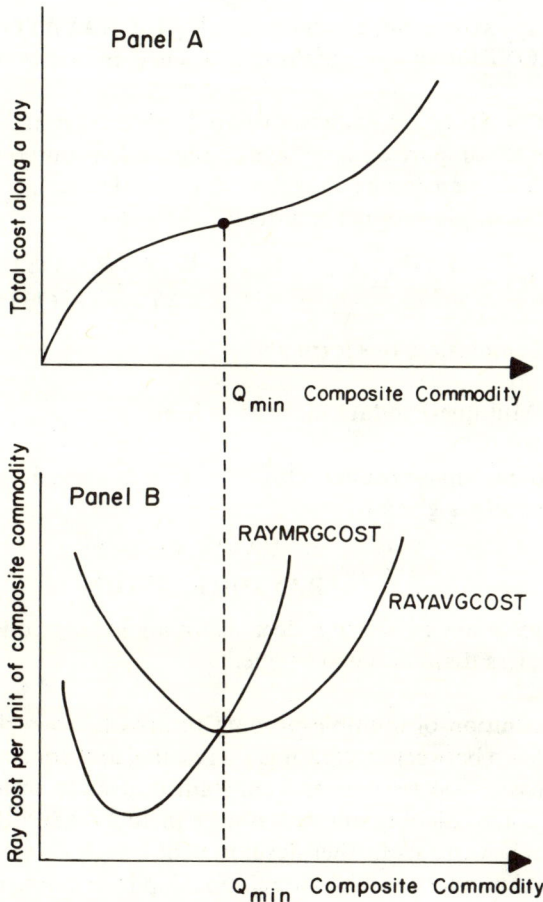

Figure 4.6 General ray cost characteristics.

on the ray and its projection on the ray cost curve:

$$\text{RAYMRGCOST}(I^*) = \frac{d\tilde{C}(I^*)}{dI^*}. \tag{4.9}$$

Definition 4.3 Ray (Composite Commodity) Average Cost Characteristics

Ray average costs are strictly decreasing at a specific level of the composite commodity if, for a small positive change ($e > 0$) in the level of the composite commodity, ray average costs decline, that is,

$$\frac{\tilde{C}(I^* - e)}{I^* - e} > \frac{\tilde{C}(I^*)}{I^*} > \frac{\tilde{C}(I^* + e)}{I^* + e}. \tag{4.10}$$

The inequalities are reversed for strictly increasing ray average costs.

Ray average cost is at a minimum (I^*_{min}) if RAYAVGCOST(I^*_{min}) < RAYAVGCOST for all levels of the composite commodity other than I^*_{min}.

The concept of returns to scale is also applicable. As in the single-product case, the idea is to compare a percentage change in the composite commodity with the associated percentage change in ray cost. Using the symbol SN for the measure of multiple-product returns to scale, then

$$SN(I^*) = \frac{dI^*/I^*}{d\tilde{C}/\tilde{C}} = \frac{\tilde{C}}{I^*} \cdot \frac{1}{d\tilde{C}/dI^*} = \frac{\text{RAYAVGCOST}(I^*)}{\text{RAYMRGCOST}(I^*)}. \quad (4.11)$$

Definition 4.4 summarizes this formally.

Definition 4.4 Multiple-Product Returns to Scale

The degree of multiple-product returns to scale at a specific level of a composite commodity is given by

$$SN(I^*) = \frac{\text{RAYAVGCOST}(I^*)}{\text{RAYMRGCOST}(I^*)}. \quad (4.12)$$

Returns to scale are increasing, decreasing, or locally constant as SN is greater than, less than, or equal to one.

From the definition of multiple-product returns to scale there is, intuitively, a relationship between decreasing, increasing, and constant ray average costs and increasing, decreasing, and constant returns to scale. Proving this point requires some calculus, and will not be included here; the result, however, is useful and warrants further development.[1]

The first step in understanding the relationship is to define the elasticity of ray average cost with respect to the composite commodity. If this elasticity is greater than zero (say it equals two), then an increase (say 10%) in the quantity of the composite commodity will require a commensurate increase in ray average cost to support it (i.e., 20%). In this example, ray average cost increases. When this is the case there are decreasing returns to scale. If the elasticity is negative and does not exceed one in absolute value, then ray average cost decreases and there are increasing returns to scale. Constant returns to scale occur if the elasticity is zero, that is, ray average cost does not change with the quantity of composite commodity. So if ray average cost

---

[1] The development follows from

$$e = \frac{I^*}{\tilde{C}(I^*)/I^*} \cdot \frac{d\left|\frac{\tilde{C}(I^*)}{I^*}\right|}{dI},$$

evaluating the derivative and then substituting in the definition of SN.

4.2 The Multiple-Product Cost Function

decreases (increases), then there are increasing (decreasing) returns to scale, respectively. Thus, the measurement of ray average cost and its rate of change provide the cost information necessary to determine the nature of returns to scale.

As in the single-product case, cost information is relevant to the question of organizational design. One aspect of this, in the current context of two products, is the number of organizational units needed to support a given requirement for both types of information. If there is a point at which ray average cost is a minimum, then there will be a single point on every possible ray where this occurs. If these minimum ray average cost points are mapped out, they form a curve that can be used to illuminate the organizational design issue. Consider Figure 4.7. The curve, labeled the M-locus, contains the minimum ray average cost points. If the requirement for both types of information is toward the origin from the M-locus, then only one organizational unit is needed. For requirements somewhere beyond the M-locus and short of two times the M-locus, two units will provide the least-cost organizational design. The same logic continues outward from here.

The last aspect of ray cost behavior is a restatement of the measure of multiple-product returns to scale (SN) in terms of the two types of information rather than the composite commodity. In order to do this, it is necessary to reconsider the nature of the composite commodity. First, the fixed proportion between the products represented by the ray was used to create weights for the individual products in the composite commodity, and second, the unit level of composite commodity was defined where the ray crosses the line connecting combinations (1,0) and (0,1). Now a more general approach will be useful.

First, the unit level of the composite commodity is clearly arbitrary; any point along the ray could be used and everything rescaled accordingly. So, define the unit level to be at that point on the ray where the sum of the quantities of this product equals one ($I_1 + I_2 = 1$). Then, for ease of exposition, label this unit level I_0^* to avoid confusion between the unit index and the index of information products. The other levels of composite commodity are

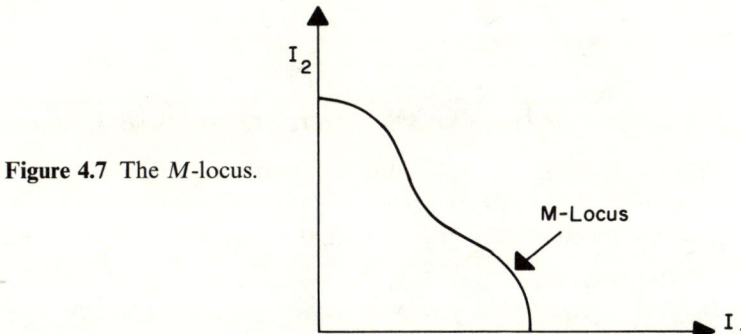

Figure 4.7 The M-locus.

now obtained from this level by scaling I_0^* up or down by a factor designated a. If a is greater than one, then composite commodity levels greater than one are obtained. If it is less than one (negative numbers are not permissible), then fractions of a unit are obtained. So, with this change of variable in mind, the ray average cost can be measured as $\tilde{C}(aI_0^*)$ divided by aI_0^*, and the original measure of ray marginal cost $d\tilde{C}/dI$ becomes $(1/I_0^*)(d\tilde{C}/da)$. Thus, the measure of returns to scale, SN, becomes

$$SN = \frac{\tilde{C}(aI_0^*)}{aI_0^*} \cdot \frac{1}{d\tilde{C}/I_0^* \, da} = \frac{\tilde{C}(aI_0^*)}{a d\tilde{C}/da}. \tag{4.13}$$

Ray marginal cost can be calculated from the marginal cost of each of the products. If at some specific point along a ray (say I_1^0, I_2^0) only one of the products (say I_1) is increased in quantity, some additional cost will be incurred. This marginal cost is denoted $\text{MRGCOST}_{cp}(I_1)$, where the specific level of information 1 from which the change occurs is I_1^0. The subscript cp is a reminder that the quantities of all other products are held constant (*ceteris paribus*). Of course there is a similar measure for information of type 2 [$\text{MRGCOST}_{cp}(I_2)$]. The only remaining step is to combine these into the ray marginal cost of the composite commodity. Since the ray represents the products in fixed proportion, these proportions are appropriate for weighing the marginal costs just developed. At the unit level of composite commodity these are I_1^0 and I_2^0, which are also the weights. So the ray marginal cost at level aI^* is

$$\text{RAYMRGCOST}(aI^*) = I_1^0 \, \text{MRGCOST}_{cp}(\hat{I}_1) \\ + I_2^0 \, \text{MRGCOST}_{cp}(\hat{I}_2). \tag{4.14}$$

Substitution in the equation for SN yields

$$SN = \frac{\tilde{C}(aI_0^*)}{aI_1^0 \, \text{MRGCOST}_{cp}(\hat{I}_1) + aI_2^0 \, \text{MRGCOST}_{cp}(\hat{I}_2)}. \tag{4.15}$$

Now aI_1^0 equals I_1 and aI_2^0 equals I_2. Also, aI_0^* can be written as I^*, using the original notation. So the result can be written as

$$SN = \frac{\tilde{C}(I^*)}{\hat{I}_1 \, \text{MRGCOST}_{cp}(\hat{I}_1) + \hat{I}_2 \, \text{MRGCOST}_{cp}(\hat{I}_2)}. \tag{4.16}$$

This relationship can be used to study the financial feasibility of multiple-product production, where a marginal cost pricing rule is required. If prices (q_1, q_2) are set equal to marginal cost, then equation (4.16) becomes

$$SN = \frac{\tilde{C}(I^*)}{\hat{I}_1 q_1 + \hat{I}_2 q_2}. \tag{4.17}$$

4.2 The Multiple-Product Cost Function

If there are increasing returns to scale ($SN > 1$), then $\tilde{C}(I^*) > (\hat{I}_1 q_1 + \hat{I}_2 q_2)$, that is, cost exceeds revenue. So the complexity of the multiple-product case does not eliminate the inherent financial infeasibility of marginal cost pricing when increasing returns to scale are present. If in an activity (e.g., computer center or software development and maintenance center) ray average cost exceeds ray marginal cost, then the imposition of a marginal cost pricing rule will almost inevitably lead to financial failure. And, as will be seen later, if a marginal cost pricing rule is not used, resources are misallocated. A classic management dilemma! A way to avoid it is to recognize the financial infeasibility and to provide a subsidy so that production becomes financially feasible for the manager responsible. This subsidy, which should equal $\tilde{C}(I^*) - \hat{I}_1 q_1 - \hat{I}_2 q_2$, must come from elsewhere in the organization. Its source will be considered later.

4.2.2 Incremental Product Cost

The next multiple-product cost-function characteristic to be studied is the incremental cost of adding (or deleting) a product from the organization's line of information products. As an example, suppose information of type 1 were to be examined for possible deletion, given that information of type two was to continue to be produced at level $\hat{I}_2$. Figure 4.8 shows the behavior of the cost function when I_2 is equal to $\hat{I}_2$. It is a part of the original multiple-product cost function shown in Figure 4.3.

Notice that costs first fall, reach a minimum, and then begin to rise. Now suppose the current operating point is $(\hat{I}_1, \hat{I}_2)$ with associated cost $\tilde{C}'$. If there is a decision to delete information 1 from the product line, the operating point will be at $(0, \hat{I}_2)$ with associated cost $\tilde{C}''$. So in this case, whatever occurs in the production process as the result of joint production results in lower cost for the composite commodity. The incremental cost of information 1 is defined as current cost minus planned cost, that is, $\tilde{C}' - \tilde{C}''$; since $\tilde{C}''$ is larger than $\tilde{C}'$, the incremental cost is negative—it costs more to produce zero type

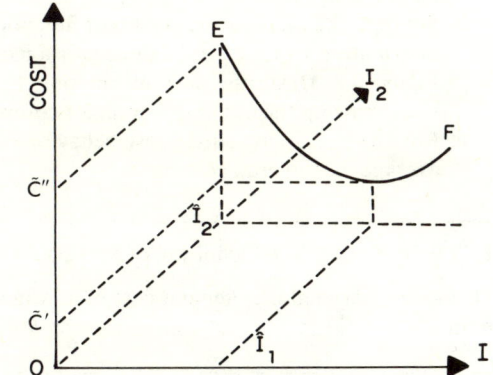

Figure 4.8 Incremental cost of information 1.

1 information than I_1 units of it. Conversely, if none of I_1 were being produced and the planned level were $\hat{I}_1$, the incremental cost would then be positive. This somewhat back-to-front way of thinking about increased cost is the result of the notion that incremental cost typically begins by rising, not falling as in the current case. Definition 4.5 formally defines a product's incremental cost:

Definition 4.5 The Incremental Cost of a Product

The incremental cost of a product in the set of all products produced, at a particular output level for each product, is for product 1:

$$\text{INC}_1(\hat{I}_1, \hat{I}_2) = \tilde{C}(\hat{I}_1, \hat{I}_2) - \tilde{C}(0, \hat{I}_2), \tag{4.18}$$

and for product 2:

$$\text{INC}_2(\hat{I}_2, \hat{I}_2) = \tilde{C}(\hat{I}_1, \hat{I}_2) - \tilde{C}(\hat{I}_1, 0). \tag{4.19}$$

Now that the complexity of multiple-product cost behavior is reduced to analysis of a single product, the usual cost concepts of average cost, marginal cost, and returns to scale can be defined and used. The only change is that these familiar concepts must be studied in a product-specific context, that is, holding production levels of all other products constant. Three of the following exercises ask for the respective definitions.

EXERCISE 4.8 The Definition of Average Incremental Cost of a Product

Define the average incremental cost [AVGINC(I_1, I_2)] of information product 1.

EXERCISE 4.9 The Diagram of Average Incremental Cost

a. For the incremental cost behavior shown in Figure 4.8 draw the average incremental cost curve.
b. Suppose the multiple-product cost function changes so that the introduction of information 1 in the product line uses a fixed cost over and above that shown in Figure 4.8. Draw the *new* information 1 incremental cost curve, including in your drawing the old one as well, for comparison.
c. For the new incremental cost behavior curve you have just drawn, draw the average incremental cost curve.

EXERCISE 4.10 The Definition of Marginal Incremental Cost of a Product

Define the marginal incremental cost of information 1 using MRGINC($\hat{I}_1$, $\hat{I}_2$) as the notation.

4.2 The Multiple-Product Cost Function

EXERCISE 4.11 The Diagram of Marginal Incremental Cost

a. For the incremental cost behavior shown in Figure 4.8 draw the marginal incremental cost curve in the same diagram in which you drew the answer to Exercise 4.9a.

b. For the incremental cost behavior you developed in Exercise 4.9b, draw the marginal incremental cost curve on the same diagram as your answer to Exercise 4.9c.

EXERCISE 4.12 The Definition of Product-Specific Returns to Scale

Define the product-specific returns to scale measure for information 1, $SN_1(\hat{I}_1, \hat{I}_2)$ at the operating point $(\hat{I}_1, \hat{I}_2)$. Be sure to include in your definition the concepts of increasing, decreasing, and constant returns to scale.

The next exercise uses your answer to Exercise 4.12 to study the financial feasibility of the sale of product 1 in the presence of returns to scale and a marginal cost pricing rule.

EXERCISE 4.13 The Financial Feasibility of Information 1 Using a Marginal Cost Pricing Rule

If use of a marginal cost pricing rule is required, state the financial feasibility (or infeasibility) of producing information 1 when (a) increasing returns to scale are present, (b) decreasing returns to scale are present, and (c) constant returns to scale are present. How would you decide which type of returns to scale are present at a specific operating point?

The study of multiple-product cost functions has so far focused on only two products. While the concepts studied are applicable to three or more products, there is a need for one change. When more than two products are produced, not only are there product-specific incremental costs, returns to scale, and so on, but incremental costs, returns to scale, and so on, for combinations of products. For example, suppose there were three products (labeled 1, 2, 3); it would then be necessary to study not only the separate products (I_1, I_2, I_3) but also the two-product combinations (I_1, I_2), (I_2, I_3), and (I_1, I_3). These ideas will not be pursued further here.

4.2.3 Economies of Scope

The next multiple-product cost concept considered is that of economies of scope—the impact of cost in joint production. Figure 4.3 shows a multiple-product cost situation where the cost of joint production is less than the cost of separate production. Geometrically, the funnel-shaped multiple-product cost function is lower in the middle than on the edges. Such situations are said to exhibit *economies of scope* and, when they occur, the joint scope of the products produced lowers the cost of production. If the situation shown in Figure 4.3 were reversed (i.e., the funnel were upside down), then the center of the multiple-product cost function would be higher than the edges. Joint production would then cost more than separate production. When this joint cost increase is strong enough, it is said that *diseconomies of scope* apply. Definition 4.6 summarizes this idea.

Definition 4.6 Economies and Diseconomies of Scope

Economies of scope exist at a particular operating point $(\hat{I}_1, \hat{I}_2)$ if the cost of joint production $[\tilde{C}(\hat{I}_1, \hat{I}_2)]$ is less than the sum of the costs of independent production of the same products $[\tilde{C}(\hat{I}_1) + \tilde{C}(\hat{I}_2)]$. If the joint cost exceeds the sum of the costs, diseconomies of scope are said to be present.

The concept involved in Definition 4.6 is that of *subadditivity*, which relates to comparing the sum of the costs of a single product produced in two activities with the cost of producing that same product in a single activity. In the multiple-product environment, the same concept decomposes *joint* production into two separate production facilities. In the case of two products, Definition 4.6 applies. If more than two products are present, Definition 4.6 and what follows need to be generalized to study the partition of the set of all products into two sets and the economies or diseconomies of scope between the sets.

It is useful to have a measure of the degree of economies of scope beyond an indication of existence or nonexistence. The most straightforward measure is to compare the difference in cost between independent production and joint production with the cost of joint production. The bigger the difference in cost between independent and joint production, *ceteris paribus*, the larger the degree of economies of scope. And the larger the cost of joint production, *ceteris paribus*, the smaller the degree of economies of scope. If the index of economies of scope is negative, then diseconomies of scope apply. Overall, the index of economies (diseconomies) of scope measures the relative decrease (increase) in cost that results from joint production instead of independent production, when production is segmented into two production facilities. In the case in which the index is zero, joint and independent production cost the same, and this is called neutral economies of scope. Definition 4.7 summarizes the discussion.

Definition 4.7 The Degree of Economies of Scope

The index for the degree of economies (diseconomies) of scope is

$$SC(\hat{I}_1, \hat{I}_2) = \frac{\tilde{C}(\hat{I}_1) + \tilde{C}(\hat{I}_2) - \tilde{C}(\hat{I}_1, \hat{I}_2)}{\tilde{C}(\hat{I}_1, \hat{I}_2)}, \qquad (4.20)$$

4.2 The Multiple-Product Cost Function

where $SC(\hat{I}_1, \hat{I}_2)$ is the index of degrees of economies of scope in producing I_1 and I_2. If $SC(\hat{I}_1, \hat{I}_2)$ is greater than zero, economies of scope apply. If it is negative, diseconomies of scope apply. If it is equal to zero, then neutral economies of scope apply.

Now consider the relationship between incremental product costs and economies of scope. If the incremental product costs are negative, as shown in Figure 4.3, then, intuitively, the sum of the costs of independent production will exceed the joint production cost. Algebraically this can be shown as follows: Using $\gtreqless$ to denote comparison in the definition of the degree of economies of scope, (4.19) can be written

$$\frac{\tilde{C}(\hat{I}_1) + \tilde{C}(\hat{I}_2) - \tilde{C}(\hat{I}_1, \hat{I}_2)}{\tilde{C}(\hat{I}_1, \hat{I}_2)} \gtreqless 0, \qquad (4.21)$$

which becomes

$$\tilde{C}(\hat{I}_1) + \tilde{C}(\hat{I}_2) \gtreqless \tilde{C}(\hat{I}_1, \hat{I}_2),$$

which in turn can be written as

$$\tilde{C}(\hat{I}_1, \hat{I}_2) \gtreqless \text{INC}(\hat{I}_1) + \text{INC}(\hat{I}_2). \qquad (4.22)$$

So if the joint production costs are positive (which seems most likely) and the product incremental costs are both negative, then economies of scope will prevail. However, if product incremental costs are positive, then there can be economies, diseconomies, or neutral economies of scope, depending on the relative magnitudes. Thus, in the likely case of positive incremental costs, the picture in Figure 4.3 is changed, and a careful numerical calculation is needed to determine the degree of economies of scope. (See Section 4.2.5, A Realistic Picture, below.)

When three or more products are present, exactly the same logic applies, but all conceivable pairwise partitions into independent production facilities must be studied.

There is a situation in which economies of scope apply for *all pairwise partitions* into independent production facilities. This is when *cost complementarity* applies. Product 1, for example, is a cost complement of product 4 if an increase in the quantity of product 4 being produced results in a decrease in the marginal cost of product 1 ($[d\text{MRGCOST}(I_1)/d(I_4)] < 0$). When the inequality is reversed, products one and four are not complements. When *all* products are pairwise cost complements, then economies of scope exist for all ways of partitioning the joint production into pairwise independent processes. While this condition is logically valid, it is difficult to imagine that it applies to more than a few special instances. So the much more tedious pairwise checking of production facilities must be undertaken in choosing the least-cost organizational design for multiple-product production.

In addition to the concept of economies of scope and its measurement, it is also important to have an idea of the underlying source of such economies.

After all, the very idea of economies of scope is opposed to a long-held and still-cherished idea—namely, that specialization of task reduces the cost of production. There are two categories of cases. In one category are the cases in which one or more of the resources used in production are shared by the products being produced. An interesting example of this is a computer system being shared by the jobs (production processes) run on it. The second category requires a new concept. Suppose there is a resource that is shared equally by all the products without any conflict—all the products can use the resource at the same time. Such resources are called collective or public resources. One example that has many characteristics similar to a collective good is that of application programs resident in a computer system library. One person's use of an application program does not interfere with or prevent any other person's use. Thus, library programs are collective goods.

When the second category applies, for example, to a computer system, then the multiple-product cost function exhibits economies of scope. From the example, it should be expected that computer centers exhibit economies of scope. At least for this one characteristic of multiple-product cost behavior, large computer centers then have a cost advantage over smaller centers. The next exercise suggests the use of these cost concepts in structuring a current issue.

EXERCISE 4.14 Mainframes or Minis?

There has been much talk of whether it pays to have a general-purpose mainframe computer or a number of minicomputers, each performing specialized functions. Structure this issue using the multiple-product cost concepts.
Hint: In structuring the issue, be sure to relate all the cost concepts to one another and then apply them.

4.2.4 Isocost Contours

The last characteristic of the multiple-product cost function to be studied here is the isocost contour. In Figure 4.3, curve *CD* is such an isocost contour that exhibits economies of scope. If there are diseconomies of scope, the isocost contour will be convex to the cost dimension, rather than concave to it as in the figure. Thus, the plot of an isocost contour can be most helpful in understanding economies of scope.

4.2.5 A Realistic Picture

Now that the basic concepts of multiple-product cost functions are understood, it is time to present a more intuitively acceptable picture of such a function. Figure 4.9 shows such a cost function. In order to validate understanding of the concepts used, the following exercises are provided.

4.2 The Multiple-Product Cost Function

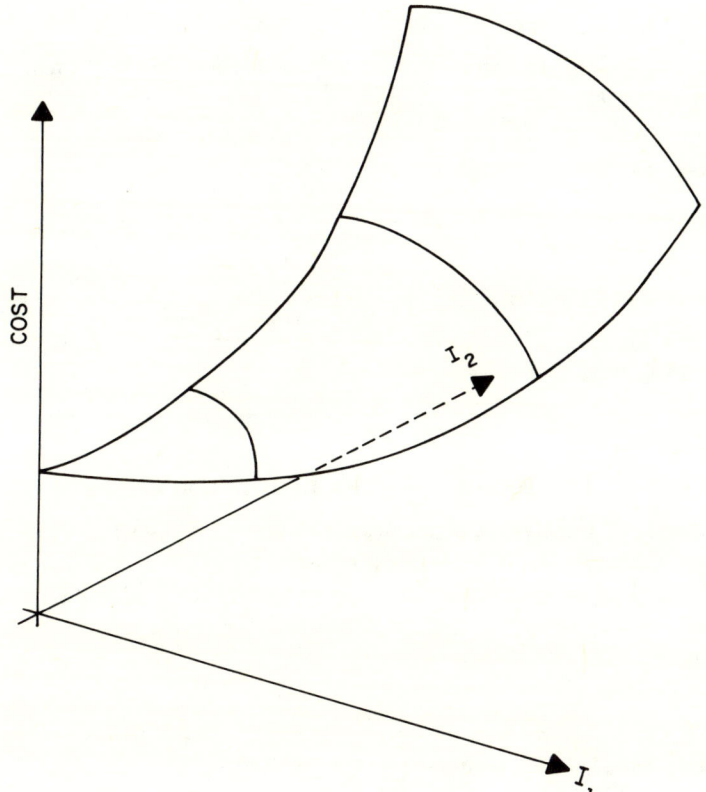

Figure 4.9 A realistic multiple-product cost function.

EXERCISE 4.15 Ray Cost Behavior

Draw pictures of the typical ray cost behavior for each of the following:

1. Ray average cost.
2. Ray marginal cost.

What type of multiple-product returns to scale are exhibited?

EXERCISE 4.16 Incremental Product Cost

Draw pictures of the typical cost behavior for each of the following:

1. Product incremental cost.
2. Average product incremental cost.
3. Marginal product incremental cost.

What type of product-specific returns to scale are there?

EXERCISE 4.17 Financial Feasibility

Is an activity exhibiting the typical cost behavior financially feasible if a marginal cost pricing rule is used?

EXERCISE 4.18 Isocost Contours

Draw a picture of the typical isocost contour.

EXERCISE 4.19 Mainframes and Minis Again

For the cost function of Figure 4.9, what is the solution to the mainframe versus minicomputer minimum-cost problem?

4.3 Analysis of Two Resources—Two Information Products

The synthesis of the two-resources/one-product and one-resource/two-product cases is designed as a series of exercises to allow readers to validate their understanding of the material. These exercises provide guidance as to what should be reviewed if it is felt that understanding of the material is not yet sufficient.

EXERCISE 4.20 The Information-Processing System Technology

Show that the production function

$$[1.51 I_1^2 + 1.51 I_2^2]^{1/2} = 6.5 R_1^{.4} R_2^{.4}$$

exhibits the following characteristics:
- **a.** Decreasing marginal physical productivity in both resources used with both products
- **b.** Isoquants convex to the origin.
- **c.** Product transformation curves convex to the origin.
- **d.** Decreasing returns to scale.

EXERCISE 4.21 The Profit Function

Develop the present life-cycle profit function for the two-resource/two-product case.

EXERCISE 4.22 The Manager's Decision Problem

State the manager's profit-maximizing decision problem for the two-resource/two-product case.

EXERCISE 4.23 The Decision Rules

For the two-resource/two-product case, develop the decision rules for determining

    a. the level of information of each type to provide.
    b. the mix of information to provide.
    c. the level of resources of each type to employ.
    d. the mix of resources to employ.

4.4 Summary of Chapters 3 and 4

Chapters 3 and 4 have presented a basic analytical approach to understanding a manager's decision making. A manager's decision must first be put in the context of the organization's incentive structure—the rewards and penalties that central management has chosen to use in planning, coordinating, and controlling the overall organization. Given a profit-maximization incentive, a manager must formulate the profit-maximizing decision problem for his/her activity. If the decisions are made by central management, the same problems and rules apply, but the value of information to the organization is the criterion rather than transfer prices.

The profit function is the present life-cycle revenue from selling information to the rest of the organization at the transfer price set by central management minus the present life-cycle cost of operations, where market prices for labor and capital services are the relevant cost drivers. The technology of information-processing systems, both current and forecasted, places constraints on the manager's actions. This technology is characterized by the nature of its marginal physical productivities (or marginal physical input requirements) and its returns to scale. The usual generic technological characteristics are decreasing marginal physical productivity and decreasing returns to scale. The manager's decision variables are the level and mix of inputs (labor and capital services) and outputs (information types).

The manager can solve the profit-maximization problem by using decision rules that identify the conditions for a technology-constrained profit-maximizing production plan. In general, the level of a resource to employ or of a product to provide is identified by the equality of the marginal revenue to the marginal cost of that resource or product, that is, by identifying the production plan where marginal profit is zero. The mix of resources (or products) is identified by equating the marginal rate of technological substitution (or the marginal rate of product transformation) to the relative marginal costs (prices) of the resources (or products). This results in an internal technological tradeoff equal to the external economic tradeoff and also identifies which profit-maximizing technology to employ. Thus, the set of decision rules provides the manager with a method of searching for and identifying the technology-constrained profit-maximizing production plan.

In studying the behavior of a technology-constrained profit-maximizing manager, the nature of costs and the cost function was also explored. The cost function was developed as a representation of the resource and product combinations which are solutions to a product-constrained cost-minimization decision problem. Thus the costs calculated from the cost function are the minimum costs associated with the output level considered. The major determinants of the shape of the cost function are the underlying technology (production function) and the market prices for resources. There is a duality between the characteristics of the cost function and the production function. The cost characteristics of returns to scale, product incremental cost, product-specific returns to scale, economies of scope, and ray costs are important tools in understanding the behavior of production costs. For additional information on the cost characteristics of multiple production, see Baumol et al. (1982) (especially Chapters 3 and 4) and/or Sharkey (1982) (especially Chapter 4).

4.5 Postscript

The concepts presented in this chapter also serve, specifically, as the basis for understanding the economic cost-value analysis of ADP equipment. In performing such an economic analysis, it is necessary to proceed in a step-by-step manner identical to the approach presented in the summary. Of course, there are variations in contexts, some of which will be considered later. Another difference is that the decision rules are sometimes stated as cost-benefit or cost-value ratios. Thus the decision rule to equate present life-cycle marginal revenue to present life-cycle marginal cost is rewritten to identify the optimal action by setting the present life-cycle marginal value (revenue) to cost ratio equal to one.

References

Baumol, William J., Panzer, John C., and Willig, Robert D. (1982) *Contestable Markets and the Theory of Industry Structure.* New York: Harcourt Brace Jovanovich.

Sharkey, William W. (1982) *The Theory of Natural Monopoly.* Cambridge: Cambridge University Press.

Chapter 5
Information System Management

The structure and process of managing an information system were discussed in Chapter 1. The generic ideas contained in Chapter 1 are as follows: (1) the structure of the system consists of physical production flows, an organizational structure, a planning and coordinating function, and flows of control data; and (2) there is a process of interaction among the system components, which is observed as the information system's systemic behavior. The idea of choosing the "best" information system was also introduced.

With the overview of Chapter 1 in mind, it is time to systematically study the management of information systems. This will be done by reconsidering each of the generic ideas in turn, using the technical tools from Chapters 3 and 4. In addition to introducing a richer set of details it is now possible to advance the understanding of the information system management process by considering systemic behavior as part of the system design problem.

5.1 Physical Flows in an Information System

While physical flows can be studied in general, the specific instance exhibited in Figure 5.1 provides a more concrete context for study. The broad flow of physical entities is from left to right, that is, from software production to computer and information services production, and then to users and managerial decision making. Any of the labeled boxes could be more closely scrutinized to reveal increasing detail. For the purpose of studying a specific information system, however, the detail in Figure 5.1 is sufficient. Within the broad flow from left to right, there are three main groupings; the software activity, the computer center, and user-manager activities. Each of these will be discussed.

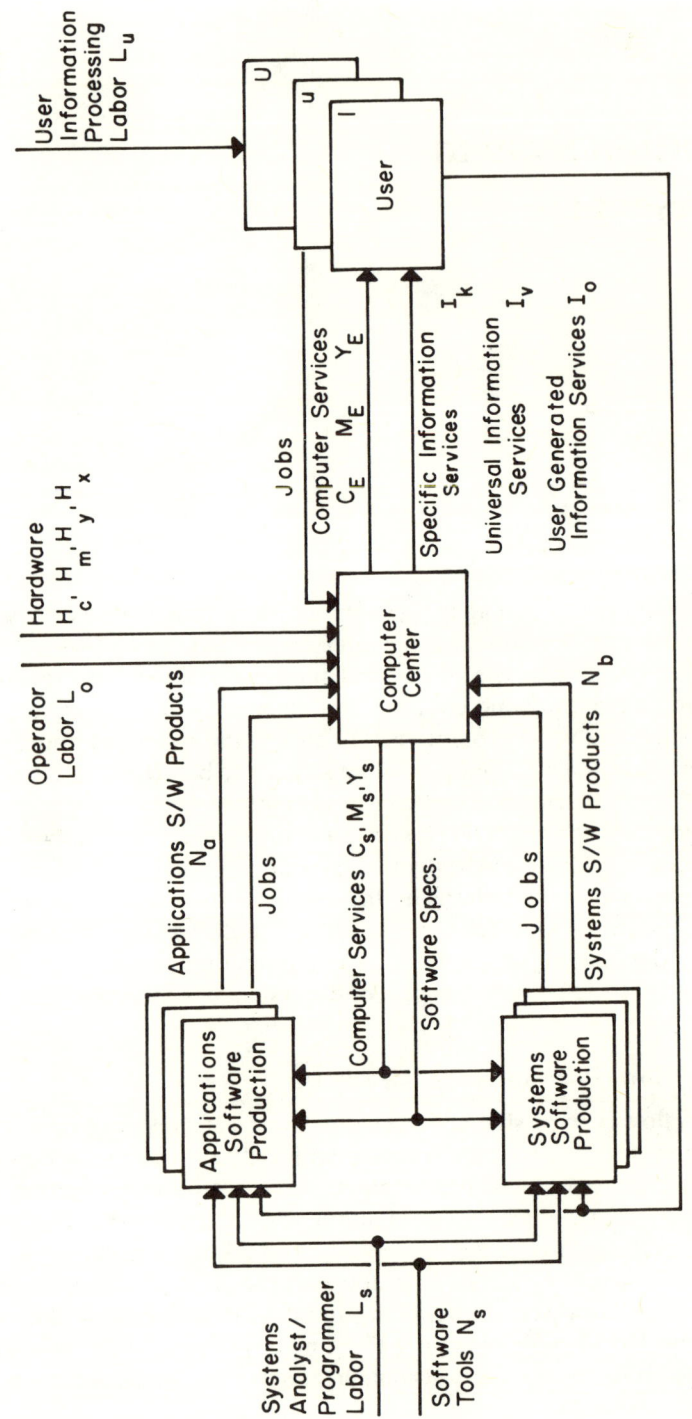

Figure 5.1 Physical flows in the information system.

5.1 Physical Flows in an Information System

Software development and maintenance involves the production of application and system software by separate production processes. In general, the development and maintenance of any software product requires resources in the form of computer services, systems analyst and programmer labor, and software development tools. The computer services used are measured in this model in three categories: central processor, memory, and input/output. For ease of exposition, systems analyst and programmer skills will be considered as being available in the same person. Their use is measured in man-years. It is assumed that a systems analyst/programmer is equally skillful whether working on applications or systems products. Last, but not least, there are software development tools. While there is no convenient measure of the quantity of such tools, it is useful to think in terms of their specifications. The specifications are usually multifaceted, but, for ease of exposition, only one specification will be used per software development tool, namely, the size of the program. The quantity is measured in the natural units of that specification, thousands of delivered source instructions (KDSI). There is also the same difficulty in measuring the quantity produced on the output side of the software development and maintenance activity. The KDSI measure is useful here too.

The production function describing software development and maintenance technology requires consideration. It is represented in Figure 5.1 by the boxes labeled application and systems software production, each box representing a single product. Separating the production of applications programs from system programs permits application of different technologies to the production of each type of software.

The computer system responds to job requests from users and from the software activity by using applications and system software in conjunction with hardware and operations labor to produce information products and computer services. Applications and system software were discussed previously. The many types of hardware are assigned here to four categories. Three of them—central processors, memory, and I/O peripherals—correspond to the services mentioned above. The fourth is telecommunications. Central processor capacity is commonly measured in millions of instructions per second (MIPS); this measure is also used here. Memory, whether random access or mass storage, is measured in megabytes (MB). Peripherals are of many types, the printer being one of the most important. Hence the representative measure of output capacity is lines printed per minute. Telecommunications channel capacity is measured in number of bits that can be transmitted per unit of time. Computer operation is the skill required of computer system labor and is measured in man-years.

Jobs are seen as being submitted either in batch mode or in interactive mode by user-managers and software developers and maintainers. While jobs can be measured in many ways, the choice here is in terms of thousands of lines of delivered source instructions used. The outputs of the computer system are threefold. There are computer services (measured in CPU time, memory utilization, and I/O quantities), information services for specific users, and information services that provide information to all users. Both types of information services can be envisioned as reports, either user-specific or universal. The available computer systems technology is expressed by a production function and is physically represented by the box labeled "computer center" in Figure 5.1.

Both user-specific and universal information services are employed by the user-manager in making decisions in his or her area of responsibility. The user-manager's activities may also involve using labor and computer services to directly produce user created information. The information production box in Figure 5.1, labeled "user," represents the user's physical program development and maintenance activities. Logically, these are represented by a production function.

Thus, Figure 5.1 represents the physical flows involved and groups them by type of activity. Note also the number and types of feedback loops. Computer services, for example, are used by many production processes, whereas all the software development and maintenance output is fed forward to the computer system. Most physical flow schematics such as Figure 5.1 are much more complicated for real situations because there are more production processes (the boxes) and/or because of more complex physical interconnections. In any case, the first step in understanding a functioning information system or in designing a new one is to complete the physical flow schematic to the level of detail needed for the decision to be made. In so doing, it is necessary to note those production processes for which an understanding of the production function is needed. When this has been accomplished, the organizational aspects can be overlaid on the physical flow schematic.

Figure 5.1 also shows users and the computer center defining software specifications and providing them to the software activity for implementation. Software specifications are the result of a management process for creating new information products. Later in this chapter, careful consideration will be given to this process of managing new products. For now, consider the software specifications as originating with users and the computer center under the managerial control of information system management.

5.2 The Organizational Structure

The physical flow of an information system must be overlaid with an organizational structure that plans, coordinates, and controls the physical flows and their associated technologies and tasks. This is the equivalent of the Industrial Dynamics model presented in Chapter 2, which views the entire organization as a network of physical flows with an information and control structure superimposed. Since the analysis here is at an aggregate level, the organizational units designated to manage the information system are them-

5.2 The Organizational Structure

selves aggregated and may include several processes. Thus the resource-product relationship for each of the organizational units, its production function, includes a measure of organizational or managerial technology in addition to the physical technology and tasks associated with the physical flows. More generally, each of the organizational units selected to manage the information system can be thought of as an information-processing activity. As such, it must organize human behavior and work flows, as well as physical technology, in order to accomplish its tasks. This organization then takes in certain resources (physical and/or data) and processes them into outputs (also physical and/or data). The resource-product relationship expressed in the production function describes this general information-processing technology in both its physical and organizational aspects.

In designing an organizational structure for managing the physical flows and technologies, the concept of task interdependence and its relationship to the type of coordination required is most useful. Thompson (1967) has identified three types of task interdependence: pooled, sequential, and reciprocal. Figure 5.2 exhibits the typical forms of these interdependencies. In the pooled case, the output of one task impacts several other tasks, while in the sequential case the tasks follow one after the other. Reciprocal interdependence is the case in which tasks mutually interact.

When tasks are pooled, the required coordination can be achieved by standardization and categorization. When the structure is of this type, each task makes a discrete contribution to the entire system and acts relatively independently of the other tasks. Hence there are few demands on the coordination processes as such, and more bureaucratic or mechanistic coordination methods can be used. An example of this in the physical flow schematic is the recruitment of systems analysts-programmers from the labor market. Since this type of labor is employed only in the software activity, its acquisition and use does not have to be coordinated with other information system activities. The same structure applies to the acquisition of computer system operators and software development tools.

Sequential task interdependence implies a higher degree of workflow interdependence. The broad sweep of the physical flow schematic from left to right demonstrates such interdependence; software development and maintenance tasks flow into computer system tasks, which feed user decision-making tasks. This chain of interdependence requires synchronization of the parts in order for the whole to function effectively. A coordinating mechanism must

Figure 5.2 Types of task interdependence.

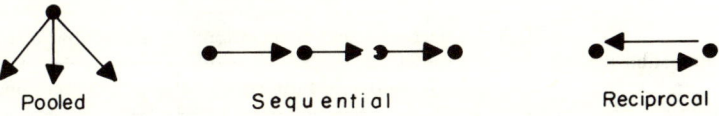

emphasize planning as well as standardization of the physical flows between tasks.

Finally, there is reciprocal task interdependence, for example, the relationship between the tasks of software production for a specific product and the computer system task. The software production task sends software products and jobs to the computer system task, which sends computer services to the software production task. Similarly, there is a reciprocal task relationship between the computer system and users via the users' information production tasks. These reciprocal relationships place great demands on coordination and control and the method of coordination must stress mutual adjustment.

Another powerful tool for information system analysis has been created by Perrow (1970), who distinguishes two aspects of tasks: variability and coping difficulty. Task variability refers to the number of exceptions to the routine method used in performing the task, while coping difficulty is the amount of search required to find a successful response to a task exception. Such coping behavior ranges from low (little search effort) to high (large search effort). Variability ranges from few to many exceptions. Combinations of the end points of these measures represent four stereotypical cases, as shown in Table 5.1. While the particular labels for the stereotypical cases are adapted for use here, they are in consonance with Perrow's concepts. Notice that the labels emphasize whether an activity is routine or nonroutine. This taxonomy of activities, often labeled programmed and nonprogrammed (Simon, 1977), is most useful.

Understanding of some of the tasks among the physical flows in the information system is enhanced by the use of these powerful ideas. Consider the task of producing computer and information services. Basically, this has low task variability, and when the exceptions occur, the coping difficulty is also low, that is, computer operations are routine or highly programmed. On the other hand, the design of software products for new information services is a task that exhibits many exceptions to the routine and, in many cases, high coping difficulty. The production task itself has been brought closer to a routine operation by the use of structured programming, structured walkthroughs, and other software engineering techniques, that is, the high variability and high coping difficulty occur at the design stage rather than the production stage. For ease of analysis that emphasizes the basic ideas, assume

Table 5.1 Degrees of Task Routine

		Task variability	
		Few exceptions	Many exceptions
Task coping difficulty	High	nonroutine search operations	nonroutine operations
	Low	routine operations	routine search operations

5.3 Planning, Coordinating, and Control Structure

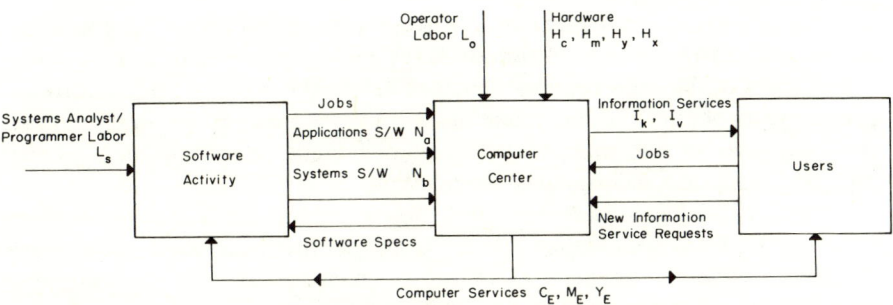

Figure 5.3 The departments in the information system.

that, except for new software product design and new computer systems hardware acquisition, the tasks in the physical flow are routine operations. The two exceptions are classified as nonroutine operations. Software maintenance should perhaps be classified as a nonroutine operation, but for ease of exposition it will be considered routine.

Standardization and programmed activity are the basis for coordination of routine operations. In the case of new software product design and computer hardware acquisition, the need is for a procedure that adjusts itself as circumstances change. As the frequency of the nonroutine tasks is small in comparison with the routine ones, the first design of the organizational overlay is in terms of the routine.

In studying the physical technologies and task flows of the routine operations, three broad technology zones have been identified, namely, software, computer system, and user. As a first cut at an organizational design, suppose there is a manager at the department level designated for each of these zones. For the software and computer center activities this designation is clear and quite common in practice. For the user activity, the prototype is a user-manager of some noninformation system functional area within the overall organization. This organizational design is shown in Figure 5.3, which aggregates the physical flows of Figure 5.1. Notice that the interconnections between organizational units in this routine world are all reciprocal. They can be coordinated in a planned, standardized, and categorized manner. The next step of the analysis is to design the information system planning, coordination, and control system.

5.3 The Information System Planning, Coordinating, and Control Structure

The organizational level involved in planning, coordination, and control is one above the department level and will be called the system level. This organizational locus will be called "information system management." Since information system management involves both producers and users (consumers) of information, the information system manager is usually part of the top echelon of the organization; this is certainly the norm recommended by practitioners of information system design. To remind us of this and to avoid the long label of information system management, this component of the information system will be called "central management."

Central management and the other organizational units must interact if the overall information system is to be balanced, that is, in equilibrium. Specifically, central management must interact reciprocally with the computer center. Each must provide the other with administrative data. As their relationship is a reciprocal one, it requires a coordination and control procedure that emphasizes mutual adjustment. Naturally, this mutually adaptive relationship must also exist for the interactions of the central management with each user and with the software activity.

What will be the nature of the coordination and control procedure? Since this book is designed to emphasize the economic and financial aspects of information systems, the procedure will have an economic-financial basis rather than a behavioral one. This is not meant to imply that the behavioral aspects are unimportant—far from it. The economic-financial approach has been chosen in order to emphasize these aspects and to sharpen the reader's understanding of them, not to downgrade the importance of behavioral aspects. Thus, the variables in the procedure comprise market prices, transfer prices, budgets, marginal costs, and a performance evaluating incentive system for the managers based on cost and profit.

In designing the system for evaluating managers' performance, each of the system components will be given a different incentive structure to permit consideration of all the managerial issues involved. The system components are the technology zones previously identified. Starting with the software activity as a cost center, the discussion will move to the computer center as a profit center, and finally to the users as budget-constrained decision makers.

5.3.1 *The Software Activity*

Designation of the software activity as a cost center implies, in addition to the technical accumulation of accounting costs for the center, that the software activity manager is charged with *minimizing* cost. This mandate to minimize cost is constrained by the output level of software that the activity is required to produce and also by the software development and maintenance technologies available. In order for the software activity manager to solve this decision problem, certain administrative information must be available.

In compliance with the earlier categorization of routine and nonroutine operation, the software to be developed must be specified in detail so that only routine tasks need be performed. To reduce the complexity of the analysis, the myriad specifications have been reduced to one—the size of the product in thousands of lines of source instructions delivered (KDSI).

5.3 Planning, Coordinating, and Control Structure

Now consider the inputs to a software production process. The resources shown in Figure 5.1 are computer services (CPU time, C_S; memory, M_S; input/output, Y_S), systems analyst/programmer labor (L_s), and software tools (N_s). The products are the sequence of jobs needed to develop and maintain a software product and, of course, the product itself measured in KDSI. The costs are the sum of computer service costs, labor cost, and software tool rental (only rental will be considered in order to reduce the complexity of the analysis). Since computer services are internally produced within the organization, central management must provide the software manager with the transfer prices for CPU time (q_{CE}), memory (q_{ME}), and I/O (q_{YE}). The software manager is presumed to know the market price of labor (p_{Ls}), although in many organizations the personnel office would provide such information. The market price of software tools (p_{Ns}) is also presumed known to the manager. Thus, by appropriately multiplying price and quantity, the manager can compute the operating cost in any one year as ($q_{CE}C_E + q_{ME}M_E + q_{YE}Y_E + p_{Ls}L_s + p_{Ns}N_s$). This formula assumes that central management foresees the future to be a replication of the present. So that the present value of cost can be computed, central management also provides the organization's cost of capital, r, and the planning period, $(0, T)$. Thus the present life-cycle cost is

$$\text{PLC} = \sum_{t=0}^{T} \frac{q_{CE}C_E + q_{ME}M_E + q_{YE}Y_E + p_{Ls}L_s + p_{Ns}N_s}{(1+r)^t}. \quad (5.1)$$

The perceptive reader will have noticed that telecommunications services do not appear in the above formulation, nor even in the list of computer services offered. The reason is that management generally does not want to penalize activities that happen to be geographically remote from the computer center and so incur higher telecommunications costs. Such penalties can be prevented either by central management assuming the communications costs, or by prorating them as overhead on the other hardware costs; in either case they will not then appear specifically in the cost functions of activities. Should it be decided that activities be charged directly for communications costs, all that is required is the addition of the cost term p_{XE}, or q_{XE}, depending on whether communications are charged at market rates or by transfer prices. Throughout this chapter, communications are included in the computer center's production functions, where they must be considered, but are ignored in production functions of other activities. These other activities do not require communications to perform their tasks—its use is imposed on them by location decisions made elsewhere—and the cost structure is designed to neutralize their effect. Note, however, that, if the computer center manager is charged with the communications costs, this presents him with the problem of optimally locating, and possibly distributing, computing resources. This issue will be addressed when the issue of centralization versus decentralization is discussed.

The technology and tasks involved in producing a software product are embodied in a production function. The quantity of computer services (C_S, M_S, Y_S) and labor (L_s) used in the development of each product will be denoted by using an additional subscript. The letter a will denote applications products and the letter b, systems products. There will be a total of A application products developed and a total of B system products. The software development tools denoted N_s can be used by anyone and there is a total of S of them. This multiple use is possible, since use by one person does not physically preclude simultaneous use by someone else. The tools can be thought of as being resident in the computer system. Hence the production functions are

$$N_a = f^{Na}(C_{Sa}, M_{Sa}, Y_{Sa}, L_{sa}, N_s),$$
$$N_b = f^{Nb}(C_{Sb}, M_{Sb}, Y_{Sb}, L_{sb}, N_s),$$
$$a = 1 \cdots A; \quad b = 1 \cdots B; \quad s = 1 \cdots S. \tag{5.2}$$

Software production is a time-consuming asset-creation process. Hence there must also be an estimating relationship for production time. A detailed analysis is given in Chapter 7, but readers should note intuitively that, as the rate at which resources are employed in any one period is increased, the length of time it takes to develop the product decreases, subject to some law of decreasing marginal productivity for each resource in the reduction of production time. If T_{Da} denotes the delivery date of product a, and T_{Ba} the project start date, then for both types of products the production times are

$$T_{Da} - T_{Ba} = f_a^T(N_a, C_{Sa}, M_{Sa}, Y_{Sa}, L_{sa}, N_s),$$
$$T_{Db} - T_{Bb} = f_b^T(N_b, C_{Sb}, M_{Sb}, Y_{Sb}, L_{sb}, N_s),$$
$$a = 1 \cdots A; \quad b = 1 \cdots B; \quad s = 1 \cdots S. \tag{5.3}$$

Notice that the sizes of the products (N_a and N_b) slipped into these equations. Intuitively, the larger the software product the more time it takes to develop it. As N_a or N_b increases, so does the production period; it decreases as the other variables increase, subject to the usual decreasing marginal productivity considerations. Software maintenance is product-specific and requires an estimate of the maintenance production capacity and the quantity of maintenance needed. The latter can be modeled as simply a fraction of the lines of source instructions needing "repair." This fraction is Z_{at} ($a = 1 \cdots A$; $t = 0 \cdots T$) and Z_{bt} ($b = 1 \cdots B$; $t = 0 \cdots T$) for applications and systems software, respectively. The maintenance production capacity is embodied in a familiar production function in which the subscript m denotes maintenance.

$$N_{am} = f^{Nam}(C_{Sam}, M_{Sam}, Y_{Sam}, L_{sam}, N_s),$$
$$N_{bm} = f^{Nbm}(C_{Sbm}, M_{Sbm}, Y_{Sbm}, L_{sbm}, N_s),$$
$$a = 1 \cdots A; \quad b = 1 \cdots B; \quad s = 1 \cdots S. \tag{5.4}$$

5.3 Planning, Coordinating, and Control Structure

Overall then, the software activity manager is presumed to know these technological relationships. Central management's system coordination responsibility requires that it inform the software manager what products to deliver (denoted $\bar{N}_a$, $a = 1 \cdots A$ and $\bar{N}_b$, $b = 1 \cdots B$) and also when they must be delivered (denoted $\bar{T}_{Da}$, $a = 1 \cdots A$ and $\bar{T}_{Ba}$, $b = 1 \cdots B$), as well as the transfer prices (q_{CS}, q_{MS}, q_{YS}). With information about technology from within the software activity, about transfer prices, what to produce and by when from central management, and about market prices from direct observation, the decision problem of the software manager can be formalized. This is Exercise 5.1.

EXERCISE 5.1 The Software Manager's Decision Problem

State the software manager's decision problem in words and symbols.

Central management, in its turn, needs some administrative data from the software activity in order to coordinate and control the system. First, the software manager must provide central management with its demand for computer services (denoted C_S, M_S, Y_S). These data are the natural result of choosing the least-cost input mix. In addition, the requirement for system coordination suggests that knowledge of the marginal cost and delivery date of each product would be most helpful. From these marginal costs, central management can develop a sense of the incremental costs of software specifications and delivery times, which can ultimately be weighed against the marginal values of specifications or delivery speedup or slowdown. Thus the software manager provides the present life-cycle marginal cost of each product and also the present life-cycle marginal cost of its delivery date, denoted PMRGCOST(N_a), PMRGCOST(T_{Da}), $a = 1 \cdots A$; PMRGCOST(N_b), PMRGCOST(T_{Db}), $b = 1 \cdots B$). As this economic/financial information is so important to system coordination, it is also the basis for evaluating the software manager's performance. Given the transfer prices, product specifications, and delivery times, the lower these present life-cycle marginal costs, the better the management performance. Before discussing the computer center, note that the submission of jobs to the computer center for product development was not included in the discussion. It was not made part of the coordination and control structure because the computer services (C_S, M_S, Y_S) and their transfer prices were included in this structure. Motivating the software manager to choose the least-cost mix of resources means that the stream of jobs submitted is already controlled by the internal pricing mechanism. To add a direct control on job submissions would significantly change the software manager's decision problem and in effect reduce the concern for software cost control.

5.3.2 The Computer Center

The computer facility is designated a profit center. As such, it buys resources (computer hardware, operations labor, and applications and systems software) and produces information services (user-specific and universal) and computer services for use by the users and the software activity. The job input shown in Figure 5.1 is not considered, since, as described in the discussion on the software activity, it is controlled by other means. Physically, however, it is still present.

The technology and tasks can again be represented as a production function. Table 5.2 displays the symbols for each type of resource and each type of output. The production function that relates these resources and products is written:

$$f^H(L_o, H_c, H_m, H_y, H_x, N_a, N_b; I_k, I_v, C_E, M_E, Y_E) = 0,$$
$$a = 1 \cdots A; \quad b = 1 \cdots B; \quad k = 1 \cdots K; \quad v = 1 \cdots V. \quad (5.5)$$

This production relationship will be further refined in Chapter 6. For now it should be thought of as having decreasing marginal physical productivities and decreasing returns to scale.

The profit over the designated planning period $(0, T)$ is computed in the same manner as in Chapters 3 and 4. The only significant difference here is the need to account for the acquisition cost of hardware, the maintenance

Table 5.2 Computer Center Resources and Products

Resources	
applications software	$N_a; a = 1 \cdots A$
systems software	$N_b; b = 1 \cdots B$
operations labor	L_o
CPU hardware	H_c
memory hardware	H_m
peripheral hardware	H_y
telecommunications hardware	H_x
Products	
user-specific information services	$I_k; k = 1 \cdots k$
universal information services	$I_v; v = 1 \cdots V$
external computer services	
CPU time	C_E
memory services	M_E
input/output services	Y_E

5.3 Planning, Coordinating, and Control Structure

cost of hardware, and last, but not least, the salvage value of hardware. To reduce the complexity of the analysis, assume that there is a market for both new and used hardware and that the computer center manager can purchase and sell hardware in that market at any time. The market price will be denoted as p_{jt} ($j = c, m, y, x$) for the specific type of hardware (CPU, memory, peripherals, telecommunications) at the date t of the acquisition or salvage. Until Chapter 6, assume that all hardware is acquired at time zero and sold or salvaged at time T. The net capital cost per unit of hardware in present value terms is

$$p_{jo} - \frac{p_{jT}}{(1+r)^T}, \quad j = c, m, y, x. \tag{5.6}$$

The maintenance cost per unit of hardware is denoted as p_{mj} ($j = c, m, y, x$). The next exercise provides the opportunity to state the center's profit function.

EXERCISE 5.2 The Computer Center's Profit Function

State the computer center's profit function, using the following symbols in addition to those already stated:

transfer prices of computer services:	q_{CE}, q_{ME}, q_{YE}
transfer prices of user-specific information services:	$q_{Ik}; k = 1 \cdots K$
transfer prices of universal information services:	$q_{Iv}; v = 1 \cdots V$
market price of operations labor:	p_o
transfer price of applications software:	$q_{Na}; a = 1 \cdots A$
transfer price of systems software:	$q_{Nb}; b = 1 \cdots B$.

With this background, it is possible to state the center's decision problem.

EXERCISE 5.3 The Computer Center's Decision Problem

State in words and symbols the computer center's decision problem.

Central management needs information to coordinate this system. Specifically, it needs the quantities of each resource required and of each product produced. In addition, it needs an economic life-cycle profit and loss statement, which is the center's profit function, using the profit-maximizing quantities of resources and products. This profit statement is also the economic and financial basis for evaluating the performance of the computer center manager. Striving for profit maximization is an integral part of conducting and controlling the information system, so the manager is rewarded for earning larger profits, given the transfer and market prices and the state of technology.

5.3.3 The Users

Managers of the functional areas in the organization, for example, marketing and manufacturing, are users of information outside the administrative flow that has been discussed. These users gather information from three sources: user-specific information services, universal information services, and user-developed and -maintained application programs. The first of these sources, user-specific information services, provides the routine batch reports and interactive queries that are tailored to a specific user. The second source generates organizationwide information, for example, general financial health. Last, but not least, programs can be developed and employed by users or users' staffs to generate information that is not organizationally routine. Each user evaluates this information by using a subjective preference—indifference relationship. There are subjective tradeoffs and substitutions among specific types of information in the user's decision process. In short, the user has a utility function for the various types of information. Including the time preference aspect, it is denoted as

$$\tilde{U}_u = \sum_{t=0}^{T} \frac{f^u(I_k, I_v, I_o)}{(1 + r_u)^t},$$

$$k = 1 \cdots K; u = 1 \cdots U; v = 1 \cdots V; o = 1 \cdots O. \tag{5.7}$$

In this utility function k, v, and o identify specific, universal, and user-developed information service, respectively, I_k denotes the amount of user-specific information services, I_v denotes the universal information service level, and I_o denotes the user-developed information services. The symbol r_u is the user's personal rate of time discount. There is one such utility function for each user, hence the subscript u on U and r and the superscript u for the functional form f.

The technology and tasks associated with the users' development and maintenance of special programs is represented by a production function. The resources are external computer services (C_E, M_E, Y_E) and the user-provided labor (L_u) used in development and maintenance. The product is an amount I_o of information of type o. The production function is

$$I_o = f^{I_o}(C_{Eo}, M_{Eo}, Y_{Eo}, L_u), \tag{5.8}$$

where the subscript E_o denotes the amount of external hardware service used in producing user-developed product o.

5.3 Planning, Coordinating, and Control Structure

Administratively, users are coordinated and controlled as elements of the system via their demand for computer and information services. The mechanism is user information budgets and appropriate transfer prices. The budgets are for the life cycle, each placing an upper bound on the life-cycle expenditures for a specific user. They will be denoted as B_{Iu}. The expenditures are obtained by summing up the expenditures on user-specific information services, computer capacity, and labor. Universal, organizationwide information is supplied free of charge by central management. Using the previous transfer price symbols and p_{Lu} as the market price of user information-processing labor L_u, the life-cycle expenditure and the budget constraint for each user u is

$$\sum_{t=0}^{T} \frac{\sum_{o=1}^{O}(q_{CE}C_{Eo} + q_{ME}M_{Eo} + q_{YE}Y_{Eo} + p_{Lu}L_u) + \sum_{k=1}^{K} q_k I_k}{(1+r)^t} \leqq B_{Iu}. \quad (5.9)$$

The users' decision problem is to maximize utility constrained by the information generation technology available to them and by their information budgets. The next exercise asks for a formal statement of this problem.

EXERCISE 5.4 The User's Decision Problem

State a user's formal decision problem.

The users' choices result in individual demand functions for each type of information service, for each measure of computer service, and for user labor. Each user's level of demand, expressed in the demand function, is determined by the transfer and market prices, the user's information budget and the user's preferences. Symbolically,

$$I_{ku} = f^{Iku}(q_{Ik}, q_{CE}, q_{ME}, q_{YE}, p_{Lu}, r_u, B_{Iu}),$$
$$C_u = C_{ku} + C_{ou} = f^{Cu}(q_{Ik}, q_{CE}, q_{ME}, q_{YE}, p_{Lu}, r_u, B_{Iu}),$$
$$M_u = M_{ku} + M_{ou} = f^{Mu}(q_{Ik}, q_{CE}, q_{ME}, q_{YE}, p_{Lu}, r_u, B_{Iu}),$$
$$Y_u = Y_{ku} + Y_{ou} = f^{Yu}(q_{Ik}, q_{CE}, q_{ME}, q_{YE}, p_{Lu}, r_u, B_{Iu}),$$
$$L_u = L_{ku} + L_{ou} = f^{Lu}(q_{Ik}, q_{CE}, q_{ME}, q_{YE}, p_{Lu}, r_u, B_{Iu}),$$
$$k = 1 \cdots K; \quad u = 1 \cdots U. \quad (5.10)$$

The general information services, computer capacity, and information-processing labor are superior goods, that is, larger budgets yield larger demands. Furthermore, an increase in the price of a service, of computer capacity, or of labor, is expected to decrease the demand for that service or resource.

The coordination and control of the information system requires central management to provide each user with the transfer prices $[q_{Ik}(k = 1 \cdots k)$,

q_{CE}, q_{ME}, q_{YE}] and his budget (B_{Iu}). The marketplace provides the price of labor (p_{Lu}). The user in turn must provide central management with the quantities of services and capacity demanded. Notice that there can be a different budget for each user, which implies that central management distributes wealth differentially among the users as part of coordinating and controlling the information system.

5.3.4 The System Manager

The system manager has organizational responsibility for managing the information system. These system management responsibilities are part of the role here called "central management" to indicate the level of authority normally needed to manage an information system, including users and information-producing resources. Hierarchically, the software development and maintenance activity and the computer center report to the information system manager. The users, however, are line managers elsewhere in the organization and, as line managers, do not report to the system manager. Nevertheless, the system manager plans, controls, and coordinates the information system by significantly impacting the users' decisions. The process of planning, coordinating, and controlling the information system results in users' information budgets and transfer prices for computer and information services. Although it is not discussed in this book, note the broader organizational design issue that arises from users' information being managed in the organization separately from their line responsibilities.

For the system manager to decide what the correct actions are on budgets, prices, and software specifications, there must be (1) an appropriate criterion and (2) a way to understand the current status of the information system. We shall defer discussion of the second of these responsibilities because the details are more easily approached after the managerial planning, coordinating, and central data flows have been described in the information system context.

The criterion for system management decisions involves the concept of central management's preference-indifference relation for the organization's effectiveness, that is, central management's utility function for its assessment of organizational effectiveness. Ideally, such a utility function would ordinally rank the preferences of the users so that information systems behavior would be derived from line management judgments. But in the organization constructed here, and not at all uncommonly in real organizations, this is not structurally possible. So the information system manager seeks instead to balance the information system and to provide the users with information they perceive to be of maximum value.

Central management prefers that the information system be balanced (balance will be discussed momentarily). When the information system is not in balance, central management judges the system to be less desirable, and, correspondingly, the utility value of an unbalanced state is lower. In a complicated multivariable information system there may be, and probably are, many system equilibria. The judgment of organizational effectiveness by central management includes the concept of ranking alternative system equilibria according to their organizational effectiveness.

The notion of balance is that every one of the many physical flows within the information system should have demand for an item equal to its supply. The system manager must measure the imbalance of every physical flow as part of the system-equilibrating process. But the physical flows are related to specific users, for example, user-specific information services. In considering the physical flows, the system manager naturally, albeit indirectly, weighs the relative importance of the users themselves to the organization's overall effectiveness. The system manager's decision problem will be further analyzed after the discussion of the data flows between organizational units.

As we noted earlier, management must be concerned with the integration of the information system into the organization. That integration is accomplished, at least in part, by establishing a life-cycle budget for the information system as a whole. This budget is denoted as B_{IS}. Actual transaction expenditures, as distinct from internal charges, may not exceed this budget over the life cycle. Exercise 5.5 asks for a statement of this information system budget constraint.

EXERCISE 5.5 The Information System Budget Constraint

Using B_{IS} as the symbol for the present life-cycle budget level, state in words and symbols the complete information system budget constraint. Assume that all hardware is acquired at time $t = 0$ and is discarded at the end of the planning horizon, $t = T$.

5.4 The Information System Planning, Coordinating, and Control Data Flows

From the discussion of each of the departments and of the system manager, a table of information flows for administrative purposes can be created, as Table 5.3 exemplifies for the routine activity in the information system. Large quantities of information are passed from one unit to another in order to provide each decision maker the data that will (1) move the information system toward a balanced equilibrium, and (2) provide an efficient and effective supply of information to users. The next section contains the material on the behavior of the iterative process of information exchange and decision making.

Table 5.3 Administrative Data Flows

From	To	Data transmitted	
central management (system manager)	typical user	budget	B_{Iu}
		cost of capital	r
		transfer prices for	
		information services	I_k
		computer services	q_{CE}, q_{ME}, q_{YE}
	computer center	transfer prices for	
		specific information	$q_{Ik}: k = 1 \cdots k$
		universal information	$q_{Iv}: v = 1 \cdots V$
		computer services	q_{CE}, q_{ME}, q_{YE}
		rental for	
		applications software	$q_{Na}: a = 1 \cdots A$
		systems software	$q_{Nb}: b = 1 \cdots B$
		cost of capital	r
	software activity	transfer prices for	
		computer services	q_{CE}, q_{ME}, q_{YE}
		cost of capital	r
		requirements and specifications for	
		applications software	$N_a: a = 1 \cdots A$
		systems software	$N_b: b = 1 \cdots B$
		delivery dates for	
		applications software	$T_{Da}: a = 1 \cdots A$
		systems software	$T_{Db}: b = 1 \cdots B$
markets	users	price of labor	p_{Lu}
	computer center	prices of hardware	$p_{jt}: j = c, m, y, x$ $t = 0 \cdots T$
		price of operator labor	p_{Lo}
	software activity	price of analyst labor	p_{Ls}
		price of software tools	$P_{Ns}: s = 1 \cdots S$
typical user	central management	computer capacity required	C_{Eu}, M_{Eu}, Y_{Eu}
		total cost of labor	$p_{Lu} L_u$
computer center		quantities supplied of	
		computer services	C_E, M_E, Y_E
		specific information	$I_k: k = 1 \cdots K$
		universal information	$I_v: v = 1 \cdots V$
		quantities to rent of	
		applications software	$N_a: a = 1 \cdots A$
		systems software	$N_b: b = 1 \cdots B$
		profit and loss statement	

5.5 Information System Behavior

Table 5.3 (*Continued*)

From	To	Data transmitted	
software activity	Central management (cont.)	computer services demanded	C_s, M_s, Y_s
		present life-cycle marginal cost of applications software	PMRGCOST $(N_a: a = 1 \cdots A)$
		systems software	PMRGCOST $(N_b: b = 1 \cdots B)$
users	markets	quantity of labor	L_u
computer center		quantity of operator labor	L_o
		quantity of hardware	H_c, H_m, H_y, H_x
software activity		quantity of analyst labor	L_s
		quantity of software tools	$N_s: s = 1 \cdots S$

5.5 Information System Behavior

Before we discuss the behavior of the system, the decision problem of central management, as the system manager, will be considered. As stated earlier, the criterion used by central management reflects its assessment of the effectiveness of the information system for the organization as a whole. By reason of the organization's structure, this subjective assessment is based on the quantities of user-specific information services $(I_k; k = 1 \cdots K)$, universal information services $(I_v; v = 1 \cdots V)$, and information-generating computer services $(C_{Eu}, M_{Eu}, Y_{Eu}; u = 1 \cdots U)$ supplied to the users. As in the case of users, there is also a time preference component in central management decision making. The utility function for central management, including the subjective trade-offs among information services and computer service variables, over time is written as

$$\tilde{U}_{cm} = f^{\tilde{U}cm}(I_k, I_v, C_E, M_E, Y_E) \qquad k = 1 \cdots k, v = 1 \cdots V. \qquad (5.11)$$

Now, in addition to the criterion and budget constraint, central management's decision problem formulation must also include a (possibly subjective) model of how information system resources such as computer hardware are related to information and computer services supplied to users. That is, central management needs a sense of the information system production function. In the familiar block diagram form, this is shown in Figure 5.4.

Suppose the production function for the information system *as seen by central management* is denoted as

$$F^{cm}(I_k, I_v, C_E, M_E, Y_E; H_j, L_o, L_s, L_u, N_s) = 0, \qquad j = c, m, y, x. \qquad (5.12)$$

The usual decreasing marginal physical productivities and decreasing physical returns to scale are applicable. Note the importance of this production model. Without some sense of how the information system operates, central

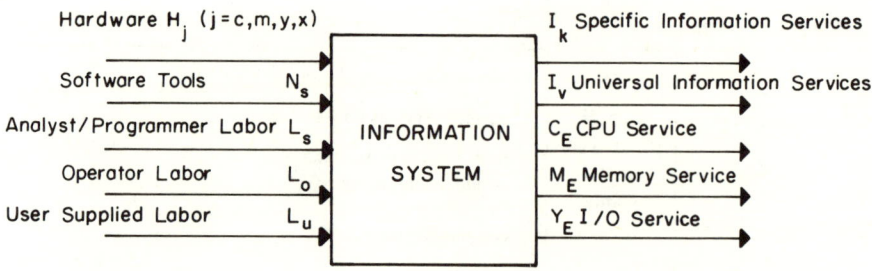

Figure 5.4 The information system production schematic.

management cannot solve its decision problem. While there are alternative designs for information systems that eliminate the need for central management to have such a sense, they are purely price-based and seem less useful in understanding information system behavior. This is so because an information system provides some universal services (I_v) used by all and is not closed, since users are not subordinate to the information system central manager.

Overall then, central management's decision problem is

$$\max f^{\tilde{U}\text{cm}}(I_k, I_v, C_E, M_E, Y_E), \quad k = 1 \cdots K,$$
by choice of $I_k, I_v, C_E, M_E, Y_E,$
constrained by

$$\sum_{t=0}^{T} \left[\sum_{u=1}^{U} \frac{p_{Lu}L_u}{(1+r)^t} + \frac{p_{Lo}L_o + p_{Ls}L_s + \sum_{s=1}^{S} p_{Ns}N_s}{(1+r)^t} \right]$$

$$+ \sum_j \left[\frac{p_{jTB}H_j}{(1+r)^{TB}} - \frac{p_{jTE}H_j}{(1+r)^{TE}} \right] \leq B_{\text{IS}}, \quad j = c, m, y, x;$$

$$F^{\text{cm}}(I_k, I_v, C_E, M_E, Y_E; H_c, H_m, H_y, H_x, L_o, L_s, L_u, N_s) = 0. \quad (5.13)$$

It is possible to analyze this decision problem in detail as we did for earlier problems, but this is not particularly helpful in understanding the equilibrium search procedure used by central management. Nevertheless, this broad picture is useful at the general level. Given the production function and the market prices of inputs, there is a multiple-product cost function for management to consider. If we suppose, as seems likely for information systems, that there are economies of scope, then in the product space (I_k, I_v, C_E, M_E, Y_E) there is a product-transformation curve for the information system budget level, concave to the origin, showing the equal cost tradeoffs of the products. The utility-maximizing point on the product-transformation curve is that at which management's indifference curve is a tangent. This is central management's ideal system equilibrium for the given budget level. Figure 5.5 shows a general picture of this for the two-product case.

5.5 Information System Behavior

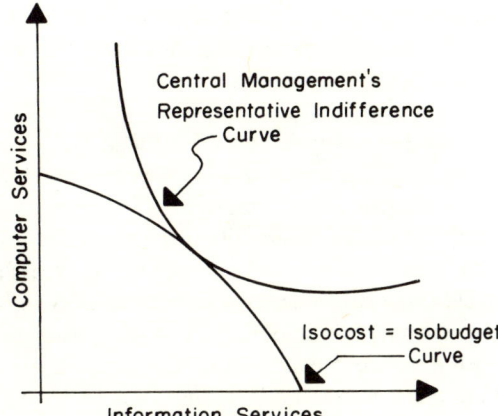

Figure 5.5 Central management's decision problem.

Once central management knows the best system equilibrium, it can set in motion a dynamic procedure to seek this equilibrium point. The procedure is stated in three steps, the first of them initializing the process. This procedure can be repeated as necessary until system equilibrium is reached. So that the goal is clear, an information system equilibrium is characterized by the following:

1. Demand equal to supply for every physical flow; this is achieved directly for controlled flows, and indirectly for the others, for example, jobs.
2. The information system present life-cycle budget is not exceeded.

If the outcome of the two-step procedure repeated after initialization is an equilibrium that is not the one chosen by central management, further adjustments are possible along the isocost (equal-budget) line exhibited in Figure 5.5. It is also possible that central management might not initially have a correct sense of the aggregate information system production function. Central management could then learn from its experience. But such ideas and adjustments, however intriguing, are beyond the scope of this book. The step-by-step procedure is as follows.

Initializing Step. The first part of the procedure is the initializing step, during which central management chooses a set of transfer prices and user budgets and provides them to the software activities manager, the computer center manager, and the users, as appropriate (see Table 5.2). It is never necessary to repeat this step in its entirety, since, in an ongoing organization, adjustments can be made from the current status of the system.

Step 1. In step 1, the software activity manager, the computer center manager and each user solve their respective decision problems as discussed earlier in the chapter. Each provides central management with his or her respective demand for quantities of physical resources or products, the marginal cost of software, and the computer center profit and loss statement (see Table 5.3).

Step 2. In step 2, central management adjusts the transfer prices and user budgets in a manner that moves the information system toward equilibrium. First, central management must determine the status of the information system. For each physical item the total demand and supply are computed. Total demand minus total supply is the excess demand. The system present life-cycle expenditure level is also compared with the budget to obtain the level of budget surplus or deficit. Assuming that there is at least one physical flow with a nonzero excess demand or there is a budget surplus or deficit, central management must adjust the transfer prices and users' budgets. These adjustments will be discussed in turn.

For each transfer price, if the total demand exceeds the supply, then the transfer price should be raised; if demand equals supply, no change should be made, and if supply exceeds demand the transfer price should be lowered. Notice that, on the demand side, all the analyses of individual user-managers, software activity management, and computer center management assume that raising (lowering) the price lowers (raises) the quantity demanded. Thus, the demand adjusts in an equilibrating way to these central management decisions. On the supply side, the computer center manager is also responsive. If an output price is raised, the profit-maximizing response is to produce more, *ceteris paribus*. Thus, the price adjustments tend to move the information system toward an equilibrium. Of course, the interaction of many prices changing simultaneously is not easy to explain, but if all the products are good substitutes, then the system will ultimately respond by moving toward equilibrium. In the case of software services, the transfer prices are set to the respective marginal costs. This assures that information system efficiency will hold at equilibrium.

The user budgets are adjusted in two circumstances: (1) If the total demand for information and computer services exceeds the supply, then the way to size the system down is to reduce all users' budgets until only relative adjustments are needed among the information and computer services; when present life-cycle expenditures on the information system exceed the budget, reducing user budgets will size the system back within total budget. (2) Conversely, insufficient demand in general or insufficient expenditures relative to the budget should lead to user budget increases. Thus, central management adjusts the prices and user budgets and provides these new prices and budgets to all.

Repetition of Steps 1 and 2. We now are at the point where repeated application of steps 1 and 2 will eventually lead the information system to an

5.5 Information System Behavior

equilibrium that is judged organizationally effective. So step 1 and step 2 are repeated until equilibrium is achieved.

Now consider a system in equilibrium. In addition to knowing that the demand for, and supply of, each item are balanced, and that information systems expenditures match the budget, the following features are of interest. First, the software activity manager will be implementing a least-cost production plan, producing software that exactly matches need. Next, the computer center manager will have a profit-maximizing production plan in operation and, allowing for central management use of a nongaming dialogue with the computer center manager, the center will also be operating at the bottom of the U-shaped average cost curve, with zero economic profit. This implies a range of output with increasing returns to scale and a range with decreasing returns to scale. The profit-maximizing production plan exhibits constant returns to scale. Finally, the users have maximized their utility, and are as well off as they can be, given the prices and their budgets. Thus, overall, without any changes in prices, user budgets, or technology, not only is the system in equilibrium, but no decision maker has any incentive to change from that equilibrium. The management process leads to an "ideal" state.

Looking at the marginal conditions and treating technical details casually, notice the outcome at equilibrium. Starting with the users and working backward through the information system flow diagram, the existence of a service, at equilibrium, implies that its users subjectively judge its marginal value at least equal to its marginal cost. Now the marginal cost to the users is the transfer price, which in turn is the marginal revenue to the computer center. Within the center, the marginal revenue equals the marginal cost of producing the service, which is determined by the market prices of the resources employed. So overall, and for all services, the prices are a device to ensure that each software manager, computer center manager, and user properly assesses, *at the margin*, the economic feasibility of demanding or supplying a service or product. Prices permit decentralized decisions in a way that puts all the separate marginal decision rules in equilibrium. If there were only one dictatorial decision maker, the same decision rule would result, that is, the

---

EXERCISE 5.6 Information System Systemic Behavior

Suppose the software manager discovers a free training program for system-analysts programmers. The program is guaranteed to increase the marginal physical productivity of these employees. Suppose further that the software manager gladly adopts this idea, as it will lower cost. What is the systemic behavior of the information system as a result of this action by the software manager? Given your answer to this question, what would you suggest that central management do?

decentralized procedure acts as if the decisions were made by central management. Exercise 5.6 is designed to provide a sense of this systemic behavior.

5.6 The Capital Budgeting System for Nonroutine Activities

Before we discuss the nonroutine part of the information system, notice how the acquisition of computer system hardware flows naturally from the operation of the routine information system management process. When the information system is moving toward equilibrium, the act of profit-maximizing by the computer center manager produces a demand for hardware (and other resources) derived from the demand for information and computer services; the timing of hardware acquisition flows naturally from demands placed on the profit-maximizing computer center. The reporting of the computer center profit and loss statement to central management, and then the comparison of present life-cycle information system expenditure (including hardware acquisition costs) to the budget, ensures that the hardware acquired is in balance with all the other activities, that is, it is part of the information system equilibrium. It would be desirable, when designing and operating the information system management process, if the nonroutine software product specification process could be similarly routinized and incorporated in the routine information system management process.

The first step in routinizing is to identify the source of nonroutineness in software product specification. The essence of the lack of routine is that software product specification is part of the information system activity that generates new services for users. The software specification process leads to the design and introduction of new information services or products.

In order to design and introduce a new software product it is necessary (1) to describe the information product so that the users can understand and approve its use, (2) to specify the changes needed in software and hardware, thereby making it possible to produce the product routinely, and (3) to organize and manage the new information product design and introduction process. The first decision—deciding what product to routinely produce—gives rise to the most uncertainty. This will be discussed first, but in a sequence that satisfies the goal of the third point.

In order to decide what products to produce, there must be some process for identifying new product ideas. In a competitive market this happens automatically. In an administrative structure with a single, monopolistic information system, this process is not automatic. Fortunately, an innovative process is not impossible within the administrative structure. First, note that in the information system studied here, users are free to choose, to design, to develop, and to use software programs created entirely by themselves. That is, there is no requirement that the central authority approve of every information product.

5.6 The Capital Budgeting System

Suppose that the system analysis activity is designated as a part of central management's staff. The systems analysts are required to study and recommend new information products to central management. They are in the business of suggesting user decision support products. One source of new information product ideas is user-generated products already in existence. If these products can be used by more than one user, that is, they are widely usable as standard products, then possibly there are cost savings to be had by routine production in the computer center and widespread distribution. The now traditional system analysis techniques of interviews, data flow diagrams and so on, may also be used to generate ideas for products not currently in use by anyone. The outcome of this system analysis effort must be well-specified information products—what information is provided, in what form, how often, what data sources are needed to generate the information, and the associated algorithms for converting data into information. For example, accounting transaction data are converted into quarterly profit and loss statements by the traditional algorithms of accepted accounting procedure.

The definition of information products must be accompanied by analyses of the economic feasibility of the products, given current prices and budgets. Central management then decides whether to proceed to the next step of the information product design and introduction process. This decision is based on the proposed product description and on economic analysis. If it makes economic sense to proceed, the computer center manager is authorized to specify and analyze the needed software and hardware changes.

Assume that such a positive decision is made. The computer center manager's first step is to do the necessary technical analysis; assume for the moment that the resources consumed in this analysis are zero, or at least negligible. The analysis involves applying the concept of marginal physical input requirements to the information product specification in order to calculate the additional hardware and software needed. Suppose this is done and it is found that additional hardware and software are required. The additional hardware and software must be specified in detailed engineering terms. If no additional resources are required, the nonroutine can immediately be reduced to the routine by central management's authorizing the production and subsequent use of the product. In this case the routine price-budget system will determine its economic feasibility.

If additional resources are required, the computer center manager can provide central management with a study of the profitability of the information product or service, given various assumptions about the service transfer price and the center's resource prices. Central management again has to decide whether to continue the development of the information product. If the business sense of central management is that it is not a good product, that is, its product incremental costs will exceed the users' marginal valuation of the product at all reasonable levels of output, then the product idea should be dropped. But suppose it is not, that is, there are at least some levels of output where product incremental costs and probable transfer prices suggest a profitable operation. Central management then authorizes the software manager to study the software specifications generated by the computer center. Organizationally, it would make sense here for the information system to allow the computer center to buy the software specification service from the software activity. This would permit the clustering of all software tasks in the software activity. In this description of the nonroutine process for creating a new product, this particular interaction will not be considered.

The software manager's analysis is aimed at estimating the marginal development and maintenance costs of the software specified. In order to do this, there must be a technical analysis, a preliminary software product design must be made, and a cost estimate must be prepared. The cost estimate would most likely conform to the current industry practice of basing the estimate on the probable size of the program, in KDSI, derived from the technical analysis. This marginal cost estimate is then provided to central management.

Finally, central management has all the pieces of data needed for making a decision: estimates of demand given prices, computer center product incremental costs at various outputs and levels of resource prices, and the software center estimate of the marginal cost of the software at various price levels of software activity resources. Central management must now put all the data together and, at least subjectively, estimate the probability distribution for the information product marginal cost in comparison to its marginal value. Again, a go–no-go decision must be made. "No-go" means that the product is dropped. If it is "go," then the software product and the information service become part of the routine system and are handled as previously described. Notice that, even then, the optimal outcome for the information system may still be not to produce the information service after it has been developed—all the analysis and wisdom in the world does not guarantee the perfect prediction of future system behavior. Notice also that old products can also be dropped as noneconomic at the current information system equilibrium. It may still be worthwhile to continue to consider dormant products in the routine management process, for at other equilibria they may be economically feasible again.

The above discussion assumed that the innovation system for a new information product was costless to operate. This is clearly not the case in reality. So central management must allocate part of the information system life-cycle budget to product innovation. Thus the number B_{IS} used in the above discussion is somewhat smaller than the total information system life-cycle budget. The difference is the operating cost of the innovation system for new information products. This operating cost includes all expenses of the technical and cost analyses, user interaction, and central management personnel involved. The dichotomy of innovation versus routine products is clearly a very important decision for central management. It can be incorporated into the original information system equilibrium decision by appropriately adjusting the original statement of the central management decision problem. This is the next exercise.

EXERCISE 5.7 The Central Management Routine and Nonroutine Decision Problems

State in words and symbols central management's routine and nonroutine decision problems.
Hint: It is a modification of the central management system equilibrium decision problem.

Finally, it must be noted that many alternative organization and management structures are possible for the nonroutine new information product decision, as is true also for the routine decisions. The ultimate choice is the one that plans, coordinates, and controls the system at least cost. The next exercise asks for a proposed alternative scheme for the nonroutine new information product decision system.

EXERCISE 5.8 An Alternative New Information Product Process

Design an alternative way to manage the creation of new information products. Be sure to explicitly use the organizational ideas of section 5.3.

5.7 Summary: The Generalized Information System Design Problem

The design of an information system was discussed in this chapter. It is a complex problem, too complex in fact for neat mathematical solution, but understanding it provides a vision of the information system to guide managerial judgment. In general, the management of the overall organization must choose the organizational structure, the associated incentive, reward and penalty structure and the information system management process so as to maximize organizational effectiveness. The constraints on the decision problem are the existing and predicted technology, the physical flows, and the budget for the information system as a whole. A step-by-step approach would be as follows:

1. State the physical technology flow schema.
2. State the desired system behavior, consisting of
    a. the nature of the system equilibrium;
    b. the time constraints on reaching equilibrium.

3. Design an organizational structure with the associated incentive-reward-penalty structure.
4. Design an information system management process.
5. Study the system's behavior by actually operating the information system if necessary, in order to ascertain the following:
    a. Does the system seek an equilibrium?
    b. How fast does the system seek an equilibrium?
    c. What are the characteristics of the equilibrium?
6. Compare actual system behavior with the desired system behavior and the cost with the budget.
7. Loop back through steps 3 to 6 as necessary in order to achieve the desired result, with the goal of seeking the least-cost system that is technically, physically, and financially feasible.

References

Perrow, Charles. (1970) *Organizational Analysis: A Sociological View.* Belmont, CA: Wadsworth.

Simon, Herbert. (1977) *The New Science of Management Decision* (revised edition). Englewood Cliffs, NJ: Prentice-Hall.

Thompson, James D. (1967) *Organization in Action.* New York: McGraw-Hill.

Chapter 6
The Computer Center

6.1 The Computer Center as an Information Resource

The function of the computer center as an information resource is to provide the organization with a central data-processing capability. To perform this role the computer center manager draws upon the software development and maintenance activity for both applications and systems software, the computer equipment markets for computer system hardware, and the labor market for operations labor. The manager generally provides information services of various types (e.g., reports and online query services from databases maintained by the center) as well as computer services (CPU time, storage, and input/output) to users throughout the organization. This last class of services will be called external computer services to distinguish it from services used internally by the computer center. Table 6.1 displays a list of the resources and products that are the variables in the computer center management problem and the symbols associated with them.

In the formalization of computer center operations exhibited in Figure 6.1, computer capacity is produced by combining operations labor, CPU hardware, and systems software products. When allocated directly to users throughout the organization, this computer capacity is referred to here as external computer services. Alternatively, the capacity can be allocated, wholly or in part, to routine transaction processing and management information systems, labeled in the diagram as production of information services. While the basic distinction is between internal and external use of computer capacity, a secondary distinction is made between specific information services and universal information services. Specific information services are services provided routinely to specific users—for example, inventory reports for the

Table 6.1 Computer Center Resources and Products

Resources	Products
INTRAORGANIZATIONAL	
applications software $(N_a, a = 1 \cdots A)$	specific information services (I_k)
systems software $(N_b, b = 1 \cdots B)$	universal information services (I_v)
EXTRAORGANIZATIONAL	
operations labor (L_o)	external computer services
CPU hardware (H_c)	CPU time (C_E)
memory hardware (H_m)	storage (M_E)
peripheral hardware (H_y)	input/output (Y_E)
telecommunications hardware (H_x)	

production manager or hours worked for the personnel manager. Universal information services provide information products required throughout the organization. Typically, they are mandated by central management: examples are balance sheets, pay scales, and planning parameters.

In a nutshell, the role of the computer center is to use hardware, software, and labor resources in a centralized activity to produce external computer services, universal information, and user-specific information in an efficient manner. This function must be coordinated and controlled by central management so that the computer center is synchronized with the rest of the organization. To accomplish this, central management is assumed to have designated the computer resource as a profit center. This being the case, the computer center manager needs certain data from central management and from the hardware and labor markets in order to perform life-cycle profit calculations.

Central management communicates transfer prices to the computer center manager for each of the internally supplied resources and the center's products. In addition, central management sets the life cycle by designating the date when computer operations will begin (T_B) as well as the date for the end of operations (T_E). The manager of the computer center also monitors the hardware markets and thus keeps informed as to the market prices for equipment acquisition and maintenance. By keeping informed about the labor market as well, the manager has knowledge of wages, salaries, and fringe benefits for operations labor.

If it is to plan, coordinate, and control the total information system in a systemic manner, central management needs, in its turn, certain data from the computer center manager. The information needed includes the quantities of all resources demanded from within the organization and products which can

6.1 The Computer Center as an Information Resource

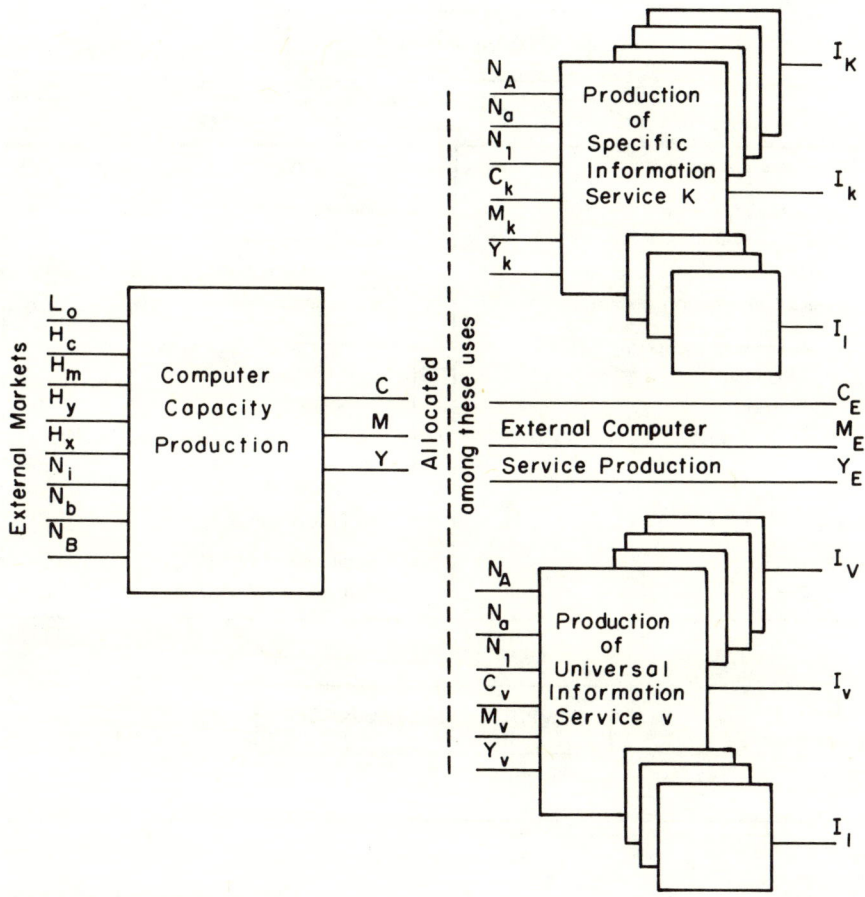

Figure 6.1 Computer center block diagram.

be supplied to the organization over the life cycle. Thus, the computer center manager must provide the quantities of application and system software demanded and the quantities of all computer services, and all universal and specific information services supplied. In addition, central management requires information on the marginal profitability of the current planned beginning and ending dates for the life cycle. Using these and other data, central management can then develop a set of transfer prices and life-cycle dates for the next iteration of the planning process. Figure 6.2 displays this data exchange.

With this model of the physical and technological relationships, the designation of the computer installation as a profit center, and the data exchange between central management and the computer center manager, it follows

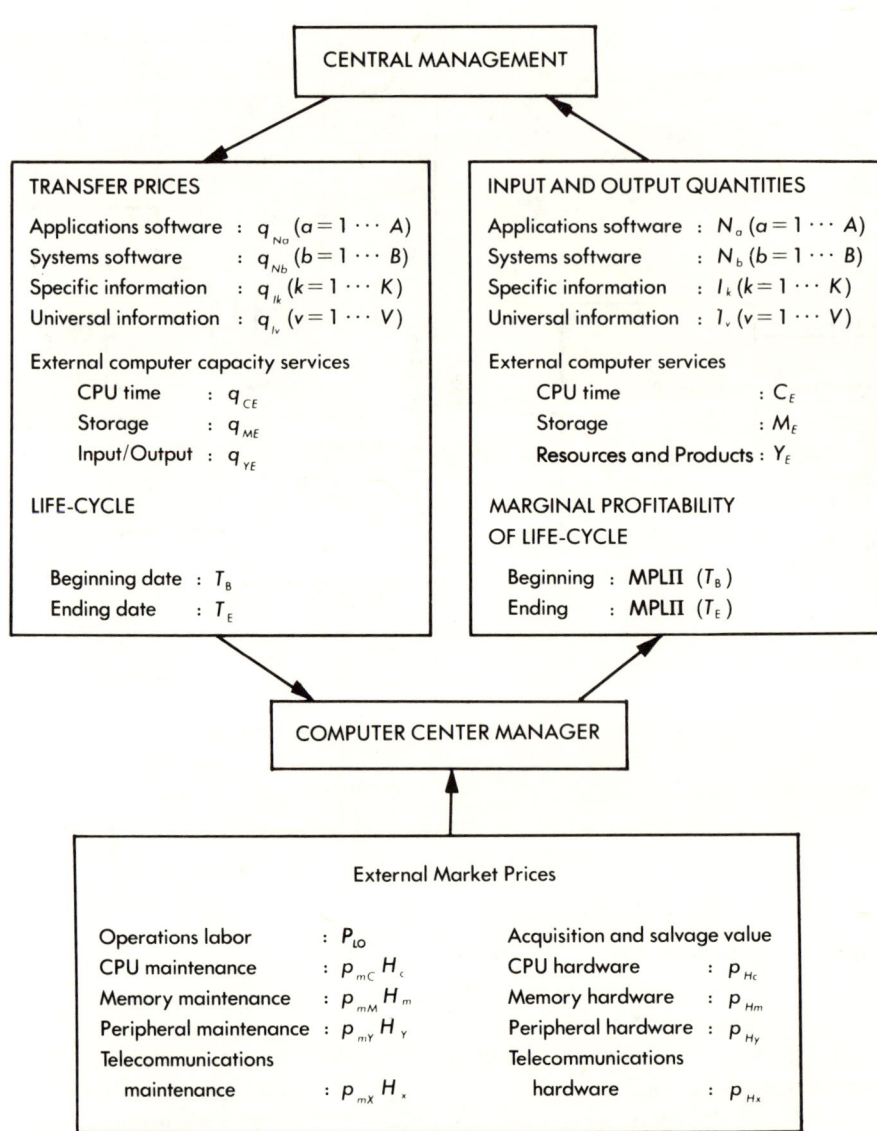

Figure 6.2 Computer center IRM system data flow.

that the computer center manager faces a profit-maximization decision problem. The criterion is maximization of the present value of life-cycle profit. The constraints and the technologies are implicit in the physical flows displayed in Figure 6.1. The decision variables are quantities of each resource to employ and quantities of products to provide. These are the variables listed in Table 6.1 either as extraorganizational resources or as products. The decision analysis begins in the next section with a model of computer center technology.

6.2 The Production Model

In the previous section, the discussion focused on the general flow of resources through the center to produce information products. Figure 6.1 displays a block diagram of that process. The production model here is similar to that in Chapters 4 and 5, but it has several structural features that deviate from the discussion there and are of special interest.

The models of production in Chapters 4 and 5 did not exhibit the two stages seen in Figure 6.1. The first phase of production here is the transformation of labor, hardware, and systems software resources into computer capacity—the ability to provide computational services as measured by CPU time, storage capacity, and input/output rates. The second stage is the transformation of this potential computer capacity into products, that is, computer services and information services, both universal and specific. This two-stage description is an example of the vertical integration of sequential production processes requiring a decision on the allocation of the first-stage product to the multiple production opportunities in the second stage.

Another feature of the structure of production in computer operations is the multiplicity of separate production processes at the second stage. Until now, the production models covered cases of both single and multiple outputs, but did not attempt to specify the way in which the products share resources. In computer operations, an operating system is employed to manage different processes, from initiation as job submissions until completion; management in this case takes the form of a mechanism for allocating computer capacity among the processes. The vertical dotted line in Figure 6.1 represents the operating system's management function. Furthermore, the specific and universal information production processes represent the relationship of computer capacity used by each process to the product provided. It is a representation of the performance of the software that executes the jobs.

A similar interpretation applies to the jobs that are completed using external computer services. The difference is that the user provides all but the computer capacity expended; in this case the computer center manager needs to think about production only in terms of the total quantity of external computer capacity expended, as it is not necessary to know what other resources are involved and the computer center is not responsible for them.

At this point it is appropriate to note that the focus in this discussion is on *planning* computer center operations. Bottlenecks, congestion, and backlogs may also be planned *and chosen* as the most profitable way to conduct operations. It is not necessarily profitable to provide all users with the perfect service they would like to have.

6.2.1 Stage 1 of the Production Model

The first stage of production is modeled as a relationship among the multiple resources and three types of products, represented by the function

$$f^H(L_o, H_c, H_m, H_y, H_x, N_b[b = 1 \cdots B]; C, M, Y) = 0. \quad (6.1)$$

This form of functional relationship is used to convey the idea that all resources are related to all the products, and there are technological substitution possibilities among the resources and also among the products. The authors know of no empirical studies which specify complex relationships of this kind. But general observation suggests that the interaction of the operations labor, hardware, and systems software products does yield alternative capacity specifications. Observation further suggests that there are alternative hardware and software configurations yielding the same output. Thus, the most reasonable technological characteristics to assume must allow for technological substitution among resources and among products during system planning. The assumed technological characteristics are

1. decreasing marginal physical productivity to each resource in the production of each product, for example,

   $$\text{MPP}(H_c, C) > 0 \quad \text{and} \quad \text{MCNB}[H_c, \text{MPP}(H_c, C)] < 0,$$

   where $\text{MPP}(H_c, C)$ is the marginal physical productivity of CPU hardware in producing CPU services and $\text{MCNB}[H_c, \text{MPP}(H_c, C)]$ is the marginal contribution of CPU hardware to $\text{MPP}(H_c, C)$.
2. decreasing returns to scale, that is, a doubling of all the inputs produces less than a doubling of output.
3. increasing marginal physical productivity of a resource in the production of any product with increasing employment of any other input, for example,

   $$\text{MCNB}[H_m, \text{MPP}(H_c, C)] > 0,$$
   $$\text{MCNB}[L_o, \text{MPP}(H_m, C)] > 0,$$
   $$\text{MCNB}[N_b, \text{MPP}(H_c, C)] > 0.$$
4. decreasing marginal physical productivity of a resource in the production of any product with increasing employment of the resource, for example,

   $$\text{MCNB}[H_c, \text{MPP}(H_c, C)] < 0,$$
   $$\text{MCNB}[H_m, \text{MPP}(H_m, Y)] < 0,$$
   $$\text{MCNB}[L_o, \text{MPP}(L_o, M)] < 0.$$

In the next chapter there is a discussion of some empirical studies related to the computer system production function.

Unlike computer hardware per se, the investigation of computer center production functions has not been a popular topic to date. Thus, there is little that can be said empirically. General observation and conventional wisdom suggest that the micro-electronics revolution has significantly improved the marginal physical productivity of hardware. One explanation of the significant reduction of the share of hardware costs in total costs is this improvement in hardware productivity. The changes in cost contributions of different resources will be further explored when the computer center cost function is discussed. Given that the previously stated assumption is consistent with informal observation, its use will continue.

Technological change has had, and will continue to have, a significant impact on initial acquisition and replacement decisions. When technological change is extremely fast, it seems as if it is not good business to acquire a new system or replacement today, as tomorrow's will be so much better—the same performance level becoming a lot cheaper. Carried through logically, this leads to the absurd conclusion that if technological change is rapid enough, it never pays to initiate or replace a system. In practice, of course, opportunity costs eventually take over and dictate a positive decision. The proper analytical approach then is to formulate the initiation/replacement decision problem as one determining the best time to act, given the opportunity costs and projected technological changes. This decision problem will be studied later in the chapter.

The concepts of average and marginal productivity for multiple products were developed in Chapter 4. In the context of technological change or of competing technologies, it is necessary to stress that marginal physical productivity is technology-specific. For example, the marginal physical productivity of hardware is considered to be greater in fourth-generation computers than in the third. That is, there is a marginal physical productivity for each resource in the production of each output in each of the technologies. Thus, productivity can be measured for a specific technology *at the margin* with the base being the current production plan.

6.2.2 Stage 2 of the Production Model

The second stage of computer center production involves the programs that are used to produce specific or universal information services. This software is employed in processes internal to the computer center. Consider first a specific information product. Activating software results in the computer system using CPU time, storage capacity, input/output capacity, and, possibly, some library programs to produce the information service. The relationship between the computer resources used and the product provided is the production model for specific information services. It is represented by the equation

$$I_k = f^{Ik}(C_k, M_k, Y_k, N_a[a = 1 \cdots A]), \qquad k = 1 \cdots K. \qquad (6.2)$$

I_k represents the kth user-specific information service offered. The function relates the resources used in producing the kth information service to the product. There is one such relationship for each type of specific information service offered. As usual, it is assumed that the marginal physical productivity of each resource is positive and decreasing with increasing resource use.

Similarly, the processes that produce each type of universal information service, v, are represented as

$$I_v = f^{Iv}(C_v, M_v, Y_v, N_a[a = 1 \cdots A]), \qquad v = 1 \cdots V. \qquad (6.3)$$

Here, also, decreasing marginal physical productivity is assumed.

6.3 The Computer Center Decision Problem

This section formulates the manager's problem of maximizing the present value of life-cycle profit constrained by the production function for generating capacity, the production functions for information services, and the allocation of capacity among internal and external services. The manager's decision variables—the levels and mixes of resources and products—are also stated. The discussion will proceed by first developing the profit function, next the constraints, and then listing the decision variables. Lastly, the manager's decision problem is stated formally.

6.3.1 The Profit Function

The first component of profit at a given point during the life cycle is revenue. The computer center generates revenue from external computer services and from internal information services. Using the symbols from Table 6.1 and Figure 6.1, the revenue from selling computer capacity externally is $q_{CE}C_E + q_{ME}M_E + q_{YE}Y_E$. The revenue from sales of specific information services is $\sum_{k=1}^{K} q_{Ik}I_k$ and the sale of universal information generates a revenue of $\sum_{v=1}^{V} q_{Iv}I_v$.

The second component of profit at a given point in time is hardware operating cost. If maintenance and rental costs of hardware of type j are denoted p_{mHj}, then hardware operating costs are $p_{mHc}H_c + p_{mHm}H_m + p_{mHy}H_y + p_{mHx}H_x$. Labor expenses are $p_{Lo}L_o$. The rental of applications software has a total cost of $\sum_{a=1}^{A} q_{Na}N_a$. Systems software rental charges are $\sum_{b=1}^{B} q_{Nb}N_b$.

The third component of profit relates to the acquisition and salvage of purchased hardware. When hardware is rented, the rental is considered an operating cost; when it is purchased, there is the problem of determining its cost at a given time. In order to do this, the manager is assumed to have the staff develop a cost-estimating relationship for hardware prices. This relationship shows the projected price of a unit of hardware at time t. After some point in time, the price estimates would be those for "reconditioned" ma-

6.3 The Computer Center Decision Problem

chines obtained from the secondhand market. This price projection relationship f for a specific type of hardware j is denoted $f^{pj}(t, p_{Hj})$ where p_{Hj} is a constant. The subscript j takes on values c, m, y, or x as in Table 6.1. Thus, the acquisition cost per unit of memory is denoted $f^{pm}(T_B, p_{Hm})$, since T_B is the beginning of the life cycle. Correspondingly, the salvage value would be $f^{pm}(T_E, p_{Hm})$. These two terms, one a cost the other a revenue, occur only at the beginning and end of the life cycle.

From the above, the operating profit at a point in time can be expressed as

$$q_{CE} C_E + q_{ME} M_E + q_{YE} Y_E + \sum_{k=1}^{K} q_{Ik} I_k + \sum_{v=1}^{V} q_{Iv} I_v - p_{mHc} H_c - p_{mHm} H_m$$

$$- p_{mHy} H_y - p_{mHx} H_x - p_{Lo} L_o - \sum_{a=1}^{A} q_{Na} N_a - \sum_{b=1}^{B} q_{Nb} N_b. \tag{6.4}$$

This is discounted to the present using the continuous-time discount factor, e^{-rt}, instead of the discrete time factor. Continuous time is used here because it facilitates development of the rules for choice of times to begin, end, and replace. The factor e^{-rt} applies in the same way as the discrete factor but works only in a continuous context and integrates over all instants of time between T_B and T_E. The continuous time symbol for this integration is $\int_{T_B}^{T_E}$ at the beginning of the term to be integrated, and dt at the end. So the present value of life-cycle operating profit is

$$\int_{T_B}^{T_E} \left[\left(q_{CE} C_E + q_{ME} M_E + q_{YE} Y_E + \sum_{k=1}^{K} q_{IK} I_K + \sum_{v=1}^{V} q_{Iv} I_v - p_{mHc} H_c \right. \right.$$

$$\left. \left. - p_{mHm} H_m - p_{mHy} H_y - p_{mHx} H_x - p_{Lo} L_o \right. \right.$$

$$\left. \left. - \sum_{a=1}^{A} q_{Na} N_a - \sum_{b=1}^{B} q_{Nb} N_b \right) e^{-rt} \right] dt. \tag{6.5}$$

In order to compute financial profit, investment costs for hardware must also be considered. The present cost of the hardware acquired at time T_B is

$$\sum_{j} f^{pj}(T_B, p_{Hj}) e^{-rT_B}, \qquad j = c, m, y, x. \tag{6.6}$$

The present value of the salvage value of hardware is

$$\sum_{j} f^{pj}(T_E, p_{Hj}) e^{-rT_E}, \qquad j = c, m, y, x. \tag{6.7}$$

so the present value of life-cycle profit is the sum of expressions (6.5) to (6.7). In general, (6.6) is larger than (6.7) and the difference is called the present life-cycle capital cost of the hardware.

6.3.2 The Constraints

The first constraints to consider are those related to the production of computer and information services. These were discussed in the last section and are reproduced here for completeness:

Computer service production

$$f^H(L_o, H_c, H_m, H_y, H_x, N_b[b = 1 \cdots B]; C, M, Y) = 0. \tag{6.8}$$

Specific information service production

$$I_k = f^{Ik}(C_k, M_k, Y_k, N_a[a = 1 \cdots A]), \qquad k = 1 \cdots K. \tag{6.9}$$

Universal information service production

$$I_v = f^{Iv}(C_v, M_v, Y_v, N_a[a = 1 \cdots A]), \qquad v = 1 \cdots V. \tag{6.10}$$

The second type of constraint to consider relates to the allocation of computer capacity among its three uses. Each type of capacity must be conserved, so the equations are

$$\sum_{k=1}^{K} C_k + \sum_{v=1}^{V} C_v + C_E = C. \tag{6.11}$$

$$\sum_{k=1}^{K} M_k + \sum_{v=1}^{V} M_v + M_E = M. \tag{6.12}$$

$$\sum_{k=1}^{K} Y_k + \sum_{v=1}^{V} Y_v + Y_E = Y. \tag{6.13}$$

The final constraint is a logical one requiring that all the decision variables be zero or greater at the profit-maximizing production plan.

6.3.3 The Decision Variables

In maximizing profits, the manager must decide on the level and mix of all resources and products. Thus the manager chooses the level and mix of computer capacity (C, M, Y) and the level and mix of the resources in the production of that capacity $(L_o, H_c, H_m, H_y, H_x, N_b[b = 1 \cdots B])$. In addition, there is the choice of the level and mix of specific information $(I_k; k = 1 \cdots K)$, universal information $(I_v; v = 1 \cdots V)$, and external computer capacity (C_E, M_E, Y_E). The level and mix of the resources must also be chosen $[(C_k, M_k, Y_k; k = 1 \cdots K), (C_v, M_v, Y_v; v = 1 \cdots V)]$. Finally, the profit-maximizing allocation of computer capacity (C, M, Y) to its uses $(C_k, M_k, Y_k[k = 1 \cdots K]; C_v, M_v, Y_v[v = 1 \cdots V]; C_E, M_E, Y_E)$ is also a choice to be made. In day-to-day operation this is frequently automated in the decision rules used by the operating system to create and execute jobs. Over the long run, however, this allocation is clearly a managerial decision.

6.3.4 The Computer Center Manager's Decision Problem

In standard form the computer center manager's formal decision problem is

$$\max \int_{T_B}^{T_E} \Bigg[(q_{CE}C_E + q_{ME}M_E + q_{YE}Y_E + q_{Ik}\sum_{k=1}^{K} I_k$$

$$+ q_{Iv} \sum_{v=1}^{V} I_v \quad \text{life-cycle revenue,}$$

$$- \sum_j p_{mHj}H_j - p_{Lo}L_o - \sum_{a=1}^{A} q_{Na}N_a - \sum_{b=1}^{B} q_{Nb}N_b)e^{-rt} \quad \text{operating cost,}$$

$$- \sum_j (p_{HjTB}e^{-rTB} - p_{HjTE}e^{-rTE})H_j \Bigg] dt, \quad j = c, m, y, x \quad \text{capital costs,}$$

by choice of

$C, M, Y, L_o, H_c, H_m, H_y, H_x, N_b,$

$I_k, I_v, C_E, M_E, Y_E,$

$C_k, M_k, Y_k, C_v, M_v, Y_v,$

$a = 1 \cdots N_a, A; \quad b = 1 \cdots B; \quad k = 1 \cdots K; \quad v = 1 \cdots V,$

constrained by

$f^H(L_o, H_c, H_m, H_y, H_x, N_b[b = 1 \cdots B]; C, M, Y) = 0$

capacity production function,

$I_k = f^{Ik}(C_k, M_k, Y_k, N_a[a = 1 \cdots A]) \quad (k = 1 \cdots K)$

specific information production,

$I_v = f^{Iv}(C_v, M_v, Y_v, N_a[a = 1 \cdots A]) \quad (v = 1 \cdots V)$

universal information production,

$$\sum_{k=1}^{K} C_k + \sum_{v=1}^{V} C_v + C_E = C \quad \text{CPU capacity,}$$

$$\sum_{k=1}^{K} M_k + \sum_{v=1}^{V} M_v + M_E = M \quad \text{memory capacity,}$$

$$\sum_{k=1}^{K} Y_k + \sum_{v=1}^{V} Y_v + Y_E = Y \quad \text{I/O capacity,}$$

all decision variables ≥ 0. (6.14)

6.4 The Computer Center Manager's Decision Rules

The computer center manager's decisions can be separated into five categories: *computer system capacity, technical efficiency, products, technology, and allocation.* Computer system capacity decisions involve the choice of the size of the system. This is a complex decision, as there is no single measure of size; but rather a multiplicity of resources and capacity measures. Furthermore, such decisions are executed only infrequently, so the upper limit on operations will be determined for extended periods of time by the size chosen. All these considerations translate into a need to carefully develop the decision rules for capacity choice. This set of decisions is sometimes called the *effectiveness* decision, to distinguish it from the *efficiency* decision. Technical efficiency decisions are concerned with choosing the technical features of hardware and software such that, at any level of resources employed, the most output is obtained. This book does not emphasize the configuration aspect of computer center management and it is not elaborated, but some discussion is provided at the end of this chapter and in Chapter 7. The product category comprises decisions about products to provide and their levels. Given a profit-maximizing orientation, only those products will be chosen which contribute to the profit goal of the computer center. The choice of technology is that set of decisions which deals with the correct mix of resources and products. The mix of resources (or products) reflects the technological tradeoffs at the profit-maximizing production plan and hence the profit-maximizing technology to employ. Finally, the allocation category is concerned with decisions about the allocation of computer system capacity to the products produced in a manner that leads the center toward its goal.

In discussing each of these categories of decisions it must be recognized that each decision rule can be discussed separately but that in actually making decisions, all the choices are highly interrelated. The manager cannot choose a capacity level independently of the products to be produced, let alone technical efficiency of the system. The need to study each decision by itself while at the same time recognizing the interdependence of all decisions, can be reconciled by assuming that all decisions but the one under study have already been made at their profit-maximizing level. Then, a choice of the last decision at the profit-maximizing level will ensure that the manager has maximized profit overall. After each decision has been studied, consistency and the assumption of optimality can be reviewed; additional iterations can be made, if necessary, until all decisions can be adopted simultaneously.

6.4.1 The Computer System Capacity Decisions

Given that all decision variables, except the amount of CPU time to acquire, have already been chosen at their profit-maximizing levels, it only remains for the manager to evaluate that one variable. Since the values of the other deci-

6.4 The Computer Center Manager's Decision Rules

sion variables are known, the profit-maximizing mix of resources to employ and products to produce is also known. Thus, by equality of marginal costs, the manager can select any resource for cost measurement and, by equality of marginal revenues, any product for revenue measurement. Suppose that operations labor becomes the cost measurement tool and external CPU time the revenue measurement tool. As shown in Chapter 4, the profit-maximizing level of CPU time is indicated by the level at which marginal profit is zero. The marginal revenue from an additional second of CPU time is calculated from the marginal revenue at each point in time, which is the transfer price q_C discounted to the present and summed over the life cycle. Thus,

$$\text{MRGREV}(C) = \int_{T_B}^{T_E} (q_{CE} e^{-rt}) \, dt. \tag{6.15}$$

The marginal cost of an additional second of CPU is the incremental requirement for operations labor—the marginal physical input requirement for labor at the profit-maximizing levels of labor and the other decision variables—multiplied by the marginal present life-cycle cost of operations labor. The marginal cost of operations labor at a point in time is the wage rate, p_{L_o}. Discounted to the present and summed over the life cycle, this yields

$$\text{MRGCOST}(L_o) = \int_{T_B}^{T_E} (p_{L_o} e^{-rt}) \, dt. \tag{6.16}$$

Thus, the marginal cost of a CPU second is

$$\text{MRGCOST}(C) = \text{MPIR}(\hat{C}, \hat{L}_o) \int_{T_B}^{T_E} (p_{L_o} e^{-rt}) \, dt. \tag{6.17}$$

The marginal profitability of CPU time, $\text{MRG}\Pi(C)$, is then the difference between equations (6.16) and (6.17). Setting this to zero yields

$$\text{MRGREV}(C) = \text{MRGCOST}(C). \tag{6.18}$$

In more formal terms the decision rule is

The computer center manager chooses the profit-maximizing level of CPU time to produce, *ceteris paribus*, by applying the decision rule:

$$\int_{T_B}^{T_E} (q_{CE} e^{-rt}) \, dt = \text{MPIR}(\hat{C}, \hat{L}_o) \int_{T_B}^{T_E} (p_{L_o} e^{-rt}) \, dt. \tag{6.19}$$

Notice that in the stable price world considered here, the production plan is replicated from instant to instant at the optimal level. Thus, the decision rule can be simplified by removing the discounting and life-cycle calculations, since every instant is exactly like every other. The decision rule is then

$$C_E = \text{MPIR}(\hat{C}, \hat{L}_o)p_{Lo}. \tag{6.20}$$

As in the previous discussions, the above analysis can be inverted to yield a decision rule for the profit maximizing level of operator labor to employ. This is the next exercise.

EXERCISE 6.1 Profit-Maximizing Quantity of Labor to Employ

Develop the decision rule for the profit-maximizing level of operations labor to employ. This is the staffing decision.

The material in Chapters 3 and 4 provides the basis for noting that all the other decision variables related to computer system capacity can be developed in the same manner as for CPU time. To ensure that the reader can readily develop the correct formulas for the decision rules, the next exercise picks out two of them for development.

EXERCISE 6.2 Profit-Maximizing Quantity of CPU Hardware and System Software

Develop the decision rule for the profit-maximizing level (1) of CPU hardware to acquire, maintain, and operate, and (2) of a specific systems software product to rent and use.

6.4.2 The Product Decisions

These decisions relate to the choice of products to provide and if a product (e.g., a specific information service) is to be provided, then at what level. The second aspect will be discussed first.

The level of information service of type k to supply is again based on the marginal profitability of that service. The marginal revenue is the transfer price, q_{Ik}, appropriately discounted to the present and summed over the life cycle, that is,

$$\text{MRGREV}(I_k) = \int_{T_B}^{T_E} (q_{Ik} e^{-rt})\, dt. \tag{6.21}$$

6.4 The Computer Center Manager's Decision Rules

The marginal cost of the service is computed by first calculating the marginal requirement for CPU time in that service, then the marginal requirement for operations labor, and finally the marginal cost of labor. This computation ensures that all decision variables, except for the service being analyzed, will be at their profit-maximizing levels; operations labor is the chosen cost measurement variable. Thus, the marginal cost of the kth computer service is

$$\text{MRGCOST}(I_k) = \text{MPIR}(I_k, \hat{C}_k)\text{MPIR}(\hat{C}, \hat{L}_o) \int_{T_B}^{T_E} (p_{Lo}e^{-rt})\, dt. \quad (6.22)$$

Putting this together as a decision rule yields:

The computer center manager chooses the profit-maximizing level of the kth computer service to provide, *ceteris paribus*, by applying the decision rule:

$$\int_{T_B}^{T_E} (q_{Ik}e^{-rt})\, dt = \text{MPIR}(I_k, \hat{C}_k)\text{MPIR}(\hat{C}, \hat{L}_o) \int_{T_B}^{T_E} (p_{Lo}e^{-rt})\, dt. \quad (6.23)$$

Again, the stable price situation considered here means that the discounting and life-cycle effects cancel out. By using these same ideas with only a slight modification, the reader can develop the decision rule for the quantity of universal information of type v to provide.

EXERCISE 6.3 The Profit-Maximizing Level of Universal Information

Develop the decision rule for the profit-maximizing level of the vth universal information service to provide.

The quantity of external CPU time to provide is also a decision of the computer center manager.

EXERCISE 6.4 The Profit-Maximizing Level of External CPU Time

Develop the decision rule for the profit-maximizing level of external CPU time to provide.

With an understanding of the profit-maximizing decision rule for the level of a service to provide, the discussion turns to the analysis of when it is optimal not to provide a service at all, that is, the profit-maximizing level is zero. Panel A of Figure 6.3 is the situation studied until now. It is optimal to provide service up to the point at which marginal profit is zero. This could occur at the zero level of production; Panel B of Figure 6.3 displays such a case. This also suggests another possibility, that shown in Panel C. Here the profit function is downward sloping throughout; that is, the marginal profitability is negative and zero marginal profitability is not achieved anywhere in the relevant region. Thus, again, the largest profit that can be earned, given the profit-maximizing level of all other decision variables, is when zero service of type k is provided. Finally, consider Panel D. Here the best profit is at some positive level of production, but it is a negative one. This situation can occur, but rarely, in that it implies that it is unprofitable to operate the computer center at all, given the existing transfer and market prices. Such information is clearly of great importance to central management. It will be discussed further when the computer center cost function is discussed.

Figure 6.3 kth computer service partial profit functions.

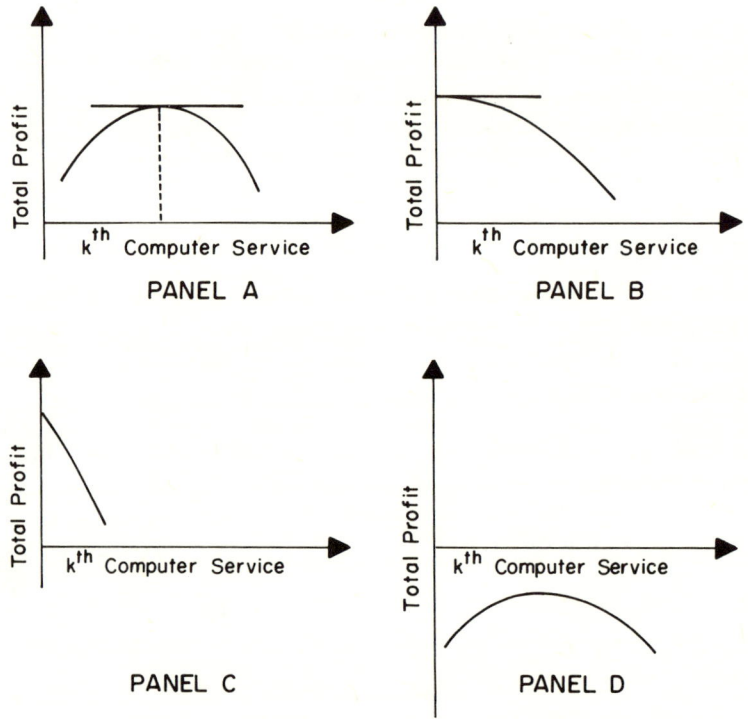

6.4 The Computer Center Manager's Decision Rules

6.4.3 The Choice of Technology

The choice of technology to employ is revealed by analyzing the tradeoffs among resources or products. These will be discussed in the following order: the mix of resources for computer capacity, the mix of products produced by computer capacity, the mix of resources for producing specific and universal information services, and lastly the mix of products to offer users.

The profit-maximizing mix of resources for computer capacity production is achieved when the marginal profitabilities of all resources are the same. The best mix of operations labor and CPU hardware would thus occur where

$$\int_{T_B}^{T_E} (q_C e^{-rt}) \, dt \, \text{MPP}(L_o, \hat{C}) - \int_{T_B}^{T_E} (p_{Lo} e^{-rt}) \, dt$$
$$= \int_{T_B}^{T_E} (q_C e^{-rt}) \, dt \, \text{MPP}(H_c, \hat{C}) - \int_{T_B}^{T_E} (p_{mHc} e^{-rt}) \, dt$$
$$- p_{HcTB} e^{-rTB} - p_{HcTE} e^{-rTE}. \tag{6.24}$$

This can be written as

$$\frac{\int_{T_B}^{T_E} (p_{Lo} e^{-rt}) \, dt}{\int_{T_B}^{T_E} (p_{mHc} e^{-rt}) \, dt - p_{HcTB} e^{-rTB} - p_{HcTE} e^{-rTE}} = \frac{\text{MPP}(L_o, \hat{C})}{\text{MPP}(H_c, \hat{C})}. \tag{6.25}$$

The right-hand side of (6.25) is, by definition, the marginal rate of technological substitution; the left-hand side contains the life-cycle marginal cost of labor in the numerator, and the life-cycle marginal cost of CPU hardware is the denominator. Thus, for the profit-maximizing mix of labor and CPU hardware, the manager sets the ratio of the marginal costs equal to the marginal rate of technological substitution. That is, profit maximization is achieved where the economic tradeoff imposed by external markets equals the internal technological tradeoff available to the center. Thus, the decision rule focuses on choice of technology.

In summary, the computer center manager chooses the profit maximizing mix of operations labor and CPU hardware, *ceteris paribus*, by applying the decision rule:

$$\frac{\int_{T_B}^{T_E} (p_{Lo} e^{-rt}) \, dt}{\int_{T_B}^{T_E} (p_{mHc} e^{-rt}) \, dt + p_{HcTB} e^{-rTB} - p_{HcTE} e^{-rTE}} = \text{MRTS}(H_c, L_o). \tag{6.26}$$

The following exercise is based on this same logic.

EXERCISE 6.5 Profit-Maximizing Mix of Computer Capacity Resources

Develop the decision rules (1) for the profit-maximizing mix of CPU hardware and a specific systems software product and (2) for the profit-maximizing mix of memory hardware and telecommunications equipment.

The mix of CPU time, storage capacity and input/output capacity to produce also trades off technology and external economic options. Using the same logic as above, the decision rule for the mix of CPU time and storage becomes:

The computer center manager chooses the profit-maximizing mix of CPU time and storage to produce, *ceteris paribus*, by applying the decision rule:

$$\frac{\int_{T_B}^{T_E} (q_{CE} e^{-rt})\, dt}{\int_{T_B}^{T_E} (q_{ME} e^{-rt})\, dt} = \mathrm{MRPT}(C, M) \tag{6.27}$$

The logic used to develop this is requested in the next exercise.

EXERCISE 6.6

Develop the logic leading to the decision rule for the profit-maximizing mix of CPU time and storage capacity.

The preceding decision rules have related to the technology of computer capacity production. The next decision relates the mix of resources to the production process for a specific information service. This is the choice that optimizes the use of software in the production of a service. Consider the mix of CPU time and storage in the production of service k. Equating the marginal profitability of CPU time and storage yields

$$\int_{T_B}^{T_E} (q_{Ik} e^{-rt})\, dt \cdot \mathrm{MPP}(C_k, L_o) \int_{T_B}^{T_E} (p_{Lo} e^{-rt})\, dt$$
$$= \int_{T_B}^{T_E} (q_{Ik} e^{-rt})\, dt \cdot \mathrm{MPP}(M_k, L_o) - \mathrm{MPIR}(M_k, L_o) \int_{T_B}^{T_E} (p_{Lo} e^{-rt})\, dt. \tag{6.28}$$

6.4 The Computer Center Manager's Decision Rules

The usual algebraic manipulation results in

$$\frac{\text{MPP}(C_k, \hat{I}_K)}{\text{MPP}(M_k, \hat{I}_k)} = \frac{\text{MPIR}(C_k, \hat{L}_o)}{\text{MPIR}(M_k, \hat{L}_o)}. \tag{6.29}$$

This in turn is, by definition,

$$\text{MRTS}(M_k, I_k) = \text{MRPT}(C, M). \tag{6.30}$$

Thus, in this case, the choice is entirely internal and the technological tradeoff within the program defining the computer service must equal the technological tradeoff available between CPU time and storage capacity in the computer system itself. Further, since there is no difference in this matter between different information services, specific or universal, then this must be true for all services. But, by the last decision rule, MRPT(C, M) is equal to the ratio of marginal present life-cycle revenues. Thus, there is still an external economic tradeoff involved, which is controlled by central management. By its choice of the relative transfer prices of external CPU time and storage, central management provides the incentive for the profit-maximizing computer center manager to use only software designed to incorporate the same tradeoff.

In summary, the computer center manager chooses a profit-maximizing mix of CPU time and storage to use in an information service production process, *ceteris paribus*, by applying the decision rule:

$$\frac{\int_{T_B}^{T_E} (q_{CE} e^{-rt})\, dt}{\int_{T_B}^{T_E} (q_{ME} e^{-rt})\, dt} = \text{MRPT}(C, M) = \text{MRTS}(C_k, M_k), \quad k = 1 \cdots K. \tag{6.31}$$

The next exercise demonstrates this same idea in a different application.

EXERCISE 6.7 Profit-Maximizing Mix of Storage and Input/Output in Information Service Production

Develop the decision rule for the profit-maximizing mix of storage and input/output in the production of an information service.

Another mix decision involves the tradeoff of applications software with CPU time in the production of an information service. Note that applications software has a unique characteristic. Its use in the production of a specific information service in no way reduces its use in the production of a different service. In fact, once an application program is resident in a computer library, it is available for all uses without being consumed or denied to other users in the process. Any good that has these characteristics is called a collective or public good in the economics literature and will receive special attention later in the context of central management's problem of coordination and control. In calculating the marginal revenue of collective goods it is necessary to account for all their uses. In the present context, the total marginal revenue of applications software is obtained by summing over the marginal revenue from each of the information services offered. Thus,

$$\text{MRGII}(N_a) = \sum_{k=1}^{K} \left[\text{MPP}(N_a, \hat{I}_K) \int_{T_B}^{T_E} (q_{Ik} e^{-rt}) \, dt \right]$$
$$+ \sum_{v=1}^{V} \left[\text{MPP}(N_a, \hat{I}_v) \int_{T_B}^{T_E} (q_{Iv} e^{-rt}) \, dt \right]$$
$$- \int_{T_B}^{T_E} (q_{Na} e^{-rt}) \, dt. \tag{6.32}$$

Using the usual logic, the formula for the decision rule pertaining to the mix of application software and CPU time can be written

$$\frac{\int_{T_B}^{T_E} (q_{Na} e^{-rt}) \, dt}{\text{MPIR}(\hat{C}_k, \hat{L}_o) \int_{T_B}^{T_E} (p_{Lo} e^{-rt}) \, dt} = \text{MRTS}(C_{k'}, N_a) + \frac{\sum_{k=1}^{K} \text{MPP}(N_a, \hat{I}_k) \int_{T_B}^{T_E} (q_{Ik} e^{-rt}) \, dt + \sum_{v=1}^{V} \text{MPP}(N_a, \hat{I}_v) \int_{T_B}^{T_E} (q_{Iv} e^{-rt}) \, dt}{\text{MPP}(N_a, \hat{I}_{k'}) \int_{T_B}^{T_E} (q_{Ik'} e^{-rt}) \, dt},$$
$$k = 1 \cdots k' - 1, k' + 1, \ldots, K. \tag{6.33}$$

where k' is the application under study.

This result is only partly familiar. The left-hand side is the familiar ratio of the marginal present life-cycle costs of the two resources. The first term on the right-hand side is the familiar technological tradeoff in service production. The last term on the right-hand side is the ratio of the sum of the marginal revenues from all information services (except the one being studied) to the marginal revenue from the service being studied. The magnitude of this term depends on the relative prices of the information services and the marginal

6.4 The Computer Center Manager's Decision Rules

physical productivity of application software in the production of those services. Its numerical value relative to the other terms can only be known in a specific use, since there are no *general* relative magnitudes.

In summary, the decision rule is as follows:

The computer center manager chooses the profit-maximizing mix of applications software and CPU time to use in an information service production process, *ceteris paribus*, by applying the decision rule

$$\frac{\int_{T_B}^{T_E} (q_{Na} e^{-rt}) \, dt}{\text{MPIR}(\hat{C}_k, \hat{L}_o) \int_{T_B}^{T_E} (p_{Lo} e^{-rt}) \, dt} = \text{MRTS}(C_{k'}, N_a) +$$

$$\frac{\sum_{k=1}^{K} \text{MPP}(N_a, \hat{I}_k) \int_{T_B}^{T_E} (q_{Ik} e^{-rt}) \, dt + \sum_{v=1}^{V} \text{MPP}(N_a, \hat{I}_v) \int_{T_B}^{T_E} (q_{Iv} e^{-rt}) \, dt}{\text{MPP}(N_a, \hat{I}_{k'}) \int_{T_B}^{T_E} (q_{Ik'} e^{-rt}) \, dt}$$

$$k = 1 \cdots k' - 1, k' + 1, \ldots, K. \tag{6.34}$$

The last category of mix decisions to study is the one for the mix of products to offer. Focusing on the products that are offered at a level greater than zero, the profit-maximizing mix is achieved, as before, where the marginal profit is the same for all the products. Specifically, consider the mix of the k_1th computer service (I_{k1}) and the k_2th computer service (I_{k2}). From the profit-maximizing logic, the equality of the marginal profits yields:

$$\int_{T_B}^{T_E} (q_{Ik1} e^{-rt}) \, dt - \text{MPIR}(I_{k1}, \hat{C}_{k'}) \text{MPIR}(\hat{C}, \hat{L}_o) \int_{T_B}^{T_E} (p_{Lo} e^{-rt}) \, dt$$

$$= \int_{T_B}^{T_E} (q_{Ik2} e^{-rt}) \, dt - \text{MPIR}(I_{k2}, \hat{C}_{K2}) \text{MPIR}(\hat{C}, \hat{L}_o) \int_{T_B}^{T_E} (p_{Lo} e^{-rt}) \, dt. \tag{6.35}$$

Algebraic rearrangement yields

$$\frac{\int_{T_B}^{T_E} (q_{Ik1} e^{-rt}) \, dt}{\int_{T_B}^{T_E} (q_{Ik2} e^{-rt}) \, dt} = \frac{\text{MPIR}(I_{k1}, \hat{C}_{k1})}{\text{MPIR}(I_{k2}, \hat{C}_{k2})}. \tag{6.36}$$

In summary, the computer center manager chooses the profit-maximizing mix of information services to provide, *ceteris paribus*, by applying the decision rule:

$$\frac{\int_{T_B}^{T_E} (q_{Ik1} e^{-rt}) \, dt}{\int_{T_B}^{T_E} (q_{Ik2} e^{-rt}) \, dt} = \frac{\text{MPIR}(I_{k1}, \hat{C}_{k1})}{\text{MPIR}(I_{k2}, \hat{C}_{k2})}. \tag{6.37}$$

Notice that the manager should equate the ratio of the marginal present lifecycle revenues to the ratio of the marginal physical input requirements (or alternatively the marginal physical productivities). Thus, the internal tradeoff dictated to the center by technology is adapted to the economic tradeoff dictated by central management. This form of the internal technological tradeoff is not expressible as a marginal rate of product transformation as in Chapters 4 and 5 because here there are two parallel but separate production processes. Nevertheless it represents a broader technological tradeoff in the software used in producing the services. The following exercise applies this same logic to the profit-maximizing mix of the kth specific information service with the vth universal information service and with external CPU time.

EXERCISE 6.8 Profit-Maximizing Mix of Products

Develop the decision rules for the mix of (1) the kth specific information service and the vth universal information product and (2) the kth specific information service and external CPU time.

6.4.4 The Allocation Decisions

The allocation decisions concern the profit-maximizing use of resources among their competing uses. Consider CPU time as an example. As opposed to the collective good, applications software, the use of some amount of CPU time to produce one service means that that amount cannot be used to produce another service. In an optimal allocation the marginal profitability of all uses must be equal. Formally,

$$\text{MRG}\Pi(C, I_k) = \text{MRG}\Pi(C, I_v) = \int_{T_B}^{T_E} (q_{CE} e^{-rt}) \, dt,$$

$$k = 1 \cdots K; \quad v = 1 \cdots V. \tag{6.38}$$

6.4 The Computer Center Manager's Decision Rules

To provide some specificity, focus on the kth specific service and the vth universal service. Then

$$\text{MPP}(C_k, \hat{I}_k) \int_{T_B}^{T_E} (q_{Ik} e^{-rt})\, dt = \text{MPP}(C_v, \hat{I}_v) \int_{T_B}^{T_E} (q_{Iv} e^{-rt})\, dt. \quad (6.39)$$

Rearranging yields

$$\frac{\int_{T_B}^{T_E} (q_{Ik} e^{-rt})\, dt}{\int_{T_B}^{T_E} (q_{Iv} e^{-rt})\, dt} = \frac{\text{MPP}(C_v, \hat{I}_v)}{\text{MPP}(C_k, \hat{I}_k)}. \quad (6.40)$$

Thus, the profit-maximizing allocation occurs where the ratio of the marginal present life-cycle revenues equals the ratio of the marginal physical productivities of the variable resource allocated in the production of its competing uses (specific and universal information service production).

In summary, the decision rule is:

The computer center manager chooses the profit-maximizing allocation of CPU time between production of a specific information service and production of a universal information service, *ceteris paribus*, by applying the decision rule:

$$\frac{\int_{T_B}^{T_E} (q_{Ik} e^{-rt})\, dt}{\int_{T_B}^{T_E} (q_{Iv} e^{-rt})\, dt} = \frac{\text{MPP}(C_v, \hat{I}_v)}{\text{MPP}(C_k, \hat{I}_k)}. \quad (6.41)$$

The following exercise permits the development of another such rule.

EXERCISE 6.9 Profit-Maximizing Allocation of CPU Time

Develop the decision rule for the profit-maximizing allocation of CPU time between direct external sale and providing the kth information service.

EXERCISE 6.10 Maximizing Profit from Computer Center Operations with Software Purchase

Reformulate the computer center manager's profit-maximizing decision problem when software is purchased instead of rented. Develop the decision rules that differ from those associated with the original formulation.

EXERCISE 6.11 Maximizing Profit from Computer Center Operations with Software Upgraded

Reformulate the computer center manager's profit-maximizing decision problem of Exercise 6.10 so that in addition to the initial purchase of software, specific systems and application software products are purchased at times T_1, T_2, and T_3 between T_B and T_E. Develop the manager's decision rules.

6.5 The Short-Run Utilization Decision Problem

Planning for computer system utilization was implicitly discussed in the last sections. Without explicit consideration, the capacity was chosen such that it would be utilized in a profit-maximizing manner. In Chapters 4 and 5 and in the previous sections of this chapter, it was assumed that the computer center manager could choose the levels for all resources so as to maximize profit. This defines a long-run situation where all resources, products, and technologies are variable. Obviously, managers frequently face situations with far less flexibility; many decisions, once made, cannot be immediately adjusted. It takes time to change computer system configurations or capacity. Once the center has undertaken to provide a certain mix of services there may be organizational resistance to changing the mix. As the number of changeable decision variables decreases, so does flexibility. Situations where some of the resources or products are not variable, but fixed, are generally called short-run situations. In this section, consideration is given to computer center utilization decisions in the short run.

Suppose the computer center manager faces a situation where all hardware is in place and cannot be changed; nor can systems software be adjusted. This leaves operations labor (number of people and number of shifts) as the only variable resource which the manager can change without running into a fixed upper bound. As has been the procedure until now, the profit function will be developed for this case, and then the constraints. These are followed by formal statement of the decision problem and development of the decision rules.

6.5.1 The Profit Function

The revenue generated from the sale of products is unchanged from the previous discussion. Costs, however, do change. First, since the hardware has been acquired and is in place there are no hardware acquisition costs, though salvage values can still be realized. The existence of fixed levels of hardware and systems software also means that certain costs become fixed. The rental cost of systems software and the maintenance cost of hardware continue, but are no longer variable with production. Notice that the fixed levels must be supported even though it may be optimal to use less than those amounts. Otherwise, the costs remain unchanged. With these ideas in mind, the reader is

6.5 The Short-Run Utilization Decision Problem

asked to develop the present life-cycle profits for this situation. Notice that the life cycle ($T_E - T_B$) is that period of time where hardware and systems software levels are fixed.

EXERCISE 6.12 Present Life-Cycle Profit from Short-Run Utilization

Develop the present life-cycle profit from short-run utilization. Identify the fixed costs involved.

Hint: Denote the fixed levels of hardware and systems software with a bar over the symbol, for example,

$$\bar{H}_c \text{ or } \bar{N}_b.$$

6.5.2 The Constraints

The previous constraints related to technology, allocation, and nonnegativity continue to apply here, since these describe the computer system production process. However, use or employment of hardware and systems software cannot exceed the fixed level. This is expressed in inequality constraints as follows:

$$\begin{aligned}
H_c &\leq \bar{H}_c \\
H_m &\leq \bar{H}_m \\
H_y &\leq \bar{H}_y \\
H_x &\leq \bar{H}_x \\
N_b &\leq \bar{N}_b \quad b = 1 \cdots B.
\end{aligned} \quad (6.42)$$

6.5.3 The Decision Variables

The decision variables for the short-run problem are the same as for long-run system planning. The difference is that in the short run there are upper bounds that cannot be exceeded for some of the variables.

6.5.4 The Manager's Decision Problem

Given the preceding discussion of the similarities and differences between the short- and long-run situations, the following exercise provides readers the opportunity to demonstrate their problem formulation skills.

EXERCISE 6.13 The Short-Run Profit-Maximizing Decision Problem

Formulate, in words and symbols, the computer center manager's short-run profit-maximizing decision problem.

6.5.5 The Manager's Decision Rules

You should satisfy yourself that if the profit-maximizing action requires less than the fixed levels of hardware or systems software, then there is no difference in the decision rules in the short and long run. However, due to the need to pay for the fixed level of hardware and systems software, the level of profits would be lower; if the level of profits were negative no operation would occur at all.

The more interesting cases arise when the fixed levels constrain the manager. In these cases, additional product could be produced and more profit earned, but this is prevented by the limited resource availability. The fixed upper bounds on hardware and software impose an opportunity cost on the manager. The fixed levels mean that some production plans are not resource feasible, so profit opportunities are foregone, that is, an opportunity cost measured by the foregone profit is imposed by the fixed resources. Any marginal profitability calculation must include this opportunity cost.

Consider the specific decision rule concerning CPU hardware. The long-run decision rule is

$$\int_{T_B}^{T_E} (q_{CE} e^{-rt}) \, dt \, \text{MPP}(H_c, C)$$
$$= \int_{T_B}^{T_E} (p_{mHc} e^{-rt}) \, dt + p_{HcTB} e^{-rTB} - p_{HcTE} e^{-rTE}. \tag{6.43}$$

In the short-run situation, maintenance costs do not vary, since all the fixed hardware must be maintained. The hardware acquisition term is not present, since the hardware is already owned. The hardware salvage value does not vary with the level of hardware usage and neither does it appear. The opportunity cost of foregone profit must appear. Denote it by Π'_{Hc}. The short-run decision rule is then

$$\int_{T_B}^{T_E} (q_{CE} e^{-rt}) \, dt \, \text{MPP}(\bar{H}_c, \hat{C}) = \Pi'_{Hc}. \tag{6.44}$$

The manager must set the marginal revenue earned by the fixed level of hardware (H_c) equal to the opportunity cost of the hardware (Π'_{Hc}).

It may be easier to think of this as if all the fixed level of hardware is needed to maximize profit. Then one proceeds to do just that. In this case the manager can measure the opportunity cost of the hardware limitation by evaluating the marginal revenue over the life cycle that is foregone because of the fixed level of hardware. This information is useful in evaluating the desirability of acquiring additional hardware. For example, suppose the marginal present life-cycle cost of acquiring new CPU hardware was less than the marginal present opportunity cost of the existing fixed level of CPU hardware. Then it would be profitable to acquire the additional hardware. Correspond-

6.5 The Short-Run Utilization Decision Problem

ingly, if the inequality was reversed it would not be profitable to acquire the hardware. In the long-run decision situation, the manager implicitly equates the marginal present life-cycle cost of acquisition to the marginal present opportunity cost of the profit maximizing level of CPU hardware.

The following exercises should be helpful in understanding these opportunity cost arguments.

EXERCISE 6.14 Opportunity Costs of Input Level Limitations

Develop the decision rules in the short-run situation for (1) memory hardware and (2) Type b (systems) software.

EXERCISE 6.15 A Modified Short-Run Decision Problem

Suppose the short-run situation is modified by a change in circumstances that do not require the maintenance of unused hardware. Suppose further that it is stored without cost. How do the decision problem and decision rules change?

The decision rule for operations labor remains unchanged in form from the long-run problem since labor is not a limited resource. The decision rule, therefore, is

$$\int_{T_B}^{T_E} (q_{CE} e^{-rt})\, dt \, \text{MPP}(\hat{L}_o, \hat{C}) = \int_{T_B}^{T_E} (p_{Lo} e^{-rt})\, dt. \qquad (6.45)$$

However, behind the scenes, the other resources are at their limiting levels which determine the total productivity curve for labor and thus partially the term $\text{MPP}(\hat{L}_o, \hat{C})$. This can be seen also in considering the mix of operations labor and CPU hardware in the short run.

Using the marginal profitability calculations expressed in (6.44) and (6.45) the mix decision rule can be written as

$$\text{MRTS}(\hat{L}, H) = \frac{\text{MPP}(\hat{L}_o, \hat{C})}{\text{MPP}(\hat{H}_c, \hat{C})} = \frac{\int_{T_B}^{T_E} (p_{Lo} e^{-rt})\, dt}{\Pi'_{Hc}}. \qquad (6.46)$$

In words, the marginal rate of technical substitution equals the ratio of the marginal present costs. The difference is that one of the marginal present costs is an opportunity cost. If this mix decision is thought of as one of minimizing present life-cycle cost constrained by a product level, then the "price" of CPU hardware is the opportunity cost of that hardware at the margin.

EXERCISE 6.16 Short-Run Profit-Maximizing Decision Rules

Develop the decision rules for (1) the quantity of CPU time to produce, (2) the quantity of the kth information service to produce, and (3) the quantity of memory to sell external users. Give an interpretation noting the effect of the short run on the decision rule.

Chapter 7 contains discussions of a number of topics arising from the analysis of computer center management together with practical techniques for assisting with some of the decisions.

Chapter 7
Computer Center Management:
Special Topics and Practical Techniques

7.1 System Initiation, Termination, and Replacement Decisions

Just as important as capacity, staffing, and technological choices are the timing decisions—when to initiate system operation, when to terminate system operation, and when to replace a system (or a system component). Initiation and termination decisions for a computer center as a whole are rare, of course, but partial initiation, termination, and replacement decisions are common. For example, a new software package is considered, which does not replace an old package; that is an initiation decision. When a service is discontinued, there is a termination decision. These decisions will now be studied: first the initiation decision, then the termination decision, and finally the replacement decision, which is a combination of the first two.

The initial timing decision is analyzed in the context of the computer center manager's long-run decision problem, for the reader should by now be familiar with it. Since profit maximization is still the goal, the manager will choose the starting date, T_B, so that the marginal profit from initiation is zero. As usual, there is a revenue and a cost side to profit. The revenue side will be considered first.

The marginal present value of revenue at the instant a project is started is the marginal present start date revenue (MPT_BREV). In symbols it is

$$\text{MPT}_B\text{REV} = \left(q_{CE}\hat{C}_E + q_{ME}\hat{M}_E + q_{YE}\hat{Y}_E + \sum_{k=1}^{K}[q_{Ik}\hat{I}_k] + \sum_{v=1}^{V}[q_I\hat{I}_v] \right)e^{-rT_B}. \tag{7.1}$$

The costs include the operating costs at the instant the project is started. These are the marginal present value of operating cost ($\text{MPT}_B\text{OPCOST}$) at the starting date. In symbols it is

$$\text{MPT}_B\text{OPCOST} = \left(p_{mHj}\hat{H}_j - p_o\hat{L}_o - \sum_{a=1}^{A} q_{Na}\hat{N}_a - \sum_{b=1}^{B} (q_{Nb}\hat{N}_b)\right)e^{-rT_B},$$

$$j = c, m, y, x. \qquad (7.2)$$

The difference between these is the marginal present value of operating profit for the starting date.

In addition to the operating cost, there is an opportunity cost concept of some subtlety and importance. Consider CPU hardware as an example. The manager has a market price estimating relationship, $f^{pc}(t, p'_c)$, that projects the market price into the future. The history of the computer hardware business suggests that equipment prices fall, in real terms, as time passes. Thus, tomorrow's price for a CPU will be lower than today's price. In this situation the manager incurs an opportunity cost by purchasing the CPU today; he or she forgoes the opportunity to buy the CPU at a lower price tomorrow. This opportunity cost is measured by the time rate of change of the acquisition price at the start date (denoted as dp_c/dT_B) times the quantity of CPU hardware acquired (denoted as $\hat{H}_c$). Thus the acquisition price change opportunity cost is denoted as $(dp_c/dT_B)\hat{H}_C$. Clearly this applies to all types of hardware, so the overall present acquisition price change opportunity cost (PAPCOST) is

$$\text{PAPCOST} = \sum_j \frac{dp_{Hj}}{dT_B} \hat{H}_j e^{-rT_B}, \qquad j = c, m, y, x. \qquad (7.3)$$

In general, there are no empirical data to suggest that all prices fall over time, in real terms. So, when applying this concept in other than computer acquisition situations, a specific price-projection relationship must be used, and some prices may rise, so that the sense of equation (7.3) is reversed. That is, there is an opportunity gain to early acquisition rather than a cost.

Finally, there is an opportunity foregone by the act of acquiring the hardware. The opportunity foregone is the alternative income-producing possibilities for the funds invested in the hardware. Because of the investment in hardware the organization, represented by the manager, cannot invest in some other internal project or some other external opportunity, say United States Treasury bills. The rate of return on these other internal and external investment opportunities has been denoted as r. The income from such investments denied to units external to the computer center is, in present-value terms,

$$r\sum_j [p_{Hj}(T_B, p_{Hj})\hat{H}_j]e^{-rT_B}, \qquad j = c, m, y, x. \qquad (7.4)$$

7.1 System Initiation, Termination, and Replacement Decisions

For the manager to choose the profit-maximizing start time, the marginal present profit (the sum of the above terms) must be zero. Thus, the manager's decision is as follows:

The computer center manager will maximize profit from initiation of operations, *ceteris paribus*, by setting the present value of marginal start time net operating income plus the overall acquisition price change effect equal to the marginal present value of external investment revenue foregone. The formula is

present value of

$\left[q_{CE}\hat{C}_E + q_{ME}\hat{M}_E + q_{YE}\hat{Y}_E \right.$ revenue from external computer services,

$+ \sum_{k=1}^{K} q_{Ik}\hat{I}_k$ revenue from specific information services,

$+ \sum_{v=1}^{V} q_{Iv}\hat{I}_v$ revenue from universal information services,

$- \sum_j p_{mHj}\hat{H}_j - p_{Lo}\hat{L}_o$ cost of computer capacity,

$- \sum_{a=1}^{A} q_{Na}\hat{N}_a$ cost of application software,

$\left. - \sum_{b=1}^{B} q_{Nb}\hat{N}_b \right] e^{-rT_B}$ cost of systems software,

$+ \left[\sum_j \dfrac{dp_{Hj}}{dT_B}\hat{H}_j \right] e^{-rT_B}$ price change opportunity cost,

$= r \sum_j [p_{Hj}(T_B, p_{Hj})\hat{H}_j] e^{-rT_B}$ opportunity cost of investments foregone.

$$j = c, m, y, x. \qquad (7.5)$$

Notice that the overall acquisition price change effect is inherently negative, since the real price of equipment has historically fallen. Note also that the discount factor e^{-rT_B} cancels algebraically, so that the decision rule only requires a computation for a specific instant of time, that is, events over time do not affect the start-time decision. When this is the case, the decision rule is called a myopic one.

Panel A of Figure 7.1 displays the partial profit function for the situation just discussed, that is, profit is maximized by starting operations at a specific date in the future. Panel B displays the case when profit is maximized by starting immediately, with marginal profit zero. In panel C, profit-maximizing requires an immediate start, but marginal profit is negative, that is, operations should have started in the past and the best that can be done is to start now. Finally, panel D shows a case where the best choice still incurs a negative profit and it does not pay to start at all.

The termination decision is similar to the start decision, except that the alternatives are to continue operations or to terminate them rather than to start operations or to continue without. With salvage values declining, delaying initiation implies an opportunity foregone to sell the equipment at a higher price. Thus, the salvage value change is analogous to the overall present acquisition price change effect. If operations are not terminated, the organization forgoes the opportunity to invest the funds from the salvage in other investment opportunities and thereby incurs an opportunity cost. The next exercise asks the reader to provide the details and to state the manager's decision rule for termination.

Figure 7.1 Start time partial profit functions.

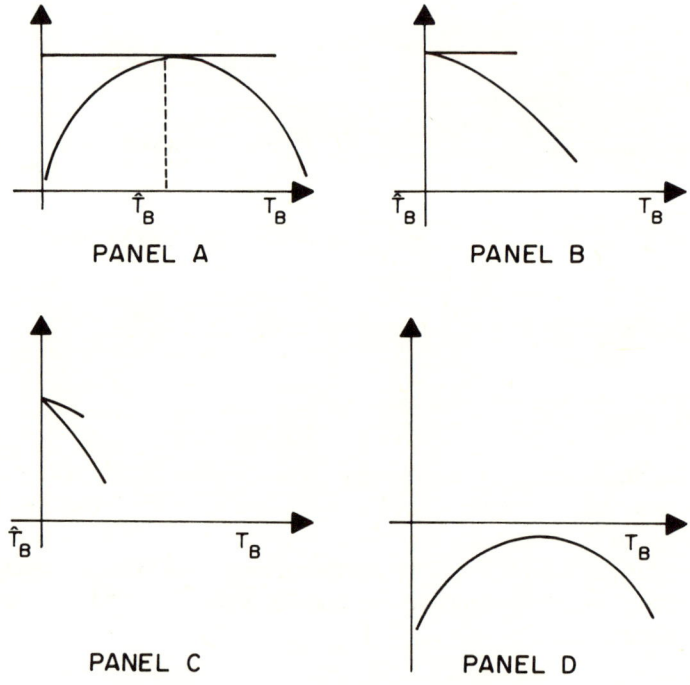

7.1 System Initiation, Termination, and Replacement Decisions

EXERCISE 7.1 The Computer Center Manager's Termination Decision Rule

Develop the computer center manager's decision rule for terminating an operation and state it formally.

The discussion now turns to replacement decisions. The context is, again, the manager's long-range decision problem. Here, however, the assumption is that there will be a sequence of systems over time. This implies a life span for at least some portion of the system less than the overall system life cycle. The first system will operate from start date T_{B1} to termination date T_{E1}. At the end of the first system's life, the second one begins operation ($T_{B2} = T_{E1}$). The second system terminates at T_{E2}. This short sequence is sufficient for the study of the replacement decision. Clearly the manager's decision problem for each system separately is exactly like the long-run situation already studied, except for the inclusion of subscripts (1 or 2) on all prices, quantities, price-projection relationships, technologies, and so on, to denote the two different time phases. The manager's overall decision problem encompassing both systems is the sequence of their two life cycles.

EXERCISE 7.2 The Manager's Replacement Decision Problem

State the manager's replacement decision problem in words and symbols.

Since the two systems, initial and replacement, are time sequenced, the decision rules applicable to the separate systems are exactly as previously developed, except for the subscripts denoting periods. The only new decision rule is the replacement decision rule, that is, when to replace system 1 with system 2. For system 1 this is a termination decision and is exactly like the termination decision rule just discussed. The decision associated with system 2 is an initiation decision and is exactly like the one discussed above. For the manager to maximize profit, the marginal profit must be zero, that is, the marginal profit from terminating system 1 minus the marginal profit from initiating system 2 must be zero. The following exercise asks for the formal development of the decision rule.

EXERCISE 7.3 The Manager's Replacement Decision Rule

Develop and formally state the manager's replacement decision rule.

With this background, the decision to replace a component can be considered. This decision problem can be formulated exactly like the overall replacement problem but is focused on the component. Suppose the CPU is under consideration for replacement. Then the only difference between the first system and the replacement system is the CPU; all other prices, quantities, and the technology are the same. Thus, the subscripts, 1 for the first system and 2 for the second, are applied only to the CPU hardware and the CPU price-projecting relationship. All other components remain unchanged, and there is no need to identify them with specific periods in the life cycle. The following two exercises complete the analysis of a component change.

EXERCISE 7.4 A CPU Replacement Decision Problem

Develop and state formally the replacement decision problem for a CPU.

EXERCISE 7.5 The CPU Replacement Decision Rule

Develop and state formally the decision rule for CPU replacement time.

The assumption of simultaneous termination and initiation in replacement was adopted above to simplify the development of the concepts of replacement timing decisions. More generally, and more realistically, a system or component can be phased in before its predecessor is dropped. The idea of stating each as part of the overall profit-maximizing decision is clear; the notational complexity, however, is acute. If one writes out the general replacement problem, its solution would include parallel operations of old and new equipment and different start-stop times for different hardware and software components, which is what happens in reality. The general problem will not be considered further, however, as the reader now has the concepts and skills to apply the ideas to specific circumstances.

7.2 Rent or Buy Decisions

In acquiring information systems equipment and software, one should consider whether to rent the items or to purchase them. While there are various versions of the two acquisition alternatives, such as lease to purchase or rent with purchase option, the basic nature of the decision can be readily studied. The long-run system planning decision problem could be modified to include two types of, say, CPU hardware—one for each method of financing. The first type would be rented (denoted as H_{cR}) and the second type bought (denoted

7.2 Rent or Buy Decisions

as H_{cB}). Both these types of equipment are identical physically and in performance—they differ only as to acquisition method. However, the modification of the long-run system planning decision problem is really unnecessary if the profit-maximizing level of CPU hardware ($\hat{H}_c$) is already known. Intuitively, if we know the level required, then the choice is dictated by the relative cost of the acquisition methods. That is, the rent-buy decision can be formulated as a minimum cost problem with a profit-maximizing level of hardware in the constraint.

The cost of renting the CPU hardware is denoted as $p_{HcR}H_{cR}$ at each instant of time. Thus, the present life-cycle cost is

$$\int_{T_B}^{T_E} (p_{HcR} H_{cR} e^{-rt})\, dt. \tag{7.6}$$

The buy alternative has a present life-cycle cost of

$$\int_{T_B}^{T_E} (pm_{Hc} e^{-rt})\, dt + p_{HcB}(T_B, \bar{p}'_c) e^{-rt} - f^{pc}(T_E, p'_{Hc}) e^{-rt} H_{cB}. \tag{7.7}$$

The constraint is that the total quantity of CPU hardware obtained must equal the profit-maximizing quantity

$$H_{cR} + H_{cB} = \hat{H}_c. \tag{7.8}$$

Note also that the price change estimating function does not distinguish between rented and purchased hardware, since it is assumed, realistically, that the price changes are of equal magnitude in both cases. The decision variables are the quantities of hardware rented and purchased. Thus, the formal decision problem is

$$\min \int_{T_B}^{T_E} (p_{HcR} H_{cR} e^{-rt})\, dt$$

$$+ \int_{T_B}^{T_E} (pm_{Hc} e^{-rt})\, dt + p_{HcB}(T_B, \bar{p}'_c) e^{-rt} - f^{pc}(T_E, p'_{Hc}) e^{-rt} H_{cB},$$

by choice of H_{cR}, H_{cB},

constrained by

$$H_{cR} + H_{cB} = \hat{H}_c,$$
$$H_{cR}, H_{cB} \geq 0. \tag{7.9}$$

The decision rule is to compare the marginal costs of the acquisition methods. Thus, if the marginal present life-cycle cost of renting exceeds the marginal present life-cycle cost of buying, the minimum-cost action is to buy, and vice versa if the inequality is reversed. If the present life-cycle costs are equal, the economic analysis is indeterminate and does not indicate a specific choice.

This same type of analysis is appropriate for make or buy decisions as well. For example, the computer capacity produced in the center could be acquired externally (bought) rather than produced internally. The next exercise asks for the statement of this make or buy decision problem as well as for the decision rule.

EXERCISE 7.6 Make or Buy Decisions for Computer Services

Formulate the long-run make or buy decision problem for computer capacity and then develop the decision rule.

7.3 Pricing Computer Services—The Supply Side

Central management, in setting the transfer prices for the products of the computer center, does so in a manner that coordinates the demand for the products with their supply. In fact, central management strives for the equality of demand and supply. The supply side of this central management decision problem is discussed here. The demand side and coordination are discussed in later chapters.

In studying the supply side, it is best to begin with an example, the decision rule for choosing the profit-maximizing quantity of the kth computer service with CPU hardware as the benchmark for costs. Assuming that overall profits are greater than or equal to zero, that decision rule is

$$\int_{T_B}^{T_E} (q_{Ik} e^{-rt})\, dt = \text{MPIR}(I_k, \hat{C}_k)\text{MPIR}(\hat{C}_k, \hat{H}_c) \int_{T_B}^{T_E} (p_{mHc} e^{-rt})\, dt$$
$$+ f^{pc}(T_B, p'_{Hc})e^{-rT_B} - f^{pc}(T_E, p'_{Hc})e^{-rT_E}. \qquad (7.10)$$

The left-hand side of equation (7.10) is the marginal present life-cycle revenue, a demand side matter as it pertains to coordination with users. The right-hand side is the marginal present life-cycle cost. Central management must consider this marginal cost figure in determining the transfer price of the product, if the computer center is to be a viable economic entity. One way to think about setting the price is to find the marginal present cost and then set the present value of price (marginal revenue) equal to it. Section 7.8 discusses some accepted practical techniques of charging for computer services.

The marginal present life-cycle cost is composed of (1) a marginal technological coefficient, which transforms the services supplied into the marginal requirements for CPU hardware, and (2) the marginal cost of that hardware. The marginal cost of the CPU hardware includes a maintenance component as well as a marginal capital cost. This latter term is the marginal economic depreciation of the hardware over the life cycle, in present-value terms. Thus, in computing the marginal cost of an asset, its economic depreciation (as distinct from accounting depreciation) is included.

Notice also that the charge to a particular user is the sum of the charges (marginal costs) for the services consumed. If a user runs a job, then, in general, there will be a charge for CPU time, storage, and input/output resources used. The user's charge could look as follows:

$$\begin{aligned}\text{TOTAL CHARGE} = &\text{MRGCOST\{CPU TIME\}} \\ &\times \text{[CPU TIME USED]} \\ &+ \text{MRGCOST\{STORAGE\}} \\ &\times \text{[STORAGE USED]} \\ &+ \text{MRGCOST\{INPUT/OUTPUT\}} \\ &\times \text{[NUMBER OF I/Os]}.\end{aligned} \quad (7.11)$$

Pricing is further discussed in Section 7.8.

7.4 Financing Considerations

The reader may be wondering about the source of the funds used for hardware acquisition. Basically, the analyses to this point assume that the organization has no shortage of capital. That is, if an internal opportunity for investment arises, and its rate of return exceeds the cost of equity capital or borrowing, then it will be profit-maximizing to obtain the funds and invest in the project. The use of the cost of capital in the discounting process ensures that profit will be maximized if the computer center earns a positive or zero profit. Thus, the financing considerations are embedded in the analysis. Choices when the capital is not readily available will be briefly discussed later as a modification to the current decision problem.

It should be stressed that the decision rules developed in this and other chapters are the optimum toward which the manager should strive. In practice, the data needed are not generally available; revenues are extremely difficult to measure, future prices and opportunity costs are unknown, changes in the cost of capital are difficult to predict, and so on *ad infinitum*. While managers should be aware that they will reach an optimum when they equate marginal costs and revenues, in practice they can only approximate these measures or evaluate them intuitively. There are practical techniques, however, based on the theory, that can assist the manager in drawing closer to the optimum. A number of such techniques for performance evaluation and configuration management aspects of computer center operations are discussed below.

7.5 Performance Evaluation

In order to implement capacity and mix decisions discussed earlier, it is necessary to measure the amount of service provided by systems and their cost. In order for such measurement to be meaningful, it must be performed on systems that are operating optimally; this is the *ceteris paribus* assumption so frequently made in this book. This section is devoted to practical techniques for evaluating the degree of optimality of system operation.

It should be noted that in discussing these issues the notation of the original articles from which the material has been drawn is generally preserved. Thus the notation will frequently be inconsistent with that of the remainder of this book as exhibited in the List of Symbols.

A number of techniques have been developed to permit the evaluation of the efficiency of computer systems operations. These techniques cover the spectrum of generality from hardware monitors, which can measure utilization of specific circuits in a system, to general management techniques for evaluating utilization of the resources invested. In increasing order of generality, these methods include hardware monitors, software monitors, accounting modules, Kiviat charts, and cost/utilization measurement.

7.5.1 Hardware Monitors

Hardware monitors are intended to collect data on computer operations by physically attaching to components of the system and collecting data on the frequency and duration of operation, or its absence. Thus, a hardware monitor is designed to provide information on the utilization of individual components or subsystems. For example, a hardware monitor might collect data on the utilization of particular registers, or of a channel, or of a disk drive. Typically, a hardware monitor is used when there is some suspicion that a particular subsystem is overutilized and is thus a bottleneck, preventing other components from being utilized more efficiently; similarly, if it is felt that some component is underutilized and cost savings might be realized by its removal, a hardware monitor might be employed to verify that this is in fact the case.

The great advantage of hardware monitors is that their use does not affect the operation of the system being monitored. Unlike most measuring devices, they do not change the values of the phenomena being measured. Furthermore, they may be attached to as large or as small a subsystem as is believed might be useful, at will, provided some hardware component physically represents that level of resolution.

The obverse side of these advantages is that monitors can *only* measure utilization of subsystems and can tell us little about the operation of the system as a whole or of the interactions between subsystems. A further disadvantage is that hardware monitors tend to generate very large amounts of data. This is due to the fact that computers operate at extremely high speeds, measured in millions of instructions per second; as a result, individual operations are performed with very high frequencies, and monitoring such operations tends to produce unmanageable quantities of data, making analysis infeasible. Thus, care must be taken in planning the use of hardware monitors so that it will be possible to make meaningful use of the data collected.

7.5.2 Software Monitors

The function of software monitors is identical to that of hardware monitors —to provide data on the functioning of a system. In form, however, it is completely different, consisting of software rather than hardware. A software monitor, then, is a program or set of programs designed to observe the functioning of a computer system. Perhaps the most common example of such a monitor is the trace routine provided by many systems to permit tracking of program execution. This highlights another feature of software monitors, namely, that they are often used for evaluating software performance as well as that of hardware.

One advantage of software monitors is their flexibility and the fact that they can be set to sample the system at any desired degree of resolution. Thus, every occurrence of a specific event may be logged (e.g., every use of a particular subroutine or every disk access) or the state of various system parameters may be logged at given intervals—be they five seconds, thirty seconds, or five minutes. If not used sparingly, software monitors, similar to hardware monitors, tend to generate enormous amounts of data, which render analysis impossible. Thus, as with hardware monitors, care must be taken to use such devices carefully, with clear objectives in mind.

The major disadvantage of software monitors is that, unlike hardware monitors, they *do* affect the phenomenon being measured. The use of a monitoring routine to gather data on the performance of a program will clearly affect the performance of the program being monitored. If the monitor is required to collect too much data, the system may spend more time serving the monitor than the production program. Consider an extreme case in which a software monitor logs the use of each instruction in a program; each such logging will require the execution of several instructions in the monitor routine for every instruction in the program being monitored. In this case, the monitor will keep the computer occupied much more than the program being observed and will, effectively, take over the machine. Not only is this likely to be wasteful, but it may well render the monitoring process useless, especially if timing considerations are being studied.

Still, one should not be frightened by the preceding caveats. When well used, a software monitor is an extremely flexible and powerful tool for observing computer system operations, and one that can be used to pinpoint the precise data required. Furthermore, software monitors are easy to use, since they do not require special equipment, as hardware monitors do, and if not available off the shelf can be written quite easily.

EXERCISE 7.7 The Decision Problem for Monitors

The major variables in the computer system monitoring problem are

how much software monitoring to perform.

how much hardware monitoring to perform.

direct cost of operating software monitors.

cost of production lost from software monitoring.

returns to software monitoring.

direct cost of operating hardware monitors.

returns to hardware monitoring.

Formally state the decision problem for how much hardware and software monitoring to perform on a given system.

Hint: This problem is an application of the principles you have learned about comparing opportunities gained to opportunities lost.

7.5.3 Software Optimizers

Software-optimizing programs are a specialized type of software monitor whose function is to analyze the performance of programs and to suggest ways of improving them. Consider the excerpt from a BASIC program in Figure 7.2.

A software optimizer would recognize the fact that there are two equivalent loops, each of which is independent of the other, and that the variable A remains unchanged throughout the loops. Thus, the program segment could

Figure 7.2 BASIC program before and after optimization.

BEFORE OPTIMIZATION	AFTER OPTIMIZATION
200 FOR I = 1 TO 5 210 LET A = B(I) 220 LET C = A ** 2 230 LET D = C + A 240 NEXT I 250 FOR I = 1 TO 5 260 LET A = B(I) 270 LET X = SQRT(A) 280 LET Y = X + A 290 NEXT I	200 FOR I = 1 TO 5 210 LET A = B(I) 220 LET C = A ** 2 230 LET D = C + A 240 LET X = SQRT(A) 250 LET Y = X + A 260 NEXT I

7.5 Performance Evaluation

be shortened as in the example. Generally, software optimizers operate at the level of machine code rather than high-level source code, but the principle is the same—elimination of unnecessary or redundant instructions. By using software-optimization programs that perform functions such as those demonstrated, considerable improvements may be achieved in program execution.

7.5.4 System Accounting

The most common form of monitoring is provided by operating system accounting modules that record the amounts of resources utilized by each job as it is run on the system. Accounting data of this kind may then be used to charge users for the resources they have utilized, to plan processing schedules, and to evaluate system utilization. An example of a report produced by an accounting module of this type is exhibited in Figure 7.3. Notice the relationship between this report and equation (7.11).

The data from accounting modules generally report the amount of each of the major system resources utilized by each job and the total utilization of each of the resources separately, for example, disk usage by each of the jobs and total usage of all jobs. However, they provide no overall picture of total

Figure 7.3 Example of accounting module output.

STEP NUMBER	1	2	3
TIME STEP INITIATED	16:54:05	16:54:57	16:55:19
STEP NAME	FOR I	INFO	GO
CPU SECONDS	25.39	1.19	11.55
TOTAL NORMAL I/O SEC	.28	4.31	.00
TOTAL CHAINED I/O SEC	.00	.36	.00
———— SPOOL I/O ————			
CARD INPUT OPS	769	0	82
SECS ∘ 2.0 MSEC/OP	1.54	.00	.16
PRT-TYPE OUTPUT OPS	942	31	149
SEC ∘ 3.5 MSEC/OP	3.30	.11	.52
TOTAL SPOOL I/O SECS	4.84	.11	.69
TOTAL I/O TIME, SECS	5.11	4.78	.69
TOTAL (CPU + I/O) SECS	31.50	5.97	12.24
REGION REQUESTED	150K	150K	150K
CHARGE AS RUN-CPU	$.50	$.02	$.21
I/O	$.09	$.09	$.01
CORE	$.59	$.11	$.23
BEST CLASS FOR STEP	0	A	0
COST IN BEST CLASS-CPU	$.45	$.02	$.19
I/O	$.11	$.08	$.01
REGION USED	148K	98K	132K

system performance. It is on data such as these that the transfer prices determined by central management would be based.

The next two techniques to be discussed attempt to integrate all the data made available by monitoring techniques in order to provide a comprehensive evaluation of system performance.

7.5.5 Kiviat Charts

Kiviat charts are a method of integrating a number of data about system performance provided by a monitoring system. The objective of such a chart is to enable the user to see at a glance whether the system under consideration is well utilized or not.

Such charts are prepared by first listing system parameters and the ideal and actual percentage utilization of the system with respect to each parameter. For an example, see Table 7.1. Note that the number of parameters for which the ideal is 0% should equal the number of those for which it is 100%. Next, the parameter values are plotted on the radii of a circle. The center of the circle represents 0% and the circumference, 100%; percentages are measured off proportionately along the radii. Each radius represents one parameter. Parameters with 0% and 100% ideal values alternate around the circle. Finally, the plots on adjacent radii are joined, and the enclosed area shaded. The example in Table 7.1 yields the chart of Figure 7.4a.

In a well-utilized system, the shaded area is star-shaped and symmetrical, with rays close to the circumference of the circle, as shown in Figure 7.4b. In the ideal case, the shaded area is reduced to alternative radii of the circle (Figure 7.4c). On comparing a number of such stars, it is usually possible to determine without difficulty which are "healthier," that is, which represent well-utilized systems and which are "unhealthy." In Figure 7.4, chart b clearly represents a better utilized system than chart a.

Table 7.1 System Parameter Utilization

Parameters	Percent utilization	
	Ideal	Actual
I. Memory used for control programs	0	10
II. Memory used for production programs	100	90
III. Bulk storage units inactive	0	20
IV. Channel utilization	100	50
V. CPU wait time	0	30
VI. CPU active	100	70
VII. CPU active on control programs	0	20
VIII. CPU active on production programs	100	80

7.5 Performance Evaluation 147

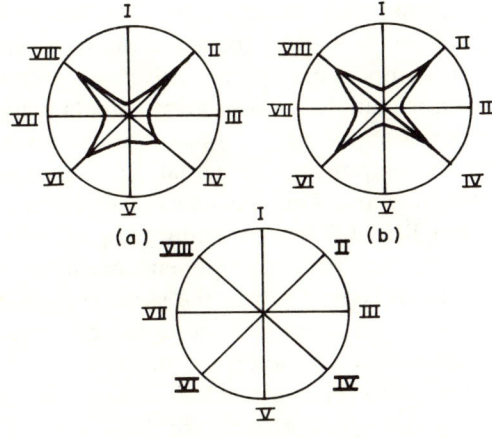

Figure 7.4 Examples of Kiviat charts.

For a more detailed discussion of Kiviat charts and the cost/utilization technique, see Borovits and Ein-Dor (1977).

7.5.6 Configuration Management

One of the problems with the visual methods of presenting utilization data is that the representations are not scaled in any absolute terms; specifically, they are not scaled in terms of the economic significance of the parameters presented. Thus, it is possible to configure a system so that, technically, utilization will be satisfactory on most dimensions, but the worst utilization may be precisely of those dimensions that are most expensive; these cost considerations are obscured in the previously discussed techniques. In general, system performance analysis is limited to technical aspects of hardware and software performance, with little attention paid to economic performance. The cost/utilization technique expands the technological aspect of system performance evaluation to include economic aspects.

The cost/utilization technique is related to the short-run decision problem discussed in Chapter 6. In that analysis, the quantity of computer capacity was assumed to be fixed (i.e., upper-bounded); it is also possible in practice that even the quantity of operations labor is fixed. In these conditions, job processing can be bottlenecked, resulting in queues of jobs awaiting processing. Rather than formulating the short-run decision problem with computer capacity and operations labor fixed, an alternative approach will now be discussed.

In the short run, the problem is to ensure that the maximum job-processing capacity is available; this is achieved when job-processing capacity is utilized in a technically efficient manner. Consider the utilization of the components of the computer system. If a particular component is utilized to the point that it becomes a bottleneck, then it may be possible to rebalance the system so as to reduce the load on the overutilized component and to increase the load on those components that are as yet not fully utilized. In the formal analysis of the short-run decision problem, rebalancing, or, more correctly, balancing, a system is adjusting the system until the marginal capacity costs are the same for all components. In actual operations, this will not usually be perfectly attainable and some bottlenecks will remain, but the system will be technically efficient. The remaining inequality of marginal capacity costs results because the various components are not infinitely divisible, the quantities of components are fixed in the short run, and components are not perfect or, usually, even good substitutes for one another; thus, perfect fine-tuning of component utilization is not possible.

The cost/utilization technique assumes the existence of performance monitoring devices to provide the basic data. These include system accounting modules, discussed above, such as IBM's MSF, Control Data's Scope, or Value Computing's Comput-a-charge. In principle, the basic model can be expanded to integrate cost-expressible data from any hardware or software monitor. Given the level of utilization of each component in a system, the cost/utilization method then weights the utilization level of each unit by its marginal capacity cost relative to marginal capacity cost of the total system. The rationale behind this weighting is that the knowledge that a card reader contributing 2% of total system marginal cost is utilized only 20% of the time is of different significance than knowledge of the same degree of utilization of internal memory contributing 25% of total system marginal capacity cost.

Assume there is a system with components, relative marginal capacity costs of components, and percentage utilizations, as shown in Table 7.2. These data can then be displayed graphically as in Figure 7.5, in which the horizontal axis represents the contribution of each unit of total system marginal capacity cost and the vertical axis represents degree of utilization. A glance at the diagram indicates immediately that some units, such as the CPU, memory, and tape drives are utilized at low levels, while other units, such as the disk

Table 7.2 Marginal Capacity Cost Contributions, and Utilization Levels of System Components

Components	Contribution to cost	Utilization
1. CPU	41%	28%
2. memory	23%	32%
3. disk drives	13%	83%
4. tape drives	12%	8%
5. card reader	2%	75%
6. printer	9%	66%

7.5 Performance Evaluation

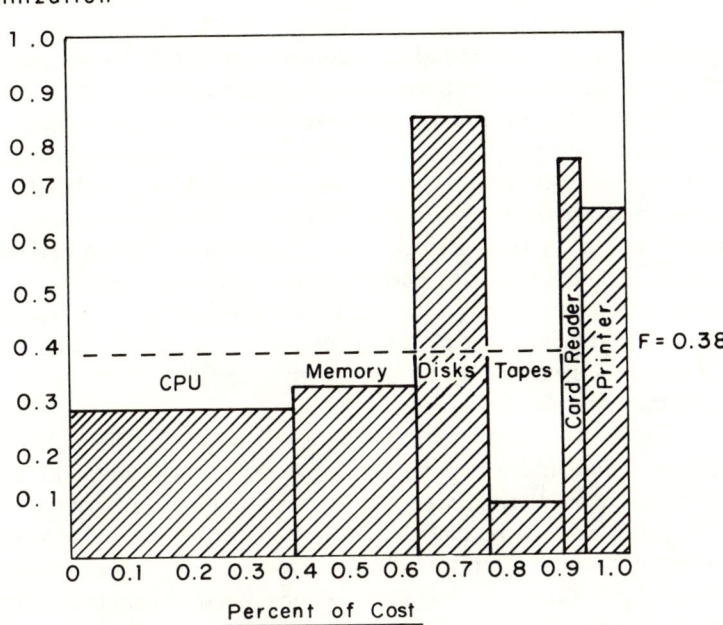

Figure 7.5 Cost/utilization histogram.

drives and printer, are close to full utilization and may be bottlenecks preventing better utilization of the other units. Lest the variances in utilization seem unrealistic to the reader, it is noted that these data were observed for a real system that had been in operation for some time.

Now that all data have been expressed in quantitative terms, it is possible to develop numerical measures of system utilization and system balance. The cost/utilization factor, F, a measure of utilization, is defined as

$$F = \sum_{i=1}^{I} p_i U_i, \qquad (7.12)$$

where p_i is the cost of the ith unit. Note that F measures the shaded area of the cost/utilization histogram and that both the shaded area and the value of F measure the extent to which the total system marginal capacity cost is utilized. F can vary from zero, in a system that is completely idle, to 1 in a fully utilized system. In actual practice, F values tend to lie in the vicinity of 0.5, with 0.75 probably about the highest value attainable in practice. In the example, $F = 0.38$, clearly a less than acceptable level of utilization.

The measure of balance, B, is defined as

$$B = 1 - 2\left[\sum_{i=1}^{I}(F - U_i)^2 p_i\right]^{1/2}, \qquad (7.13)$$

where, F, U_i, and p_i are as previously defined. The expression inside the parentheses measures the variance of the degree of utilization of the individual components (U_i) around their weighted mean (F). Multiplying these squared deviations by the relative marginal capacity costs of the components gives the variance of utilization of marginal capacity cost rather than of physical units. The square root of this number measures the standard deviation of utilization of marginal capacity cost. The scaling factor, 2, normalizes B so that it varies between 0, for a perfectly balanced system, and 1 for a maximally unbalanced system: by subtracting this measure from 1, B then varies from 0 for complete imbalance to 1 for perfect balance. Note that F and B are relatively independent, since a system can be very poorly utilized and yet perfectly balanced (in fact an idle system is perfectly balanced, by definition); on the other hand, a system may be poorly balanced but yet quite effectively utilized. In the example, $B = 0.466$.

The distribution of the measure of balance, B, varies for different values of F. Clearly, very high and very low values of F require rather high measures of balance. It has been determined, however, that for every level of cost utilization, F, balance tends to be distributed as a beta distribution. For relevant values of F, the mean of B tends to about 0.75, with standard deviation ± 0.1. In general, values of B above 0.65 may be considered acceptable, with values above 0.85 extremely good. Values below 0.65 indicate a level of imbalance, requiring remedial action. In the example above, the measure of balance is clearly unsatisfactory, supporting a similar intuitive evaluation prompted by the cost/utilization histogram.

The cost/utilization technique may be used in a variety of ways to evaluate the technical efficiency of computer system utilization in the short run. The system may be represented at any desired level of detail; for example, each disk drive might be differentiated or all disk drives may be considered as a single unit. Thus, any desired degree of resolution is attainable. By tracking the development of the cost/utilization histogram and the F and B values over time, it is possible to see whether system utilization is improving or deteriorating, and the development of potential bottlenecks may be identified sufficiently early to prevent their becoming serious impediments. This is a powerful tool for monitoring the efficiency of computer use and for indicating circumstances that require corrective action.

The remaining difficulty is the measurement of marginal capacity costs of components. This is usually not directly available. A practical alternative is to substitute the marginal acquisition cost. If the system is such that the marginal capacity cost of a component exceeds the marginal acquisition cost, *ceteris paribus*, then one or more additional units should be acquired. If the relationship is reversed, then, *ceteris paribus*, the appropriate decision is to dispose of some units, or at least not to obtain additional units. In the short run, it is not an unreasonable assumption that the marginal acquisition cost approximately equals the marginal capacity cost. However, if, after balancing is

7.6 The Computer Cost Function

attempted, one or more components are still clear bottlenecks, then this assumption is no longer valid. A complete acquisition analysis of additional computer capacity is then appropriate, for this condition probably indicates that marginal capacity cost for the system exceeds marginal acquisition cost.

The discussion of cost/utilization has centered on the achievement of efficient utilization of computer systems by an appropriate mix of components. This technique is easily expandable to the decisions on technology mix discussed in the analytical model. If, in addition to hardware components, personnel are included as a cost element in the cost/utilization diagram, then it becomes clear whether or not there is a correct balance between hardware and personnel.

EXERCISE 7.8 Cost/Utilization

a. Develop an example of data for the technology mix decision, including personnel. Compute F and B and analyze the management implications.
b. How might the cost/utilization technique be modified to help in analyzing the job mix performed by a computer system?

7.6 The Computer Cost Function

The assumption was made in Chapter 6 that computers exhibit diminishing returns to scale. This assumption is contrary to the conventional wisdom in the computer economics literature and requires some clarification. The conventional wisdom is known as Grosch's law—an intuitive assertion by the highly respected computer scientist, Herbert Grosch, dating back to the 1940s.

This law states that the costs of computer systems increase as the square root of their capacity. Thus, if the cost of a system is c, and its capacity w, then

$$c = f(w^{0.5}). \qquad (7.14)$$

The value 0.5, or its empirically found equivalents, are referred to below as Grosch's coefficient. The law is frequently stated in a slightly different form, with both sides divided by w, and then

$$\frac{c}{w} = f(w^{-0.5}), \qquad (7.14a)$$

where c/w is a measure of the average cost for a level of capacity.

It is important to note that Grosch's law is a statement about the computer hardware production function—the literature, however, refers to this law as predicting economies of scale in computers. It is necessary, therefore, to distinguish carefully between these two concepts. Economies of scale describe a

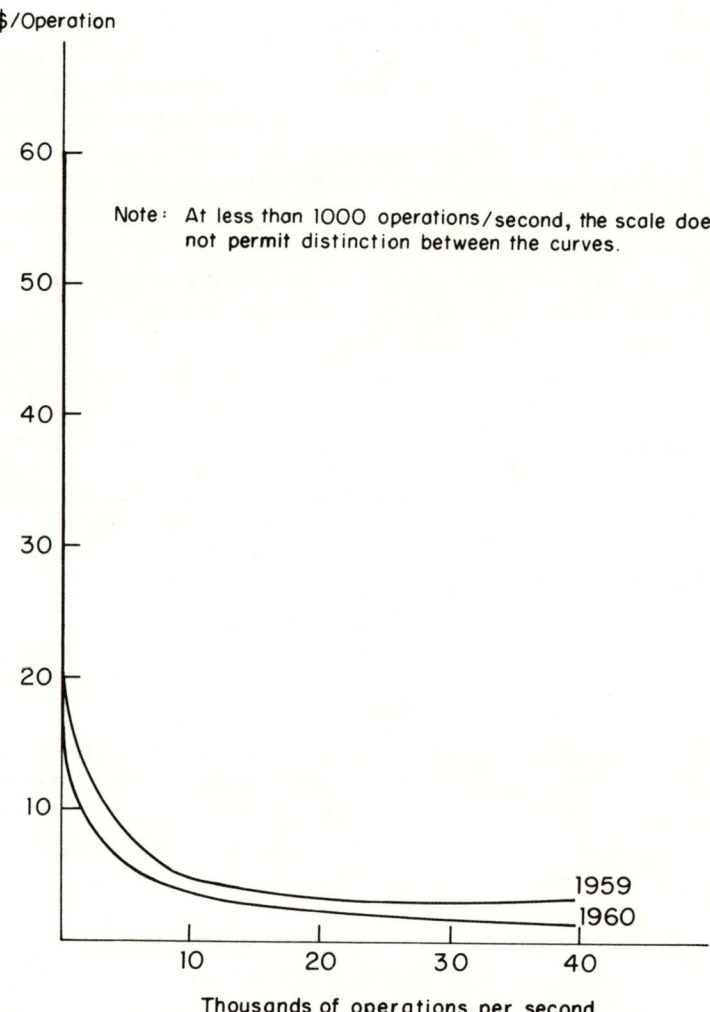

Figure 7.6 Representative computer cost functions: 1959 and 1960. *Note*: At less than 1000 operations/second, the scale does not permit distinction between the curves.

situation in which, when *all* resources are increased in the same proportion, the product increases more than proportionately. But Grosch's law, and the empirical work done on it, refers only to the computer itself, and not to the other resources associated with it, namely, labor, software, and physical facilities.

The validity of Grosch's law has been examined periodically, beginning in the early 1960s. Two major problems have been encountered in attempts to

7.6 The Computer Cost Function

Table 7.3 Average Annual Rate of Technological Improvement for Constant Cost

Year	Average annual rate of technological improvement	
	Scientific computing	Commercial computing
1950–1962	81%	87%
1963–1968	115%	160%

Source: Knight, Kenneth E. "Changes in Computer Performance." *Datamation* (September 1966): 40–54; "Evolving Computer Performance 1963–1967." *Datamation* (January 1968): 31–35.

test Grosch's law empirically. The first is to find a satisfactory measure for computer system capacity or performance. The second problem is to distinguish between improvements in cost by reason of computer capacity from those by reason of technological improvements over time; the extremely rapid rate of technological improvement in computers contaminates the data significantly.

The earliest studies of the computer production function were by Knight (1966, 1968). Knight examined the costs relative to power of virtually all computers on the market in the period 1950–1962 and again for those between 1962 and 1966. In terms of the earlier discussion of methods for evaluating computer power, Knight employed an analytical model appropriate to the relatively simple machines then in existence; it is the subject of Exercise 9.9. Because this model is no longer valid for current machines it is not discussed here in detail. The problem of technological change was solved in Knight's studies by assuming that all machines introduced in a given period represented the same technology. The periods defined were 1950–1952, 1953–1954, 1955–1956, 1957–1958, and each of the years 1959 through 1965.

The major findings of Knight's studies were as follows: (1) Over a wide range, the average cost of processing decreases with the increase in system power. Eventually, the cost curve began to rise again. The curves for two representative years, 1959 and 1960, are exhibited in Figure 7.6. (2) There was a consistent shift of the curve from one period to the next, indicating an improvement in cost/performance, which reflected the advance of technology. The rate of technological improvement is exhibited in Table 7.3, which indicates an amazing average improvement of over 100% per year. There is reason to believe that this rate has persisted to the time of writing and will continue into the future. (3) The shape of the average cost curves are close to those predicted by Grosch. The values found by Knight for Grosch's coefficient are exhibited in Table 7.4. Note that Grosch's coefficent is negative because cost *decreases* as power *increases*.

A second major study of economies of scale in computers was that by Solomon (1966). The problem of data contamination owing to technological change was neutralized in his study by referring to one series of machines, all

Table 7.4 Grosch's Coefficients: 1950–1966

Period	Scientific computing	Commercial computing
1950–1962	.519	.459
1962–1966	.322	.404

Source: Knight, Kenneth E. "Changes in Computer Performance." *Datamation* (September 1966): 40–54; "Evolving Computer Performance 1963–67," *Datamation* (Jan. 1966): 31–35.

introduced at the same time, namely, the IBM System/360, models 30, 40, 50, 65, and 75. Performance of the machines was evaluated by timing kernel programs for a few basic functions. The programs used were matrix multiplication and evaluating square roots, examples of scientific computation, and a field scan to represent commercial data processing. As an additional test of performance in scientific computation, Arbuckle's standard instruction mix was evaluated for each of the systems. Table 7.5 summarizes Solomon's findings. This table also exhibits coefficients that are close to those predicted by Grosch.

The empirical findings of Knight and Solomon strongly support Grosch's assertion concerning the computer system cost function. A later study by Cale et al. (1979), which adopted a somewhat different approach, was not as

Table 7.5 Grosch's Coefficients for IBM/360

Program	360/30	360/40	360/50	360/65	360/75	b
SCIENTIFIC						
MATRIX MULTIPLY						
$/1M executions	5162	2937	1729	677	601	
microsc/1M xqts	408803	109446	34239	8577	4756	−0.4935
FLOATING SQ RT						
$/1M executions	94.24	45.45	21.23	9.81	9.82	
microsc/1M xqts	7464	1694	420	124	78	−0.4783
ARBUCKLE'S MIX						−0.6319
COMMERCIAL						
FIELD SCAN						
$/1M executions	298	231	198	96	139	
microsc/1M xqts	23589	8616	3924	1211	1101	−0.6817

Source: Solomon, Martin B. Jr. "Economies of Scale and the IBM System/360." *Communications of the ACM* 9, 6 (June 1966): 435–440. © 1969, Association for Computing Machinery, Inc.

7.6 The Computer Cost Function

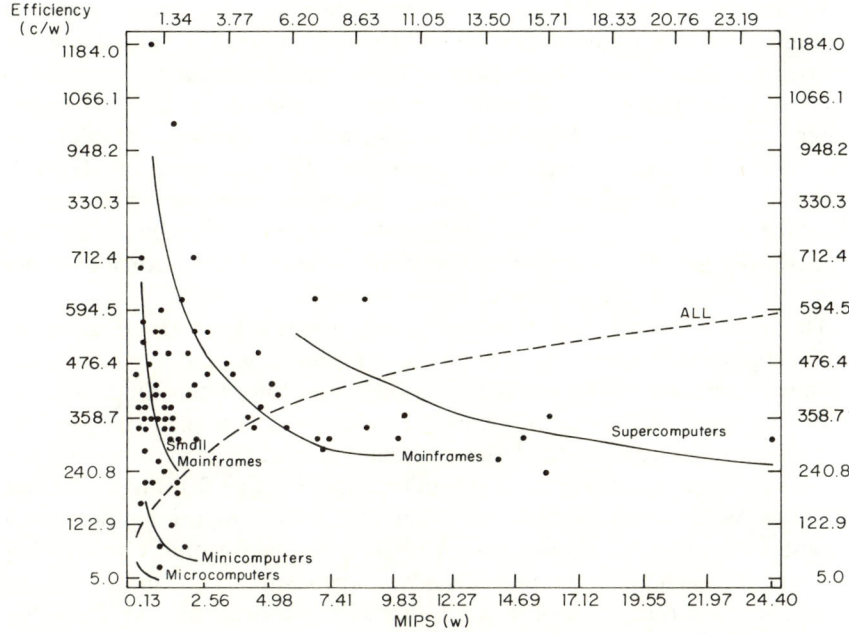

Figure 7.7 Relationship between power and efficiency by computer groups. *Source*: Ein-Dor, P. from *Communications of the AMC*, forthcoming. © 1985, Assoc. for Computing Machinery, Inc.

conclusive as Knight and Solomon, but did not categorically refute Grosch's law. Ein-Dor (forthcoming) recently concluded a study of this issue for 106 computers on the market in 1981. As the data all relate to computers that were on the market at the same time, it was assumed that all the computers in the sample represent the same level of technology. MIPS (millions of instructions per second) was chosen as the measure of computer power.

Using the same model as that employed by Knight and Solomon, the value found for Grosch's coefficient was $+0.3$. Contrary to expectations based on Grosch's law, not only was effectiveness not found to improve with the increase in power, but, rather, it decreased as the cube root of the power. The raw data, together with a graph of the regression, are exhibited in Figure 7.7.

This finding, considered against the background of known technological trends during the last twenty years, raises the hypothesis that computers can no longer be regarded as one homogeneous product, and they must be divided into groups for analytical purposes. Perusal of the data, with reference to common usage by professionals, resulted in the division of the data into five categories, identified as microcomputers, minicomputers, small mainframes, mainframes, and supercomputers.

An analysis of the relationship between computer power and computing cost indicated that Grosch's law held *within* each group. The value found for Grosch's coefficient was -0.55, close to, but slightly lower than, the predicted value of -0.5. The graphs of returns to scale for each of the groups of computers are also shown in Figure 7.7, together with the regression graph for all the data. The graph for each group appears within the range of MIPS, in which there are computers in that group. The model employed in this analysis of the data accounts for about 93% of the variance. Although the analysis related only to CPUs and not to complete systems, there is some evidence that the findings apply to complete systems also.

The main conclusions of this latest study are as follows. First, since the initial studies were made of the computer cost function, many technological changes have occurred that have led, among other things, to a differentiation into five groups of computers, instead of the original homogeneous product. The primary implication that follows is that it is most effective to accomplish any task on the *smallest* type of computer capable of performing it. Indeed, the observed tendency to decentralize and distribute computing power is apparently the practical application of this conclusion. Second, Grosch's law holds within each group, so that it is advantageous to use the most powerful computer, within a group of its kind, that suits the organization. Thus, one big microcomputer is preferable to two small microcomputers; in turn, a number of microcomputers are preferable to a minicomputer that has the combined power of the micros.

It is clear that there are many factors working against the tendency to decentralize, including economic reasons such as communication expenses in distributed systems. There are also organizational control considerations, security considerations, and other factors that work against extreme decentralization. It is reasonable to assume that in many instances the optimal solution will be integration of different sized computers, but only in extreme cases of large-scale computation or storage needs will it be more advantageous to use the largest computers. The tendency to decentralize will surely become stronger as the power of the smaller systems increases and their price falls.

Finally, the most important conclusion of this study of the computer cost function is that, overall, computers exhibit increasing average cost with scale, and therefore almost certainly diminishing, returns for a single output. It is quite possible, however, that locally, within specific categories of computers, increasing returns to scale are exhibited. These findings clearly affect decisions concerning computer system centralization and decentralization.

7.7 The Economics of Centralization and Dispersion of Computers

Before embarking on a discussion of the relative economic advantages of centralization versus dispersion of computing facilities, it is necessary to stress that this is not an either-or question. Rather there are degrees along a

7.7 The Economics of Centralization and Dispersion

continuum; one extreme is complete centralization, which would imply one computer system, generally at organization headquarters. The other extreme is complete dispersion, which would imply the employment of only the smallest computers available at a large number of sites. In practice, organizations choose an optimal degree of centralization, which frequently entails one or a small number of large computer centers together with a fairly large number of mini- and microcomputers dispersed throughout the organization. As small computers become ever cheaper and more powerful, and as more potential users acquire a sufficient background in computers, the observed tendency is away from extreme centralization and toward a higher degree of dispersion. The word "dispersion" is used here advisedly because it implies geographical distribution but centralized control; "decentralization" conveys a sense of distribution of control. It should also be stressed that the issue of centralization versus dispersion applies not only to the computers themselves, but also to software activities. Thus, computing facilities may be centralized, with dispersed analysis and programming services, or vice versa. Here the discussion centers on the hardware aspects only.

The discussion to this point implies a general formulation of the "optimal dispersion" issue. As just noted, this issue includes (1) a choice of an information management planning, control, and coordination system, with its attendant transaction costs, (2) a choice of system technology (hardware, software, and communications) and its spatial dispersion, and (3) a choice of the organization's most effective information system balance. Thus, all the material in earlier chapters can be used to formulate the issue, which is clearly most complex. One approach to reducing this complexity is to take the current information management planning, control, and coordinating systems as given, along with whatever information system balance exists. This permits the focussing of attention on the choice of system technology and dispersion. The following is one approach to studying this reduced optimal dispersion problem.

An economic model of the optimal degree of hardware dispersion was developed by Streeter (1973) in the early 1970s. This is a parametric cost-estimating model, which takes into account the effect of economies of scale on operating costs, communications costs between dispersed computers, communications costs between users and computers, and service interruption costs. The analytical formulation of these factors follows. For all factors, the decision variable that determines cost is the number of computers employed, N.

Economies of scale. Streeter adopted Grosch's law, discussed in the previous section, as the model of the computer system cost function. For a given workload, the more powerful the computer employed, the fewer of them are necessary; given Grosch's law, the total cost declines quadratically. This is then expressed as

$$\text{hardware cost} = K_0 N^{1/2}, \tag{7.15}$$

where N is the number of installations,

K_0 is a constant of proportionality between costs and number of installations.

For multiple installations, it is assumed that there is one computer per installation, and all computers are the same size. These are somewhat unrealistic and restrictive assumptions, but make for a conveniently simple model.

Interinstallation communication costs. Assuming all installations to be linked to all other installations, the number of communication links is

$$\frac{N(N-1)}{2}. \tag{7.16}$$

Assume total traffic to be determined by the number of installations and of magnitude $N - 1$ (i.e., the amount of traffic grows linearly with the number of installations). The larger the number of links, however, the smaller the volume of traffic on each link. This is given by

$$\text{traffic per link} = \frac{\text{total traffic}}{\text{total links}} = \frac{N-1}{N(N-1)/2} = \frac{2}{N}. \tag{7.17}$$

Assume further that there are the same economies of scale in communications as there are in computing. The cost per link then decreases quadratically with the amount of traffic per link and is given by

$$\text{cost per communication link} = K_1 \sqrt{\frac{2}{N}}, \tag{7.18}$$

where K_1 is the constant of proportionality.

Total communication costs are determined by the product of relative cost per link and total links:

$$\text{interinstallation communication cost} = K_1 \sqrt{\frac{2}{N}} \frac{N(N-1)}{2},$$

$$= K_1 \sqrt{\frac{N}{2(N-1)}}. \tag{7.19}$$

User communication costs. One of the major advantages of dispersed systems is that users are closer to the computers they use and may even interact with them directly. Thus, the greater the number of computers, that is, the more dispersed the computing capacity, the lower the cost of user-computer communications. Again assuming a quadratic relationship, this cost, as a function of the number of computers, is given by

$$\text{user-computer communications} = K_2 N^{-1/2}, \tag{7.20}$$

7.7 The Economics of Centralization and Dispersion

where K_2 is the constant of proportionality between user-computer communications costs and number of computers.

Cost of service interruption. Finally, assume that the cost of service interruption is proportional to the probability of a complete service disruption, that is, of all computers being nonoperational at the same time. This is given by

$$\text{cost of service interruption} = K_3(P)^N, \quad (7.21)$$

where P is the probability of failure of any computer in the system,

K_3 is the constant of proportionality.

Cost of centralization for N installations. The relative cost for a given workload of a number of computers, N, is the sum of the hardware, computer communications, user communications, and service interruption costs detailed above. Thus,

$$\text{COST}(N) = K_0 N^{1/2} + K_1 \sqrt{\frac{2}{N(N-1)}} + K_2 N^{-1/2} + K_3(P)^N, \quad (7.22)$$

where K_0 through K_3, N, and P are as defined above.

Given equation (7.22) and values for K_0 through K_3, each of the costs individually and the total cost can be computed and the least-cost number of computers found. Streeter assumed the values

$$K_0 = 4$$
$$K_1 = 4$$
$$K_2 = 0.5$$
$$K_3 = 100$$

for the proportionality constants and $P = 0.1$ for the probability of failure of a computer. This yielded the values of Table 7.6, which are exhibited graphically as Figure 7.8. These results clearly call for a high degree of centralization. Thus, while Streeter's basic model is appealing, his finding of an optimal value of 2 for the number of installations, does not seem intuitively correct at the time of this writing, when the tendency to dispersion is so obvious. This apparent discrepancy is best explained by the fact that the constants of proportionality have changed over the last decade and by the findings in the previous section concerning the changes in computer system production functions. Assume there are the following changes.

Hardware cost. As stated in Section 7.6, the production function now favors small computers and the cost per computation *decreases* with the decrease in computer capacity, that is, with the increase in number of

Table 7.6 Relative Costs for N Installation Computing Networks

		Installations: Units of workload			
Cost element	K_1	1:16	2:8	4:4	16:1
Hardware	4	4	5.66	8.00	16.00
Computer communications	4	0	4.00	16.97	169.70
User communications	0.5	0.5	0.35	0.25	0.13
Service interruption	100	10	1.00	0.01	0.00
Total		14.5	11.01	25.23	185.83

installations. The factor found was -0.3, rather than the $+0.5$ assumed by Grosch's law. In addition, the cost of hardware has decreased dramatically in the last 10 years. This changes the constant of proportionality, K_0. Assuming a drop of 90% in hardware prices is probably a conservative estimate. These changes yield the hardware cost-estimating function $0.4N^{-0.3}$ instead of $4N^{0.5}$.

Figure 7.8 Minimization of centralization or dispersion costs. *Source*: Streeter, D. H. "Centralization or Dispersion of Computing Facilities." *IBM Systems Journal*, 12, 3 (1973): 283–301. Reprinted with permission from International Business Machine Corp.

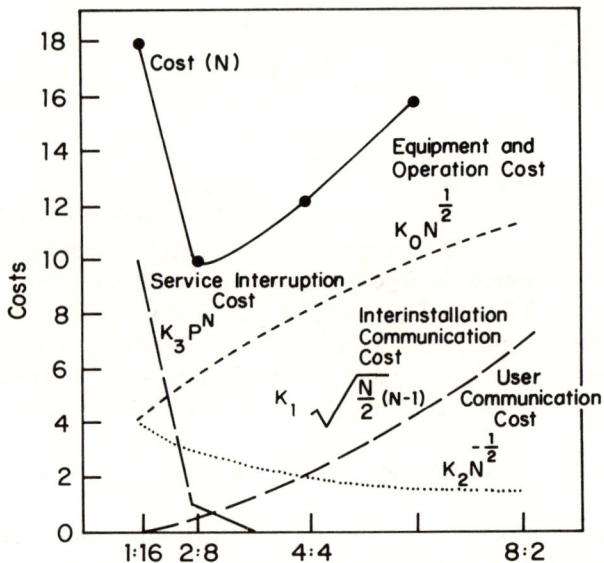

7.7 The Economics of Centralization and Dispersion

Interinstallation communications. Given the great improvements in quality and speed of data communications over the last decade and considerable competition in the field, it is not unreasonable to assume that communications costs have declined by a factor of 4. This would give a value of 1.0 for K_1, rather than 4 as in the original model. Maintaining Streeter's original model for the amount of communications, the cost relative to the number of computers is now given by $[N/2(N-1)]^{1/2}$ instead of $4[N/2(N-1)]^{1/2}$.

User-computer communications. As the use of online real-time systems has increased, users have become much more dependent on computers, which would very substantially raise the relative importance of this cost item. Furthermore, salaries have risen considerably during the period under discussion. Thus, a constant of proportionality of 20 is assumed, yielding $20N^{-0.5}$, instead of $0.5N^{-0.5}$.

Service interruptions. With the increasing role of online real-time systems, the cost of service interruptions also becomes much more significant. It is assumed here that the weight of this item has risen sixfold. This is somewhat counterbalanced by the fact that hardware has become more reliable. It is assumed, therefore, that the probability of failure has dropped from 0.1 to 0.05. This changes this cost-estimating factor to $600(0.05)^N$ instead of $100(0.1)^N$.

The result of these new assumptions are exhibited in Table 7.7 and Figure 7.9. The optimum number of computers is now 8, rather than 2 as in Streeter's original model. It should be recalled that Streeter's computer installation is also a unit of workload. Thus, the revised value of 8 for the number of installations is best thought of as 8 computerized locations, with possibly a number of computers handling the workload in each location.

It is not claimed that the proportionality constants assumed in the revised version of the model are currently correct; what has been demonstrated is that the model is sufficiently general to accommodate changes in technologies

Table 7.7 Relative Costs for N Installation Computing Networks: Revised Assumptions

Cost element	K_1	Installations: Units of workload				
		1:16	2:8	4:4	8:2	16:1
Hardware	0.4	0.40	0.32	0.26	0.21	0.16
Computer communications	1.0	0.00	1.00	2.45	3.50	10.95
User communications	20	20.00	14.14	10.00	7.07	5.00
Service interruption	600	30.00	1.50	0.00	0.00	0.00
Total		50.40	16.96	12.71	10.78	16.11

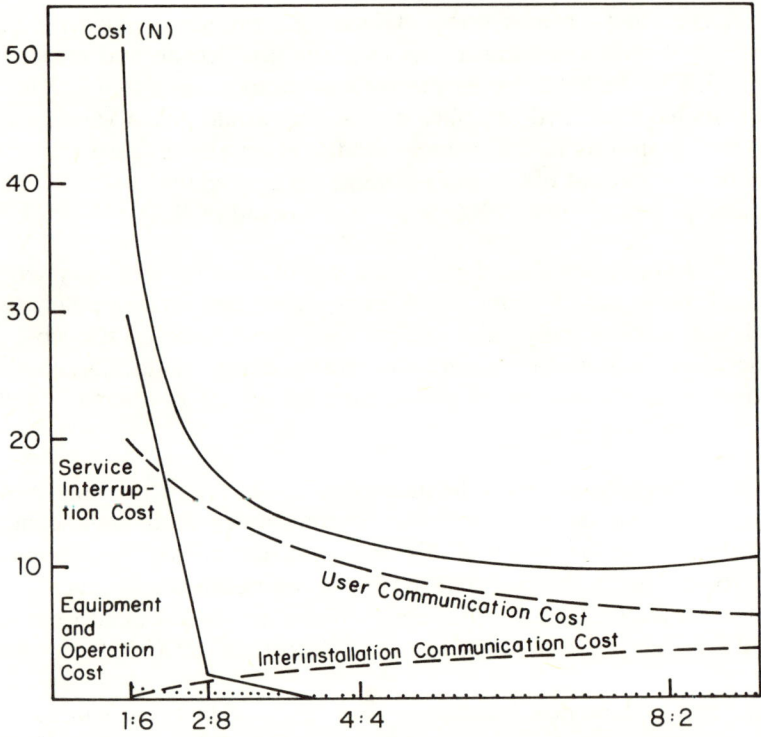

Figure 7.9 Minimization of centralization or dispersion costs: revised model.

and relative costs, and is therefore a useful tool that can be used for evaluating optimal centralization in real organizations, and has been used for this purpose in at least one case.

7.8 Establishing Transfer Prices

Virtually all the models developed in this book require the establishment of transfer prices by central management. No hint has yet been given as to how this might be done in practice. Before providing such hints, it is necessary to distinguish between two different traditional philosophies, which provide the context for discussing methods of charging for computer services. The first concept is that users should be charged so that costs are fully covered—for example, the computer center is viewed as a profit center and nonnegative profit implies that costs are fully covered. This full-cost approach is also adopted in discussing the software activity. "Pricing models, on the other hand, are not primarily motivated by a philosophy that costs of computing services should be recovered, but by the recognition that it is of greater im-

7.8 Establishing Transfer Prices

portance to coordinate demand for a resource with its availability and to allocate computing resources in a rational and effective manner" (McKell et al., 1979). Here the information system resource allocation effect of prices is emphasized.

In fact, these two traditional philosophies are not in contention. The inability to cover costs is a strong indication that the activity is uneconomic, and that resources should not be allocated to it. Thus, prices, based on marginal values and costs, also provide information on the larger resource allocation issues. For example, suppose that there are *diseconomies* of scale and that prices based on marginal values and costs cannot finance the activity; the activity is then not economic to operate. When there are *economies* of scale, on the other hand, it will not be possible to finance the activity on the basis of marginal value and cost-based prices. But this does not then imply that the activity is uneconomic; it means that a very special technology is involved, the advantages of which can be exploited only when a subsidy is provided. A subsidy may be used instead of raising the prices so that internal information system resource allocation can proceed correctly. Thus, it is clear that the correct pricing scheme is to carefully measure the marginal cost of a particular product or service and use the iterative process between central management and the activities and users to arrive at a balanced system. Since internal allocation is based on relative prices only, the ratios are important and can be adjusted to provide any subsidies necessitated by economies of scale, or such subsidies can be obtained from elsewhere in the organization, for example, an access charge or a flat fee to all users, which must come from their information services budgets.

A good survey of current costing and pricing methods and thoughtful discussions of their advantages and disadvantages are to be found in the paper by McKell et al. (1979). If the reader pursues this article, care must be taken to keep in mind the pricing principles just discussed.

On reading such a survey, which is highly recommended in this case, one is struck by the relative abundance of conceptual approaches as to how prices of computer services *should* be determined, together with a dearth of practical techniques that may actually be implemented. The conceptual approaches include the use of prices to establish priorities; the use of budgets as a basis for pricing, with prices as a means of transmitting information to users (Kanter et al., 1968); direct priority mechanisms (Marchand, 1968); two-component schemes, for example, budget/price components (Smidt, 1968, a,b), and fixed and variable components (Nielsen, 1968, 1970); and an accounting approach (Selwyn, 1970). Brief descriptions and evaluations of these conceptualizations are contained in Table 7.8.

Many of the conceptual methods require establishing internal marginal costs and marginal revenues, which must almost inevitably break down under the weight of measurement problems. A feasible alternative is market-based pricing, under which internal transfer prices are established on the

Table 7.8 Summary of Computer Service Pricing Models

Reference	Methodology	Advantages	Disadvantages
Kanter, Singer, & Moore	Use of budgets as basis for pricing; prices used as a means of transmitting demand information to user.	Computer usage is rationed by pricing mechanism.	Requires tight monitoring of demand information; prices may fluctuate widely.
Marchand	Prices first and second moments of individual priority streams.	Develops optimal prices based upon user preferences vis-à-vis waiting time.	May not result in excess capacity; assumes CPU only limiting resource; results in conflict between technical performance and economic efficiency.
Smidt	Uses two components, budget and price; budget is allocated so that marginal satisfaction to each user is same for all users; prices are set at marginal cost to the organization; the use of flexible pricing is suggested.	Prices will be high when demand is high, low when demand is low.	No information provided on how priority and price continuums should be partitioned for optimal and practical implementations.
Nielsen	Utilizes a two-component pricing model: fixed component for initiating service; variable component corresponding to marginal cost of the resource.	Approaches an optimal pricing mechanism in terms of the value of computing done.	Difficult to implement; increases system overhead.
Selwyn	Accounting approach; allows a primary user to support a system of subusers imposing any pricing structure desired.	Very flexible; desirable for support of computing utility systems.	Little guidance provided as to how prices should be determined.

Source: McKell, Lynn J., Hansen, James V., and Heitger, Lester E. "Charging for Computer Resources." *Computing Surveys* 11, 2 (June 1979): 105-120. Copyright (1979), Association for Computing Machinery Inc.

basis of external market prices. The rationale for the market-based approach is that the information resource, as a profit center, should be viable in an open competitive market. Some problems with this approach are (1) it may be difficult to obtain appropriate market prices, (2) in many cases it may be impractical to run jobs externally so that the competition is ineffective, and (3) there may be other than economic considerations in maintaining an internal computer center, for example, privacy, response time, and control.

This issue is perhaps best summarized in the words of McKell et al. (1979), who wrote: "Measurement tends to be a prohibitive factor in applying many models which are conceptually desirable.... On balance, the weaknesses or impracticality of most proposed models seem sufficient justification for concluding that considerable work is still needed to provide organizations with mechanisms which are conceptually sound, yet not impossible to implement."

7.9 Capacity Management

Capacity management consists in planning ahead for hardware needs so that increments to the hardware system can be acquired in an orderly, timely, and economic manner. Note that the discussion here is in terms of increments to systems, rather than initiation and termination. This is the way that capacity is usually changed—by upgrade rather than total replacement. Conceptually, there is no difficulty in thinking of each upgrade as initiation of a new system to replace the old system, which can be thought of as terminated. The dates of upgrades are then identical to the initiation and termination dates in the formal analysis. The capacity management model presented below is based on Ein-Dor (1977).

Future hardware needs are, of course, a function of services to be provided and programs to be written in the future. In the simplest case, no new software is anticipated, and growth is purely a function of increases in the existing workload. In this case, predicting future requirements is relatively simple, since predicted increases in amount of processing to be done will produce roughly proportional increases in the computer time required. This may be illustrated as in Figure 7.10.

In this figure, the horizontal axis represents the time line, with t_0 the current time and t_i representing the ith year in the future; the vertical axis represents system capacity and workload requirements in terms of a reference workload—full capacity of the current system. Assuming there is a current level of utilization of 70%, then C_0 and U_0 represent the current capacity and utilization. Further assume there is an anticipated annual increase of 15% in the workload; then the straight lines C and U represent the changes in utilization and capacity over a number of years. This description indicates that the system will begin to approach saturation within two years and will be completely saturated within three. Thus, an upgrade in system capacity should be

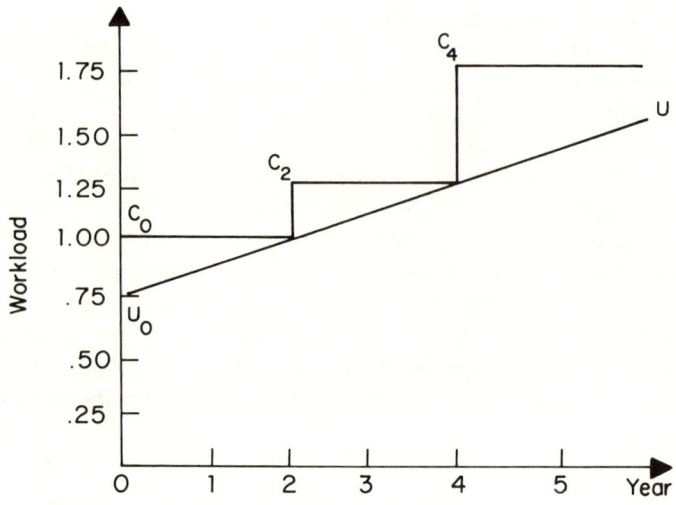

Figure 7.10 Projected hardware capacity requirements.

planned for about two years from the present in order to permit unimpeded execution of the anticipated workload. Capacity after the upgrade will depend on the replacement systems available on the market and on the degree of slack planned. If an increase of 30% is planned in capacity, to be installed at t_2, then capacity after t_2 will be C_2, allowing for considerable additional growth in workload. Two years later, the new system will approach saturation and will be replaced in its turn by a newer system with capacity, say, C_4, which will suffice for several more years. Thus, capacity management may be regarded as consisting of forecasting increases in workload and planning the "steps" in capacity enhancement accordingly. The better the forecast and the planning, the closer capacity will be to actual utilization and the less unnecessary slack there will be in the system.[1]

EXERCISE 7.9 Capacity Management Assumptions

What is the hidden assumption in Figure 7.10?

In a more realistic example than that discussed above, growth in workload will probably be a function both of natural growth in existing applications

---

[1] The emphasis here is on *unnecessary* slack, since some slack is essential in any system to allow for peak periods, unplanned maintenance, and higher growth than predicted.

7.9 Capacity Management

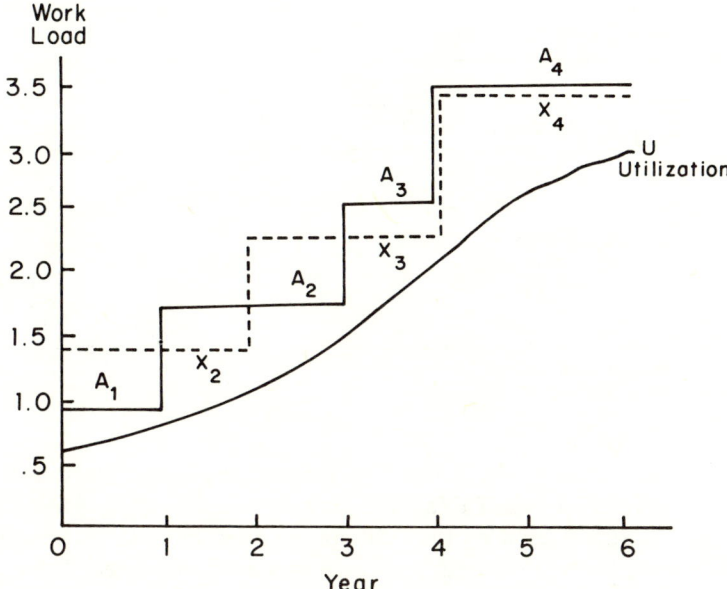

Figure 7.11 Analysis of configuration requirements.

and of new applications to be developed over the planning period. For organizations undergoing rapid growth in computer utilization, the capacity utilization forecast may look like the curve labeled U in Figure 7.11, rising rapidly as planned additions to workload are implemented, and then becoming less pronounced as the development plan is completed and additional increases stem from natural growth in transaction volumes.

In order to fit a hardware configuration to the projected growth in workload, it is useful to think of the workload as expressed in units of the capacity of the existing system. This is a convenient unit because, based on past experience with an existing system, it is a known quantity that can serve as a basis for forecasting the capacity of replacement systems under consideration. Thus, the capacity of the current system is always 1; in the example, the current workload is 0.85. The workload projected at the end of the five-year planning horizon is 2.95 units of the capacity of the existing system. The projected workloads in each of the intervening years are specified in Table 7.10.

Given the workload projection, it is now necessary to compare the performance of feasible systems with that workload. The computer system capacities and their costs proposed by two vendors are exhibited in Table 7.9. Notice that the data, adapted from those for real systems, fall into four quite distinct categories in terms of capacity and cost; we refer to these categories as classes of systems.

Table 7.9 System Capacities and Costs

		Class of system			
Vendor		1	2	3	4
ABC					
	capacity[a]	1.0	1.3	2.6	3.5
	cost[b]	60	82	100	115
XYZ		—	1.4	2.3	3.4
	cost[b]	—	82	93	116

[a] In units of reference workload.
[b] Monthly rental charge in $'000.

If the system capacities in Table 7.9 are compared to the yearly workload requirements detailed as in Table 7.10, it is easy to see what the growth paths are for the systems offered by the different vendors. In order to simplify the analysis a little, we will assume that systems must be replaced at the beginnings of years in which they would otherwise become saturated. For vendor ABC, system A1's capacity of 1.0 would be inadequate to meet year 2's requirement of 1.1 units of workload. Thus, if the decision is to remain with ABC, system A1 will need to be replaced at the beginning of year 2. The capacity will then be 1.8, which is sufficient for years 2 and 3, in both of which the requirement is less than A2's capacity. In year 4, it is necessary to upgrade to system A3, since the requirement of 2.1 units of workload is beyond A2's capacity. The following year, it will be necessary to move up to system A4, which is then sufficient until the end of the planning horizon. A similar analysis for vendor XYZ indicates that the configuration should be managed so

Table 7.10 System Growth Paths: Projected Workload of Figure 7.9

Year	Workload (year end)	Vendor					
		ABC			XYZ		
		system	capacity	rental[a]	system	capacity	rental[a]
1	0.85	A1	1.0	720	X2	1.4	984
2	1.10	A2	1.8	984		1.4	984
3	1.55		1.8	984	X3	2.3	1176
4	2.10	A3	2.6	1200		2.3	1176
5	2.65	A4	3.5	1380	X4	3.4	1392
6	2.95		3.5	1380		3.4	1392

[a] Rentals are annual rental charges in thousands of dollars.

7.9 Capacity Management

Table 7.11 Computation of Present Costs

Year (t)	Discount factor: $1/(1+4)^{**}t$	System A nominal outlays[a]	System A discounted outlays[a]	System X nominal outlays[a]	System X discounted outlays[a]
1	0.833	720	600	984	820
2	0.694	984	683	984	683
3	0.579	984	570	1176	681
4	0.482	1200	578	1176	567
5	0.402	1380	555	1392	560
6	0.335	1380	462	1392	466
Total			3448		3777

[a] Thousands of dollars annually.

that system X2 is available in years 1 and 2, system X3 in years 3 and 4, and system X4 in years 5 and 6.

In order to reach a conclusion as to which vendor's offerings permit optimal management of capacity over the planning period, the cost of each growth path must now be considered. The annual cost data in Table 7.10 show that in some years system A is the cheaper, and in other years system X. In order to establish the overall cost, it is necessary to compute the present cost of the outlay streams associated with each of the systems, as has been shown in the analytical development throughout this book. The calculation of the present cost is contained in Table 7.11, which assumes a discount rate of 20%. This calculation shows that for the workload growth anticipated, system A, offered by ABC, is the most economic choice, and evolution of the system configuration should be based on that determination.

It is important to note that the conclusion reached in the previous paragraph in no way implies that ABC's products are superior to XYZ's in any general sense. The only implication is that ABC's product line is better suited than XYZ's to the particular circumstances described. This conclusion is, in fact, quite sensitive to any change in the assumptions, whether about anticipated workload or about the interest rate. Table 7.12 assumes a different growth path than in the previous analysis and leads to different conclusions about the optimal solution. At a 20% discount rate, the present cost of the outlays associated with System ABC is $3.66M, while for System XYZ it is only $3.62M; given a different projected growth path, the relative advantages of the systems are reversed. Thus, the values of the decision variables are a function of the problem parameters, as shown in the discussion of sensitivity analysis in the formal model.

Table 7.12 System Growth Paths: For Workload Projected in the Table

Year	Workload (year end)	Vendor ABC			Vendor XYZ		
		system	capacity	rental[a]	system	capacity	rental[a]
1	1.10	A2	1.8	820	X2	1.4	820
2	1.30	—	1.8	683	—	1.4	683
3	1.90	A3	2.6	695	X3	2.3	681
4	2.10	—	2.6	578	—	2.3	567
5	2.20	—	2.6	482	—	2.3	473
6	2.35		2.6	402		2.3	394
Total				3660			3618

[a] Annual rental charges in thousands of dollars, discounted at 20%.

Note, furthermore, that the decision to acquire a system that will not be fully utilized is perfectly consistent with the analytical model that chooses levels of utilization. In selecting a system to meet its needs for a number of years, management implicitly decides on the level of utilization for the system in each year of its operation.

As the discussion suggests, the capacity management problem is usually solved as if the workload is defined as a constraint which must be met; the choice then is of the cheapest system that meets the constraint. The decision to upgrade a system at a certain time implies that, at that point, the marginal operating cost plus the marginal capacity cost of the new system is less than the combined operating and capacity costs of the old system.

EXERCISE 7.10 Capacity Management Decision Problem

State the capacity management technique discussed in the text as a formal decision problem.

References

Borovits I., and Ein-Dor P. (1977) "Cost/Utilization: A Measure of System Performance." *Communications of the ACM* 20, 3 (March):185–190.

Cale, E. G., Gremillion, L. L., and McKinney, J. L. (1979) "Price/Performance Patterns of U.S. Computer Systems." *Communications of the ACM* 22, 4 (April):225–232.

Ein-Dor P. (Forthcoming) "Grosch's Law Revisited Again: CPU Power and the Cost of Computation." *Communications of the ACM*.

References

Ein-Dor, P. (1977) "Dynamic Approach to Computer Selection." *Datamation* 23, 6 (June):103–108.

Kanter, H., Moore, A., and Singer, N. (1968) "The Allocation of Computer Time by University Computer Centers." *Journal of Business* 41 (July):375–384.

Knight, Kenneth E. (1966) "Changes in Computer Performance." *Datamation* (September):40–54.

Knight, Kenneth E. (1968) "Evolving Computer Performance 1963–1967." *Datamation* (January):31–35.

Marchand, M. (1968) "Priority Pricing With Application to Time Shared Computers." In *AFIPS 1968 Fall Joint Computer Conference*. Vol. 33. Washington, DC: Thompson, pp. 511–519.

McKell, Lynn J., Hansen, James V., and Heitger, Lester E. (1979) "Charging for Computer Resources." *Computing Surveys* 11, 2 (June):105–120.

Nielsen, R. (1968) "Flexible Pricing: An Approach to the Allocation of Computer Resources." In *AFIPS 1968 Fall Joint Computer Conference*. Vol. 33. Washington, DC: Thompson, pp. 521–531.

Nielsen, R. (1970) "The Allocation to Computer Resources—Is Pricing the Answer?" *Communications of the ACM* 13, 8 (August):468–474.

Selwyn L. L. (1970) "Computer Resource Accounting in a Time-Sharing Environment." In *AFIPS 1970 Spring Joint Computer Conference*. Vol. 36. Montvale, NJ: AFIPS Press, pp. 119–130.

Smidt, S., (1968a) "Feasible Pricing of Computer Services." *Management Science* 14, 10 (June):B581–B599.

Smidt, S. (1968b) "The Use of Hard and Soft Money Budgets, and Prices to Limit Demand for Centralized Computer Facilities." In *AFIPS 1968 Fall Joint Computer Conference*, Vol. 33. Washington, DC: Thompson, pp. 499–509.

Solomon, Martin B., Jr. (1966) "Economies of Scale and the IBM System/360." *Communications of the ACM* 9, 6 (June):435–440.

Streeter, D. N. (1973) "Centralization or Dispersion of Computing Facilities," *IBM Systems Journal* 12, 3:283–301.

Chapter 8
The Software Development and Maintenance Activity

8.1 Software Development and Maintenance in the Information System

The purpose of the software development and maintenance activity is to provide the information system with applications and systems software products. The manager of the activity is responsible for providing applications and systems software products to the computer center manager. To perform this role the software activity manager draws upon the computer center for computer time, the labor market for systems analysts and programmers, and the market for software development tools for development software. Part A of Table 8.1 displays a list of the resources and products employed in the software activity and the symbols associated with them.

Since the software activity manager is responsible for many applications products and many systems products, the activity is conceptualized as a number of project teams, each working on a specific product. These systems analysis and programming teams each require computer time, systems analysis and programming labor, and the use of software development tools. Figure 8.1 displays the block diagram of the software development and maintenance process. By allocating the software activity's resources (computer usage, systems analysis and programming labor, and software development tools) among the individual software projects, the manager produces the required software products to meet scheduled completion dates. All the resources except the software development tools share the characteristic that use by one project precludes their simultaneous use by another. Consequently, these resources are accounted for by a subscript for the specific project. Software development tools, on the other hand, are analogous to the applications software used in the computer center. Their use in one project does not

8.1 Software in the Information System

preclude their concurrent use on another project. Thus, the software tool variable appears in all the projects. It has the characteristics of a collective (or public) good. These internal variables and their associated symbols are displayed in Part B of Table 8.1.

In planning, coordinating, and controlling the information system, central management designates the software activity as a cost center. As such, central management must inform the software manager of the transfer prices for computer resources used in software activities: CPU time (q_{CS}), memory (q_{MS}) and input/output devices (q_{YS}), the transfer prices for the products—q_{Na}

Table 8.1 Software Activity Variables and Symbols

Part A		
RESOURCES		
Computer usage		
CPU time	C_s	
memory	M_s	
inputs/outputs	Y_s	
Labor		
system analysts/programmers	L_s	
Software tools		
software development tools	$N_s(s = 1 \cdots S)$	
PRODUCTS		
application software products	$N_a(a = 1 \cdots A)$	
systems software products	$N_b(b = 1 \cdots B)$	
Part B		
Type	Application products ($a = 1 \cdots A$)	System products ($b = 1 \cdots B$)
INPUTS TO PRODUCT DEVELOPMENT		
CPU time	C_{Sa}	C_{Sb}
memory	M_{Sa}	M_{Sb}
inputs/outputs	Y_{Sa}	Y_{Sb}
system analysts/programmers	L_{Sa}	L_{Sb}
software development tools	N_s	N_s
OUTPUTS FROM PRODUCT DEVELOPMENT		
application products	N_a	($a = 1 \cdots A$)
system products	N_b	($b = 1 \cdots B$)

applications products and q_{Nb} for systems products—and the required activity performance level. Performance of the software activity manager will be measured by the products produced, N'_a ($a = 1 \cdots A$) and N'_b ($b = 1 \cdots B$), their delivery time to the computer center, T'_{Da} ($a = 1 \cdots A$) for applications software, and T'_{Db} ($b = 1 \cdots B$) for systems software—and their marginal cost. In addition, the planning period, that is, the overall life cycle of operations (T_B to T_E), is provided. In turn, the software manager supplies central management with the computer requirements (C_S, M_S, Y_S), the present life-cycle marginal costs of software products, PMRGCOST (N'_a; $a = 1 \cdots A$), PMRGCOST N'_b; $b = 1 \cdots B$), and the present life-cycle marginal cost of the required delivery date, PMRGCOST (T'_{Da}; $a = 1 \cdots A$), PMRGCOST (T'_{Db}; $b = 1 \cdots B$). Central management uses this information to adjust the performance required from the software activity in coordination with the computer center so that the present life-cycle marginal revenue generated by the requirements equals the present life-cycle marginal cost. This is so that present marginal life-cycle profit for the organization *as a whole* will be zero and hence the organization's overall activity optimized. This is done by setting the transfer price of software (q_{Na}; $a = 1 \cdots A$) (q_{Nb}; $b = 1 \cdots B$) equal to the present life-cycle marginal cost. See Figure 8.1.

The manager of the software activity is knowledgeable about the labor market for systems analysts and programmers and therefore knows the wage and salary rates, including fringe benefits (p_{Ls}). It is assumed that the software tools will be rented, and the manager also knows the rental rate (p_{Ns}; $s = 1 \cdots S$) in the marketplace. Thus, the software manager will minimize present life-cycle cost of operations in his or her activity, constrained by the technology available for software development, the products required, and delivery times. The manager will accomplish this cost minimization by appropriate choice of the level of each resource to employ and the mix and allocation of these resources to the various projects. The next section discusses the nature of software and the technology for developing it.

8.2 Software Development and Maintenance Technology

Software development and maintenance technology is frequently discussed in terms of computer support required, software tools available, and personnel skills needed. Here the focus is on identifying a relationship between the resources employed in the development process and the product itself. The discussion of this perspective will begin with the identification of measurements for the resources and products.

Computer use is measured in the same manner as in the computer center. CPU time is frequently measured in seconds, memory in kilobytes per unit of time, and the inputs and outputs by a count (e.g., lines printed or disk accesses). The multiple dimensions of the input/output variable are reduced

8.2 Software Development and Maintenance Technology

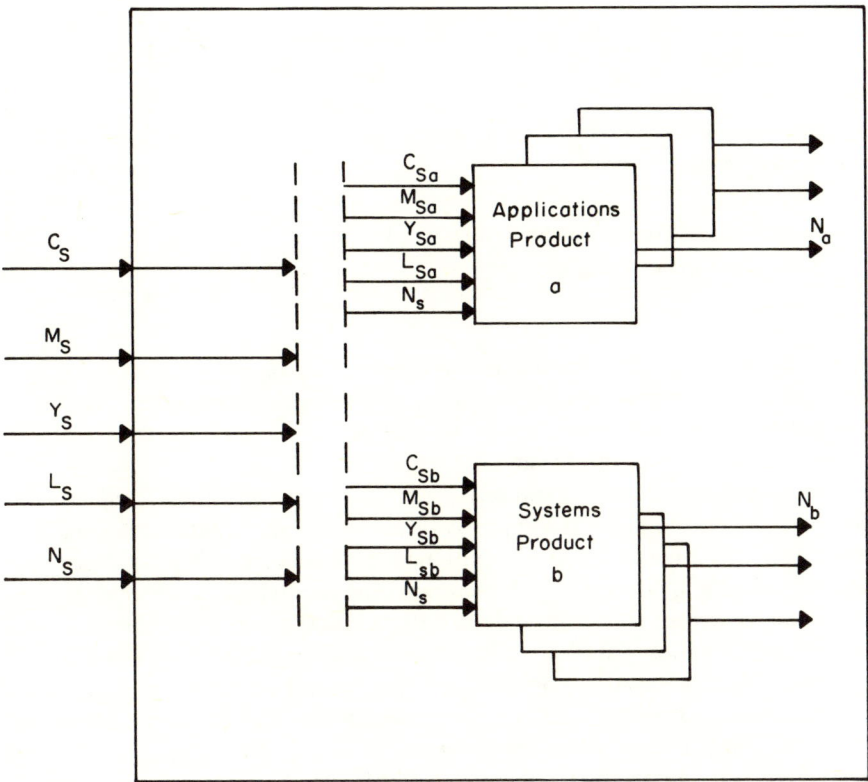

Figure 8.1 Software development and maintenance activity block diagram.

here to one measure for convenience of exposition. Labor is measured in man-months (usually considered to be 152 working hours to allow for vacations, sick leave, etc.). The software product itself can be considered a collection of attributes such as the number of source instructions, the number of types of transactions to be processed, and the number of manipulations of each transaction. That is, the software specifications themselves define the software to be developed and hence constitute a set of attributes. For ease of understanding, this multiplicity of attributes will be reduced to the program size, that is, the number of source instructions measured in thousands. This particular choice follows the work of Boehm (1981) and Putnam (1978).

The life cycle of software development has been partitioned into different stages by various authors. Table 8.2 displays a sequence that begins with "a gleam in the eye" and ends with the product being superseded and removed from use. For simplicity, all products will be considered to be useful until the end of the planning horizon (T_E). In conformance with the work by Boehm and Putnam, the project development cycle will be considered to begin at the

Table 8.2

- Product Idea
- Feasibilty Analysis
- Requirements Determination (Specifications Set)
- Product Design
- Coding
- Integration and Testing (And Product Delivery)
- Product Use and Maintenance

end of the requirements determination process and to end when delivery occurs upon the completion of integration and testing. Maintenance begins at this point in time and continues to the end of the planning horizon and is a function required by central management.

The nature of software is somewhat unique among products used in business and government. Software is a capital asset in an organization just like plant and equipment and must be managed as such. Yet it is an asset that does not physically depreciate. A program once written does not change with use. Thus, software is an infinitely durable capital asset. Now this does not mean that the value of such a capital asset is unchanged forever. The value of a capital asset is the life-cycle product incremental revenue minus product incremental maintenance and operating costs, where the life cycle is measured from the point in time when the evaluation occurs. As technology changes and other software products become available, marginal revenue will usually decline, so the capital asset value of software tends to decline with time. In these terms, one can study the optimal replacement time; this will not be done here, but the reader can easily apply the concepts of Section 7.1 to this analogous decision problem.

The maintenance aspects of software include two separate activities. First, the correction of logical or coding errors in programs is a maintenance activity. Software packages are never completely reliable, so some of this activity always occurs after products are delivered. Thus, there is a cost of corrective maintenance for each product beyond its delivery date. The second aspect is the creation of new software products by modification of old ones. This is not really maintenance, but the exact dividing line between correcting an error and upgrading a product is never perfectly clear in practice. For example, a single change in a payroll program is induced by a tax law change; is this maintenance or development? And what if an old error is corrected at the same time? While strictly speaking this is development (because the specifications change), the full management aspects of development are not invoked. Such a change would usually be managed as a maintenance project. Thus, some of the projects in the software activity are development activities with "old" software as a resource input, that is, evolutions of existing software

8.2 Software Development and Maintenance Technology

rather than *de novo* development. This will not be further emphasized, and "old" software will not be mentioned explicitly as a resource but is "behind the scenes" for some projects.

With this background, the production relationships for development and maintenance will be discussed in turn. Significant work in this area has been performed by Boehm (1981) and Putnam (1978); their models, while differing in detail and possibly in forecasting accuracy, are alike in generic concept. Boehm provides a conceptualization that is easily understood and is generally also consistent with Putnam's estimation procedure for software costs. Boehm calls his model COCOMO for *constructive cost model*. In the notation used here the basic equations of his model for product i are:

$$L_{si} = 2.4 N_i^{1.05}, \quad i = a, b. \tag{8.1}$$

$$T_{Di} - T_{Bi} = 2.5 L_{si}^{0.38}, \quad i = a, b. \tag{8.2}$$

Remember that software products, N_i, are characterized by the number of lines of source code which they comprise. As a first step in generalizing these resource requirement equations the constants will be labeled by letters, since for applications software these are organization- and product-specific. Thus,

$$L_{si} = A_i N_i^{Gi}, \quad i = a, b. \tag{8.3}$$

$$T_{Di} - T_{Bi} = D_i L_{si}^{Ei}, \quad i = a, b. \tag{8.4}$$

Clearly there are other impacts on the quantity of labor needed to produce source instructions. These are called cost drivers. In the present context they relate to computer use (C_S, M_S, Y_S) and software tools (N_s). They can be expressed as multipliers on the right-hand side of (8.1) and (8.2). Each of these effort multipliers is, in general, a function of the level of the cost driver employed. Thus,

$$L_{si} = A_i N_i^{Gi} f^{CSi}(C_{Si}) f^{MSi}(M_{Si}) f^{YSi}(Y_{Si}) f^{Ns}(N_s), \quad i = a, b; \tag{8.5}$$

$$T_{Di} - T_{Bi} = D_i L_{si}^{Ei}, \quad i = a, b. \tag{8.6}$$

This suggests, and empirical data support the idea, that an increase in a cost driver decreases the quantity of labor needed to produce a given program of fixed size. Correspondingly, the decrease in labor decreases the product's development time. The input requirement equation (8.5) can be written as a production function, that is,

$$N_i = \frac{1}{A_i f^{CSi}(C_{Si}) f^{MSi}(M_{Si}) f^{YSi}(Y_{Si}) f^{Ns}(N_s)} L_{si}^{1/G_i}, \quad i = a, b. \tag{8.7}$$

Rather than dealing with this complex specific relationship, the following general relationship is convenient for our purposes here:

$$N_i = f^{Ni}(C_{Si}, M_{Si}, Y_{Si}, L_{si}, N_{si}), \quad i = a, b. \tag{8.8}$$

Based on the empirical data of Boehm (1981), Putnam (1978), and Brooks (1975), this production function exhibits decreasing marginal physical productivity to each input (C_{Si}, M_{Si}, Y_{Si}, L_{si}, N_s) and, from the data in Boehm's work, generally decreasing physical returns to scale for each project.

Intuition (and the relationship discussed) suggests that there are long-run substitution possibilities among the resources for a fixed number of source instructions produced. However, the product development time will decrease as other inputs are substituted for labor; this is not a reasonable result. Furthermore, for fixed levels of source instructions produced, increases in the total resources used should decrease product development time, at least up to some point. But this is not expressed in the relationship discussed. A different relationship for product development time is necessary.

Boehm's equations [(8.1) and (8.2)] can be combined to begin the search for a more realistic model. Equation (8.9) results from combining (8.1) and (8.2).

$$T_{Di} - T_{Ri} = 2.5(2.4N_i^{1.05})^{0.38}, \qquad i = a, b. \qquad (8.9)$$

Thus, the size of the project directly affects product development time. However, it also highlights the difficulty of using the computer, labor, and software tools to reduce development time for a fixed project size. Clearly what is needed is a way for the resources (C_S, M_S, Y_S, L_s, N_s) to directly impact on development time. A general relationship that can do this and includes the effect of project size is

$$T_{Di} - T_{Bi} = f^{Ti}(N_i, C_{Si}, M_{Si}, Y_{Si}, L_{si}, N_s), \qquad i = a, b. \qquad (8.10)$$

As used previously, an incremental change in one of the determinants of the schedule (e.g., N_1) will also change the schedule itself incrementally. In earlier discussions this concept was labeled as the marginal physical productivity. Here, since the result is the project's schedule, the concept is called marginal physical schedule productivity. In the relationship of equation (8.10), the marginal physical schedule productivity of product size is positive [MPSchP(N_i, $T_{Di} - T_{Bi}$) > 0; $i = a, b$]. The basic resources have marginal physical schedule productivities that are negative [e.g., MPSchP(C_{Si}, $T_{Di} - T_{Bi}$) < 0; $i = a, b$].

These two marginal physical schedule productivities are clearly separate ideas. Yet, there is also an overall impact on the product development time due to a change in C_{Si}, M_{Si}, Y_{Si}, L_{si}, N_s ($i = a, b$), since these inputs have an indirect impact via the product size, N_i, as well as a direct impact. These two effects are additive, at least for rather small changes. Overall, the net marginal physical schedule productivity (NETMPSchP) is the algebraic sum of the two components. The indirect effect is the product of the effect of increasing the product size [MPSchP(N_i, $T_{Di} - T_{Bi}$)] and the effect on product size of a change in C_{Si}, M_{Si}, Y_{Si}, L_{si}, or N_s [e.g., MPP(M_{Si}, N_i)]. So the equation for

8.2 Software Development and Maintenance Technology

the net marginal physical schedule productivity of CPU time is

$$\text{NETMPSchP}(C_{Si}, T_{Di} - T_{Bi}) = \text{MPP}(C_{Si}, N_i)\text{MPSchP}(N_i, T_{Di} - T_{Bi})$$
$$+ \text{MPSchP}(C_{Si}, T_{Di} - T_{Bi}), \qquad i = a, b. \tag{8.11}$$

There are similar relationships for M_{Si}, Y_{Si}, L_{si}, and N_s. By the previous discussion the first term on the right-hand side is positive, while the second term is negative. The effect of an increased use of labor on the product development time is then an empirical question about the relative magnitudes of these two terms. Certainly, the folklore of software development is full of tales about project managers who believed the second term to be greater than the first—only to find out that this was not the case; for an example see Brooks (1975). Of course it is possible, and even likely, that at some level of use of labor (or any other resource) the second term is also negative. Again, the point of inflection from positive to negative is an empirical question. Brooks (1975) suggests that he found that inflection point and went beyond it.

In summary, there are two general technology-based relationships that describe the software development process. Of course, depending on the software specifications (e.g., complexity or computational difficulty) there can be differences in details. If "old" software is adapted to new specifications, the associated demand for resources will be less than in *de novo* development. The purpose of the general relationships is to capture the general picture in which the details are included. The relationships are

$$N_a = f^{Na}(C_{Sa}, M_{Sa}, Y_{Sa}, L_{sa}, N_s), \qquad a = 1 \cdots A. \tag{8.12}$$

$$N_b = f^{Nb}(C_{Sb}, M_{Sb}, Y_{Sb}, L_{sb}, N_s), \qquad b = 1 \cdots B. \tag{8.13}$$

$$T_{Da} - T_{Ba} = f^{Ta}(N_a, C_{Sa}, M_{Sa}, Y_{Sa}, L_{sa}, N_s), \qquad a = 1 \cdots A. \tag{8.14}$$

$$T_{Db} - T_{Bb} = f^{Tb}(N_b, C_{Sb}, M_{Sb}, Y_{Sb}, L_{sb}, N_s), \qquad b = 1 \cdots B. \tag{8.15}$$

The maintenance production function can be developed in the same manner. That is, the number of source instructions that can be maintained is a function of the resources C_S, M_S, Y_S, L_s, and N_s. Each of these resources would be expected to have positive marginal productivities. To permit a general discussion, these will be assumed to be different to the development functions. Thus,

$$N_{am} = f^{Nam}(C_{Sam}, M_{Sam}, Y_{Sam}, L_{sam}, N_s) \qquad a = 1 \cdots A. \tag{8.16}$$

$$N_{bm} = f^{Nbm}(C_{Sbm}, M_{Sbm}, Y_{Sbm}, L_{sbm}, N_s) \qquad b = 1 \cdots B. \tag{8.17}$$

The fraction of the total number of source instructions that require maintenance at any moment of time is denoted as z. This fraction will most likely decline as a function of time, so the number of source instructions requiring maintenance at time t is $Z_i(t)N_i$ ($i = a, b$). Notice that the fraction requiring maintenance is product-specific.

8.3 The Manager's Long-Run Decision Problem

The software manager's long-run decision problem is to minimize the present life-cycle cost of producing the required applications and systems software by the specified delivery dates, as constrained by the available software development and maintenance technology. In accomplishing this, the software manager can choose the quantities of resources to employ

$$(C_S, M_S, Y_S, L_s, N_s),$$

the allocation of these resources to specific product development projects,

$$\{(C_{Sa}, M_{Sa}, Y_{Sa}, L_{sa}, N_s) \quad a = 1 \cdots A;$$
$$(C_{Sb}, M_{Sb}, Y_{Sb}, L_{sb}, N_s) \quad b = 1 \cdots B;$$
$$(C_{Sam}, M_{Sam}, Y_{Sam}, L_{sam}, N_s) \quad a = 1 \cdots A;$$
$$(C_{Sbm}, M_{Sbm}, Y_{Sbm}, L_{sbm}, N_s) \quad b = 1 \cdots B;\},$$

and the time to begin each specific project,

$$(T_{Ba}, a = 1 \cdots A; T_{Bb}, b = 1 \cdots B).$$

These last decision variables permit the choice of the products' development periods to meet the delivery dates fixed by central management.

The software development and maintenance cost equation, expressed as a present value, is composed of a set of terms for development costs and another set for maintenance costs. Development costs consist of the costs of computer usage, labor, and software tools. The expression for this is

PLC DEVELOPMENT

$$= \sum_{a=1}^{A} \left\{ \int_{T_{Ba}}^{T_{Da}} [(q_{CE}C_{Sa} + q_{Me}M_{Sa} + q_{YE}Y_{Sa} + p_{Ls}L_{sa})e^{-rt}] \, dt \right\}$$

$$+ \sum_{b=1}^{B} \left\{ \int_{T_{Bb}}^{T_{Ba}} [(q_{CE}C_{Sb} + q_{ME}M_{Sb} + q_{YE}Y_{Sb} + p_{Ls}L_{sb})e^{-rt}] \, dt \right\}$$

$$+ \int_{T_B}^{T_E} [p_{NS}N_s e^{-rt}] \, dt. \qquad (8.18)$$

The maintenance costs can be calculated from

PLC MAINTENANCE

$$= \sum_{a=1}^{A} \left\{ \int_{T_{Da}}^{T_E} [(q_{CE}C_{Sam} + q_{ME}M_{Sam} + q_{YE}Y_{Sam} + p_{Ls}L_{sam})e^{-rt}] \, dt \right\}$$
$$+ \sum_{b=1}^{B} \left\{ \int_{T_{Db}}^{T_E} [(q_{CE}C_{Sbm} + q_{ME}M_{Sbm} + q_{YE}Y_{Sbm} + p_{Ls}L_{sbm})e^{-rt}] \, dt \right\}.$$

(8.19)

The cost of software tools for maintenance is already included in the development cost, since software tools have the characteristic of a collective good. The sum of (8.18) and (8.19) is the present life-cycle cost of software development and maintenance (PLCSw).

The technology available to the manager was discussed in the last section. Equations (8.12) to (8.17) express these technological possibilities.

Central management requires the software manager to produce specified products [applications (N'_a, $a = 1 \cdots A$) and systems (N'_B, $b = 1 \cdots B$)] at specified delivery dates [(T'_{Da}, $a = 1 \cdots A$), (T'_{Db}, $b = 1 \cdots B$)].

These components of the manager's decision problem are combined to express the formal decision problem. This is the first exercise of this chapter.

EXERCISE 8.1 The Software Manager's Formal Decision Problem

State in symbols the formal software decision problem.

8.4 The Manager's Long-Run Decision Rules

The manager's decision rules will be developed, using the procedure for product-constrained minimum-cost problems developed in Chapter 4. The first decision rules concern (1) the mix of resources in the production of a specific software product, (2) the allocation of resources in the production of alternative products, and (3) the allocation of resources in the production of a specific product and its maintenance. After that, the levels of all the resources will be considered. The last topic is the development of a measure of the present life-cycle marginal cost of a product and its scheduled delivery date.

8.4.1 The Decision Rule for the Mix of CPU Time and Memory in the Development of Applications Software Product a

Assuming that all other resources and mixes of resources are at their cost-minimizing values, the minimum cost mix of CPU time and memory will occur where the marginal product per dollar expended is the same for both resources. That is where

$$\frac{\text{MPP}(C_{Sa}, N'_a)}{\text{MPLC}(C_{Sa})} = \frac{\text{MPP}(M_{Sa}, N'_a)}{\text{MPLC}(M_{Sa})}. \tag{8.20}$$

Algebraic rearrangement and recognition of the ratio of the marginal physical products as the marginal rate of technical substitution yields

$$\frac{\text{MPLC}(C_{Sa})}{\text{MPLC}(M_{Sa})} = \frac{\text{MPP}(C_{Sa}, N'_a)}{\text{MPP}(M_{Sa}, N'_a)} = \text{MRTS}(C_{Sa}, M_{Sa}). \tag{8.21}$$

The present life-cycle marginal cost of CPU time (and, analogously, of memory) is composed of two parts. The first part is the present life-cycle marginal cost of the rental of CPU time. The formula for this is

$$\text{MPLC}(C_{Sa} \text{ RENTAL}) = \int_{T_{Ba}}^{T'_{Da}} [q_{CE} e^{-rt}] \, dt. \tag{8.22}$$

The second part is the impact on the product development schedule of a marginal change in CPU time allocated. In computing this impact, the net marginal physical schedule productivity measures the marginal change in the time to begin the development (the decision variable for development time, since the delivery date is fixed) from a marginal change in CPU time used. The formula for this is, from (8.11),

$$\begin{aligned}\text{NETMPSchP}(C_{Sa}, T'_{Da} - T_{Ba}) \\ = \text{MPP}(C_{Sa}, N'_a)\text{MPSchP}(N_a, T'_{Da} - T_{Ba}) \\ + \text{MPSchP}(C_{Sa}, T'_{Da} - T_{Ba}).\end{aligned} \tag{8.23}$$

The cost of incrementally increasing the development time of a project is the incrementally incurred project operating cost discounted to the present, that is,

$$[(q_{CE}C_{Sa} + q_{ME}M_{Sa} + q_{YE}Y_{Sa} + p_{Ls}L_{sa})e^{-rT_{Ba}}].$$

Collecting all these formulas yields the manager's decision rule:

The manager of software development and maintenance should choose, *ceteris paribus*, the mix of CPU time and memory to employ in the development of application software product *a* by applying the following formula:

$$\text{MRTS}(C_{Sa}, M_{Sa}) = \frac{\text{MPLC}(C_{Sa})}{\text{MPLC}(M_{Sa})}. \tag{8.24}$$

8.4 The Manager's Long-Run Decision Rules

where

$$\text{MPLC}(C_{Sa}) = \int_{T_{Ba}}^{T'_{Da}} [q_{CE} e^{-rt}] \, dt$$

$$+ (q_{CE} C_{Sa} + q_{ME} M_{Sa} + q_{YE} Y_{Sa} + p_{Ls} L_{sa}) e^{-rT_{Ba}} [\text{MPSchP}(C_{Sa}, T'_{Da} - T_{Ba})$$

$$+ \text{MPP}(C_{Sa}, N'_a) \text{MPSchP}(N_a, T'_{Da} - T_{Ba})]. \tag{8.25}$$

$$\text{MPLC}(M_{Sa}) = \int_{T_{Ba}}^{T'_{Da}} [q_{ME} e^{-rt}] \, dt$$

$$+ (q_{CE} C_{Sa} + q_{ME} M_{Sa} + q_{YE} Y_{Sa} + p_{Ls} L_{sa}) e^{-rT_{Ba}} [\text{MPSchP}(M_{Sa}, T'_{Da} - T_{Ba})$$

$$+ \text{MPP}(M_{Sa}, N'_a) \text{MPSchP}(N_a, T'_{Da} - T_{Ba})]. \tag{8.26}$$

This decision rule is rather more complex than those studies heretofore. Note that the second term of the present life-cycle marginal cost calculations can be positive, zero, or negative, and hence, so could MPLC itself. The managerial interpretation of these cases is the next exercise.

EXERCISE 8.2 Interpreting the C_{Sa}, M_{Sa} Mix Decision Rule

Provide a managerial interpretation of the C_{Sa}, M_{Sa} mix decision rule for all logical cases.

The following exercise asks the reader to develop and interpret other product development input mixes.

EXERCISE 8.3 Product Development Resource Mixes

Develop and interpret the decision rules for the following mixes of resources in development of applications software products:

1. the mix of C_{Sa}, L_{Sa};
2. the mix of M_{Sa}, Y_{Sa}.

8.4.2 The Decision Rule for the Allocation of CPU Time Between the Development of Application Software Product a and Systems Software Product b

The products here are alternative products, not technologically substitutable products. If the software activity were a profit center, the logic of equal marginal revenues would be applicable. But it is not. Therefore, this decision rule is not developed by an application of the usual logic of mix decisions. The next exercise requires some consideration of the underlying nature of the software activity. Remember that the activity is organized as a set of parallel production processes, though some time displacement is possible.

EXERCISE 8.4 The Allocation Between C_{Sa} and C_{Sb}

Develop the logic and interpret the allocation decision for allocation between C_{Sa} and C_{Sb}.

8.4.3 The Decision Rule for the Allocation of Labor Between Development and Maintenance

As shown in the last case, the routine application of a logical procedure can lead to the wrong result. The manager's situation here includes a requirement to maintain the products developed and delivered. The maintenance workload, $Z_a(t)$, is assumed to be a function of the product's size, in source instructions, that declines with time (Z_a decreases as t increases). Thus, the manager's only choice is the cost-minimizing mix of inputs to provide the maintenance function. As the manager's choices do not include decision variables that can affect the maintenance workload, there can be no tradeoff between development and maintenance. The next exercise requires this decision situation to be modified to include such a tradeoff.

EXERCISE 8.5 The Development–Maintenance Tradeoff

Modify the software manager's decision problem to permit a development–maintenance tradeoff. Develop the relevant decision rule for this modified decision problem.

8.4.4 The Cost-Minimizing Level of Each Resource to Employ

The cost-minimizing level of each resource to employ is computed by using the mix decision rule in combination with the appropriate description of the software production function. The total level to employ is the sum of the

8.4 The Manager's Long-Run Decision Rules

levels from the individual projects. The details of this are left to the reader to develop.

8.4.5 The Present Life-Cycle Marginal Cost of a Product and Its Schedule

Assuming that the cost-minimizing mixes and levels have been set, the marginal cost of a product can be determined by the usual procedure. Let C_{Si} be designated as the cost measurement resource, the numeraire, for product i ($i = a, b; a = 1 \cdots A; b = 1 \cdots B$). A marginal increase in the required output, N_i, will require additional resources. This is measured by the MPIR (N'_a, C_{Sa}). The MPLC(C_{Sa}) has already been found [equation (8.25)]. So the value of the MPLC of N_i is

$$\text{MPLC}(N'_i) = \text{MPIR}(N'_i, C_{Si})\text{MPLC}(C_{Si}), \qquad (8.27)$$

$$i = a, b; \quad a = 1 \cdots A; \quad b = 1 \cdots B,$$

where

$$\text{MPLC}(C_{Si}) = \int_{T_{Bi}}^{T'_{Di}} [q_C e^{-rt}]\, dt$$

$$+ (q_{CE}C_{Si} + q_{ME}M_{Si} + q_{YE}Y_{Si} + p_{Ls}L_{si})e^{-rT_{Bi}}[\text{MPSchP}(C_{Si}, T'_{Di} - T_{Bi})]$$

$$+ \text{MPP}(C_{Si}, N'_i)\text{MPSchP}(N_a, T'_{Da} - T_{Ba}). \qquad (8.28)$$

In the discussion leading to equation (8.28) for MPLC(C_{Si}) the MPLC(T_{Bi}) was explained as the marginal present life-cycle cost of the product development schedule, that is, $T_{Di} - T_{Bi}$. Hence it is the MPLC of the delivery date as well. Thus,

$$\text{MPLC}(T'_{Di}) = (q_{CE}C_{Si} + q_{ME}M_{Si} + q_{YE}Y_{Si} + P_{Ls}L_{si})e^{-rT_{Bi}}. \qquad (8.29)$$

$$i = a, b; \quad a = 1 \cdots A; \quad b = 1 \cdots B.$$

The numbers computed from (8.27) and (8.29) are the numbers transmitted to central management so it can set the transfer price for software and coordinate the schedules of new products between the software activity and the computer center.

8.4.6 The Decision Rule for the Level of Software Tools to Rent

Software tools are universally available to all and, for simplicity, are assumed to be used by all projects once a rental agreement has been signed. If they are not universally used then either a specific tool is universally used by a subset of the projects or it is project-specific. In any case, the development here or the previous development can easily be applied.

From the perspective of central management, the marginal cost of a software product must be made equal to the marginal revenue it can yield for the organization as a whole. That is, the marginal cost of a software product is a measure of the marginal revenue foregone when the organization is coordinated as a whole. Thus, a product's marginal cost can be understood as an opportunity cost. Using this idea, the next exercise deals with development of the decision rule for software tools.

EXERCISE 8.6 The Decision Rule for the Use of a Software Tool

Develop and interpret the decision rule for the level to rent of a software tool (N_s).

8.5 The Software Manager's Short-Run Decision Problem

As previously discussed, *the* short-run decision problem does not really exist. However, an interesting short-run situation to explore is where the availability of software tools is fixed (N'_s, $s = 1 \cdots S$), the quantity of labor is upper-bounded,

$$\sum_{a=1}^{A} L_{sa} + \sum_{b=1}^{B} L_{sb} \leq L'_s,$$

and the computer center's system is memory-bound so that the software activity has an allocation

$$\sum_{a=1}^{A} M_{Sa} + \sum_{b=1}^{B} M_{Sb} \leq M'_S.$$

It is possible that not all the labor and memory will be used in a cost-minimizing operation. But central management requires that they must nevertheless be paid for at the full quantity level. With this definition of the short run, the next exercise asks for a formal statement of the decision problem

---

EXERCISE 8.7 The Short-Run Decision Problem

State in symbols and words the software manager's short-run decision problem.

8.6 The Software Manager's Short-Run Decision Rules

Since this type of logical development has become familiar, if not routine, it will be presented as a sequence of exercises. In doing the exercises, do not forget that the upper bounds imposed imply that there is an opportunity cost present in the manager's decision making.

EXERCISE 8.8 The Short-Run Mix Decision Rules

Develop and interpret the decision rules for the mix of

    a. CPU time and memory in the development of application product a.
    b. memory and labor in the development of application product a.

EXERCISE 8.9 The Short-Run Level Decision Rules

What is the logic used in finding the levels of C_{Sa}, M_{Sa}, and L_{sa} to employ?

EXERCISE 8.10 The Marginal Cost of Product and Schedule

Develop and interpret the formula for the present life-cycle marginal cost of product N'_a and schedule T'_{Da}.

8.7 Special Topics

This section of the chapter contains discussions of several special topics. They include some advanced software development and maintenance models not mentioned before, central management issues (financing, charging for software products, making or buying software products, and the optimal time to replace software products), the software development and maintenance cost function and the related subject of software product cost estimating, estimating software conversion costs, and productivity measurement in a software development and maintenance activity.

8.7.1 Advanced Models

Only one type of labor has been defined in the model of software development and maintenance developed here. In practice, a software activity employs many types of labor. One direction to increase the realism of the software activity management model is to treat systems analysis labor and programmer labor as distinctly different skills. In addition, the applications and systems software can present different types of development and maintenance problems, so that labor specialization to one or the other can be productive. The following exercise is designed to permit the reader to develop and study an advanced labor specialization model.

EXERCISE 8.11 An Advanced Labor Specialization Model

Develop and interpret a software development and maintenance model that includes labor specialized by systems analyst skills, programmer skills, and also by type of software developed—applications or systems. Also develop and interpret the decision rules that differ from the original model. In particular, what is the managerial issue involved in these exercises?

Another aspect of labor not modeled until now is experience. The quantitative expression of the long-known fact that workers become more productive with experience in performing a task is called a learning curve. Suppose that the learning affects both marginal and average physical productivity. One way to model this idea is to use the symbols $1(t)L_{si}$, where the symbol L_{si} ($i = a, b; a = 1 \cdots A; b = 1 \cdots B$) was used in the original model. This notation qualifies the amount of labor employed (L_{si}) by its effectiveness $1(t)$ to yield effective labor, denoted as $l(t)L_{si}$. As time passes, the worker becomes more experienced—$l(t)$ increases as t increases, and hence the effective man-hours available are increased. L_{si} man-hours are employed in an accounting sense, but in terms of productivity equivalents, there are $l(t)L_i$ man-hours employed. In Figure 8.2 the effect of experience gained by labor can be seen as an increase in software produced and/or maintained. That is, in order to produce an output level of N_{it} it is necessary to use L_s man-hours. The L_s man-hours can be obtained by either hiring L_s man-hours of "inexperienced" labor or L'_s man-hours of "experienced" labor, which at time t' effectively generates L_s man-hours; $l(t')L'_s = L_s$. This also means that the marginal physical productivity of experienced labor is effectively higher than that of inexperienced labor (compare the respective slopes on the total productivity curve). Thus the marginal physical productivity of labor is $l(t)\mathrm{MPP}[l(t)L'_{si}, N'_i]$ ($i = a, b; a = 1 \cdots A; b = 1 \cdots B$).

Figure 8.2 Labor learning curve: total software production.

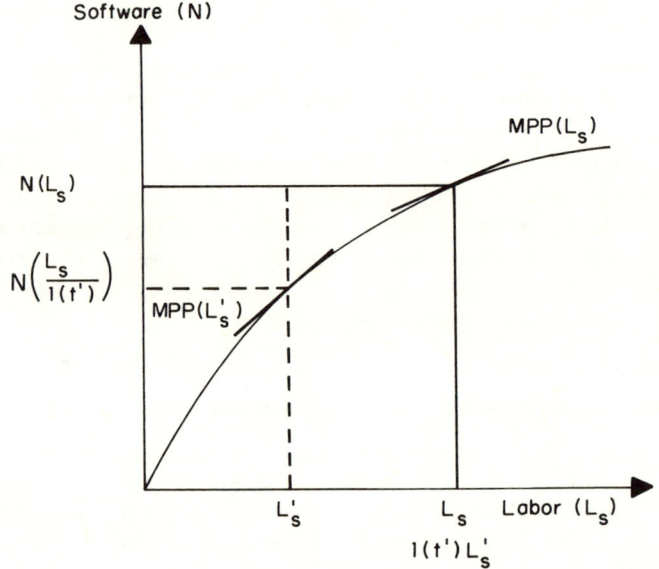

8.7 Special Topics

Putting all this in a formal model is straightforward but somewhat inconvenient. Assuming that this has been done and that more experienced personnel command a higher wage rate (and fringe benefits), then the managerial issue is the tradeoff at the cost-minimizing point between inexperienced and experienced labor. The next exercise asks for a discussion of this issue.

EXERCISE 8.12 The Mix of Experienced and Inexperienced Labor

State the formal decision rule for the cost-minimizing mix of experienced and inexperienced personnel and interpret it.

Another area in which the original model could be advanced is to relax the requirement that future years in the plan replicate the present. The projections of technology and prices might then show variations over time. Some hints at these ideas were given in earlier discussions. For example, the projected transfer price of CPU time may be a function of time, for example, $q'_{CE} = f^q(t, C'_E)$ where C'_{CE} represents the parameters in the projection or estimating relationship. The empirical work of Boehm (1981) and Putnam (1978) shows that manpower is employed in software product development projects in a pattern that follows a modified Rayleigh distribution over time. Boehm's COCOMO estimating equation for the quantity of labor needed at a particular point in time (in the symbols of this chapter) is

$$L_{si}(t) = L_{si}^{\text{total}} \left(\frac{0.15(T'_{Di} - T_{Bi}) + 0.7t}{0.25(T'_{Di} - T_{Bi})^2} \right)$$

$$e^{\left[-\frac{(0.15[T'_{Di} - T_{Bi}] + 0.7t)^2}{0.5(T'_{Di} - T_{Bi})^2} \right]^{1/2}},$$

$$i = a, b; \quad a = 1 \cdots A; \quad b = 1 \cdots B, \tag{8.30}$$

where L_{si}^{total} is the total quantity of labor used on the project. Boehm's procedure uses the size of the product, $N'_i(i = a, b; a = 1 \cdots A; b = 1 \cdots B)$, with some additional cost drivers as required to estimate the needed L_{si}^{total} [see equation (8.1)]. In turn, L_{si}^{total} is used in equation (8.30) and the estimating equation for $T'_{Di} - T'_{Bi}$ [see equation (8.2)] to compute $L_{si}(t)$. This is an appropriate approach for estimating software product development costs. Figure 8.3 shows the result pictorially.

Figure 8.3 also suggests that the description of product development technology used in the model in this chapter [equations (8.8) and (8.10)] should be modified to be explicit about time effects. An easy way to accomplish this is to ensure that a specific development technology applies at each point in time and that the required output *at that moment in time* $[N'_i(t), i = a, b]$ is set

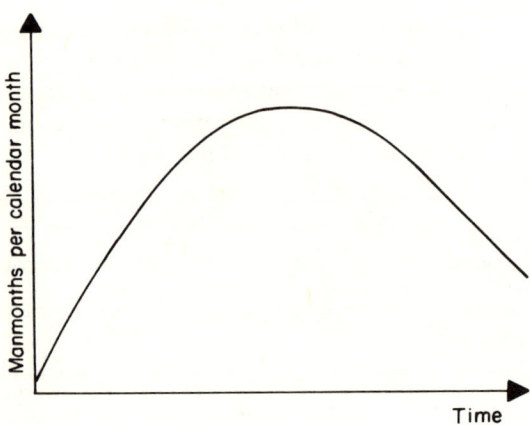

Figure 8.3 A software project manpower loading curve.

before the manager's cost-maximization problem is solved. Central management, or at least the software activity manager, would set $N'_i(t)$ on the basis of the "immmutable laws" of development time history. More generally, the software activity manager minimizes cost by choosing (1) the time path of $N'_i(t)$ such that N'_i is delivered on date T'_{Di}, and (2) the time paths of $L_{si}(t)$ and other resources. The analysis of such a situation is beyond the scope of this book, but it is the next level of software development management that should be studied.

8.7.2 Central Management Issues

Since the software activity is designated as a cost center, this activity itself cannot be the focus of any analyses as to whether it is economically viable; financing issues must be handled at a higher organizational level. However, the central management issue of whether to have an in-house software activity (the make-or-buy software decision) is related to economic viability. If the overall organization is at least to cover costs, then the combination of the computer center *and* the software activity must be jointly profitable. If this is the case, then central management can formulate and solve the decision problem as to whether it is less expensive to make or buy software.

EXERCISE 8.13 The Make or Buy Software Decision

Formulate and interpret the decision problem to make or buy software and develop and interpret the decision rule.

8.7 Special Topics

Given an in-house operation, the appropriate transfer price for software is set by central management so that MRGCOST (SOFTWARE) equals MRGREV (SOFTWARE) across the organizational boundary between the software activity and the computer center. The formulas (8.27) and (8.29) provide the information on the supply side. One implication of this is that the make-buy decision can only be made for a specific quantity of software to produce where the software activity and the computer center are coordinated with regard to the quantity of software demanded and supplied. Note also that the correct transfer price involves the long-run marginal cost, not the short-run. However, a most advanced model may include, for example, some near-term upper bounds on resource quantities as well as a future ability to vary the quantities of these resource availabilities. Thus, a more advanced model shows a rather constrained near-term with a flexible future. In such an advanced model, the long-run marginal cost of a product, that is, the present life-cycle marginal cost, is the appropriate measure of marginal cost to use in pricing decisions. It includes the effect of near-term opportunity costs imposed by constraints on inputs as well as future substitution and acquisition flexibilities. It is also the case that the marginal cost of a software product in such a model will vary with time, being higher in the near term than in the future [compare equations (8.27) and (8.29) with the answers to Exercise 8.10]. Also, long-run average cost is lower than short-run average cost except at the point of tangency with the U-shaped short-run average cost curve. That is, the minimum average cost production method for a given level of product is at least as great in the short run as in the long run. Geometrically, the long-run average cost curve is the "envelope" of the short-run average cost curves.

8.7.3 The Software Cost Function

The cost function for the software development and maintenance activity is different from the cost function for a specific project. Since a project has a single product to produce at a specific delivery date, the project cost function is analogous to the cost function developed in Chapter 4. The difference is that it is exactly like the Chapter 4 case only for a fixed delivery date. Such a function parametrized for delivery date can be written as

$$C_{Ni} = f^{CN}(N_i; T'_{Di}, q_{CE}, q_{ME}, q_{YE}, p_{Ls}, p_{Ns}, r, T_B, T_E),$$

$$i = a, b; \quad a = 1 \cdots A; \quad b = 1 \cdots B. \quad (8.31)$$

In the rest of this discussion the prices of the units, the discount rate, and the overall planning horizon ($T_E - T_B$) will be suppressed. The average and marginal cost of a software product measured by its size will exhibit the usual U-shape, provided there are decreasing marginal physical productivities to each resource and a range of increasing physical returns to scale, followed by a range of decreasing returns to scale. However, the discussion in Chapter 6 on the computer center cost function shows that the idea of physical returns to scale is a stronger assumption about a software development project than is needed. That is, projects would tend to be expanded (or contracted) in a way that uses the cost-minimizing mix of resources. Hence average cost might decrease for a cost-minimizing change, even if it did not do so for a proportionate change to all resources. Thus, it is possible for the technology to have decreasing physical returns to scale and yet exhibit increasing scale economies, since scale economy is defined locally as average cost divided by marginal cost. There is no empirical evidence on the degree of scale economies for software development projects. The usual argument for small teams suggests the possibility of negative scale economies, while the use of large teams in practice suggests the possibility of positive economies of scale. Clearly this is an important matter because sizing a project is dependent on knowledge of the average cost curve. In particular, suppose a project is sized at the bottom of the U-shaped curve (if it is U-shaped at all!). This can mean that the overall software product must be partitioned into modules that constitute a set of cost-minimizing projects. This type of decision was not included in the model explored earlier in the chapter.

Another aspect of the project cost function to explore is the effect of changing the delivery date. That is, it is of interest to understand how the cost-minimizing solution varies with the delivery date. This type of analysis is called comparative statics and involves comparing the cost-minimizing solution for T'_{Di} with the cost-minimizing solution for, say, T''_{Di}. If a schedule stretch-out for a fixed size of the software product reduces the resources needed (fewer resources for a longer time) the present life-cycle costs will decrease and so the average cost curve will shift down (i.e., for a given product size the stretched-out average cost curve is below the original). Correspondingly, an earlier delivery date will do the opposite. This information can be used by central management to set schedules in a coordinated fashion with the computer center and its associated marginal revenue. When the model used is an advanced one with variation in resource levels, it is possible that the above results can change, so a detailed analysis is required. This is beyond the scope of this book.

Given that all projects are governed by cost functions that exhibit U-shaped average cost curves, the next step is to study the cost function for the software activity itself. The project cost functions are the product incremental costs for the software activity and product-specific returns to scale are the scale attribute of the project cost function. If the projects were not "linked" by the use of software tools, the overall costs would be the sum of the project costs and, intuitively, there would be little ground for economies of scope. Thus, the grouping of the projects in a software activity would not generate lower costs. However, they are linked by the universality of software tools, so there is reason to expect that there are economies of scope. That is, it is less expensive to operate the projects jointly and pay for the software tools once, rather than pay for them on each and every project.

The degree of scale economies for the software activity as a whole has not been studied empirically. However, it is known that if an increase in one product decreases or leaves unchanged the marginal cost of all other products, then there will be positive economies of scale. In the software activity case, there is no reason to expect such an interaction between projects as long as the resources can be employed freely. Thus, scale economies are expected to be present in the software activity. Overall, it appears that a software activity, as an organizational entity where essentially independent multiple projects are located, is economically more viable than separate project organizations. On the other hand, several authors, most notably Brooks, have noted that coordination costs among projects in large software units, and especially within large projects, increase exponentially. This coordination cost may eliminate or even overwhelm any economies of scale. Thus there is still a serious question of empirically determining the magnitude of these effects and using them to structure software projects, that is, to determine the size and number of projects, and to provide minimum-cost products by appropriate mixes of resources.

8.7.4 Software Product Cost Estimating

As mentioned earlier in this chapter, software cost estimating is a fairly well-developed discipline, thanks to the efforts of Putnam and Boehm. This short discussion will outline a general procedure for estimating the costs of a specific software product. Equations (8.1) and (8.2) are Boehm's basic estimating equations.

$$L_{si} = 2.4 N_i^{1.05}. \tag{8.1}$$

$$T_{Di} - T_{Bi} = 2.5 L_{si}^{0.38}. \tag{8.2}$$

The general procedure is to estimate the number of source instructions and then use this to find the total labor needed $\hat{L}_{si}$. This in turn is used to estimate the length of the project. Then using the manpower-loading relationship [equation (8.20)] with $\hat{L}_{si}$ and $T_{Di} - T_{Bi}$, the best time pattern of the manpower loading for the project may be obtained. This can then be converted to a true budget requirement by multiplying by the average cost of labor, including fringe benefits. The present life-cycle cost is obtained by discounting this time series of costs to the present. At a more advanced level, there are separate procedures analogous to the above for different categories of software, including an adjustment for software conversions.

Another advanced model is the adjustment of the general procedure for the impact of the nature of the product, the nature of the computer system, the details of project organization and planning, and the nature of the personnel.

Each of these is detailed, and, for each detailed category, a point rating scale is used to develop an "effort" multiplier to be used to adjust the numbers obtained by the basic procedure. This adjusts the labor, development time, and manpower loading for the specific product in a given context, yielding a better estimate of the cost of a software product. For those involved in such activities, details can be found in Boehm (1981) and Putnam (1978).

8.7.5 Computer System Conversion Costs: Estimation and Analysis

Given that the life cycle of software products is generally longer than that of hardware systems, the conversion of software from one system to another is a frequent requirement. This aspect of software management is notorious among professionals for the technical problems it poses and the consequent high costs incurred. In this section, a computer system conversion cost model is discussed. It is based on the work of the Naval Data Automation Command and the General Accounting Office. Data collected and analyzed by these organizations are then synthesized to provide an estimation method for the total cost of conversion. The software conversion costs are discussed first, then their relationship to other nonhardware conversion costs. Finally, total conversion costs are considered. The reader should be aware of the fact that this discussion is based on very limited data and should not be considered a universal model. It is included in order to demonstrate the kind of data required and what can be done with limited data when available.

A considerable amount of work on software conversion costs has been performed by the Conversion and Project Management Group at the Naval Data Automation Command (NAVDAC). This group, which is undoubtedly responsible for some of the most advanced exploratory work in this field, has developed a flow model of the software conversion process. The group has collected data on manpower costs associated with converting over 150 application systems and has developed a parametric cost-estimating equation for software conversion costs. The result of this work has been formalized in a Project Management Control System (NAVDAC; GSG, 1980). It is recognized by all users of the System that additional work is necessary to evolve improved cost-estimating parameters.

The dependent variable in the NAVDAC study is the number of man-days invested in the conversion process. This variable is, of course, readily convertible into dollar costs, using an organizationally appropriate manpower costing model. The estimating algorithm is a linear model, the parameters of which are derived from quantitative attributes of the inventory of software to be converted. This model is

$$MD = aL + bP + cM + dF + eN, \qquad (8.32)$$

8.7 Special Topics

where MD = estimated man-day resource requirements for conversion,

L = number of lines of code/1000,
P = number of programs,
M = number of independent runs plus number of job streams,
F = total number of files,
N = number of individual applications.

(The notation used here is that of the original studies and is unrelated to the general notation in this book as exhibited in the List of Symbols). To date, the linear regression coefficients for this model have been estimated as:

$$a = 2.39$$
$$b = 6.17$$
$$c = 5.69$$
$$d = 2.26$$
$$e = 9.34$$

Equation (8.32) was derived from a study of four site conversions comprising more than 150 applications, over 1500 individual programs, and nearly 1 million lines of code. The total manpower effort expended was some 100 man-years. The equation derived from these data account for some 95% of the total variance with some 90% explained by the number of programs (P) alone. Thus, the remaining independent variables contribute only marginally, albeit significantly, to the accuracy of the predictions based on this model. The purpose of this equation is to predict the man-days required for a specific conversion. Hence the overriding criterion is the correlation between manpower requirements and the linear combination of software attributes. The work to date is most helpful in this regard.

Total system conversion costs. The General Accounting Office (GAO) has collected data on total costs experienced by five government agencies that recently undertook major computer system conversions (GAO, 1980). These data are contained in Table 8.3, exhibiting absolute dollar costs, and Table 8.4, which exhibits the relative cost contributions within projects.

Table 8.3 is interesting in that it provides the order of magnitude of costs involved, ranging from about $7 million in the least expensive case to $25 million in the most expensive. These numbers lend some support to the argument that computer system conversions are a major cost item and deserve close examination. Of particular interest in this table are cases III and V, representing hardware systems of nearly identical cost in two different installations of the same agency, both operating on a service bureau basis. In the

Table 8.3 Costs of Converting Five Computer Systems in Government Agencies ($'000)

	Case number				
Cost factor	I	II	III	IV	V
Computer hardware	17,268	10,388	5,388	4,852	5,084
Software conversion	3,412	3,331	4,575	1,492	1,004
Dual operation	3,655	2,899	2,788	606	439
Site modification	582	1,252	726	484	322
Training	151	1,833	520	235	121
Total	25,068	19,703	13,997	7,669	6,970

one case, all nonhardware costs amounted to about $1.9 million, and in the other to about $6 million. An explanation for this anomaly is offered later in this chapter.

Unfortunately, the size of the sample provided by the five cases exhibited is not sufficient to permit rigorous statistical analysis. However, an examination of the data and a comparison of the distribution of the costs for the individual cases with their weighted mean leads to the hypothesis that there is consistency in the cost distributions. Furthermore, values for each of the individual cases for each factor are within or just beyond one standard deviation from the mean for each factor. If this consistency hypothesis holds, then it is possible to extrapolate from the software conversion costs estimated by equation (8.32) to nonhardware conversion costs. Applying the weighted average of software conversion costs to all nonhardware costs developed in Table 8.4 $(100.00/45.4 = 2.2:)$ yields

$$\text{nonhardware conversion costs} = 2.2 \times MD \times CMD \qquad (8.33)$$

Table 8.4 Percent of Nonhardware Conversion Cost Contributed by Cost Factors[a]

	Case number					Average	
Cost factor	I	II	III	IV	V	Weighted	Unweighted
Software conversion	43.7	35.8	53.1	53.0	53.2	45.4	47.8
Dual operation	46.9	31.1	32.4	21.5	23.3	34.1	31.0
Site modification	7.5	13.4	8.4	17.2	17.1	11.1	12.7
Training	1.9	19.7	6.0	8.3	6.4	9.4	8.5
All Nonhardware	100.0	100.0	99.9	100.0	100.0	100.0	100.0

[a] Note that not all totals are exactly 100.0% because of round-off errors.

8.7 Special Topics

where MD = number of man-days, from equation (8.32),

CMD = average cost per man-day
(salary + fringe benefits + retirement).

The relationship between hardware and nonhardware costs in conversions is exhibited in Table 8.5. Again, remarkable uniformity in the relative costs is evident for cases I, II, IV, and V. The lone exception, case III, is apparently *sui generis* and exhibits much higher relative costs for nonhardware items than do the other cases. The difference for this case is so great that its relative costs are nearly three standard deviations from the means for the other cases. The substantive difference between case III and the other four, which apparently caused the differences noted, is that it involved the conversion of a database management system (DBMS), which the others did not. It is interesting that in spite of the great differences in the relative costs of hardware and nonhardware items for case III, within the nonhardware category its costs behave very much like those for the other cases. Considering nonhardware items only, case III is consistently within two standard deviations of the means for the remaining cases, and for no factor does including the data for case III increase the variance. On the contrary, for three of the four factors, adding the data for case III reduces the variance.

Total computer system cost estimating and analysis. Assuming case III to be representative of a special class of conversions and omitting it from the analysis, the total cost of a computer system conversion that does not involve a DBMS can be estimated as

$$TC = HW + NHW, \qquad (8.34)$$

Table 8.5 Percent of Total Cost Contributed by Cost Factors[a]

| Cost factor | Case number | | | | | Weighted average |
	I	II	III	IV	V	I, II, III, V
Software conversion	13.6	16.9	32.8	19.5	14.4	15.6
Dual operation	14.6	14.7	20.0	7.9	6.3	12.8
Site modification	2.3	6.4	5.2	6.3	4.6	4.4
Training	0.6	9.3	3.7	3.1	1.7	3.9
All nonhardware	31.1	47.3	61.7	36.8	27.0	36.7
Hardware	68.9	52.7	38.3	63.3	72.9	63.3
Total	100.0	100.0	100.0	100.1	99.9	100.0

[a] Note that not all totals are exactly 100.0% because of round-off errors.

where
$$TC = \text{hardware cost,}$$
$$HW = \text{nonhardware costs.}$$

But
$$HW = 1.72 NHW,$$
so that
$$TC = 2.72 NHW. \qquad (8.35)$$

Also, from equation (8.33),
$$NHW = 2.2 \times MD \times CMD,$$
so that
$$TC = 2.72(2.2 \times MD \times CMD),$$
$$= 5.98 \times MD \times CMD,$$

which, from equation (8.32),
$$= 5.98(2.39L + 6.17P + 5.69M \times 2.26F + 9.34N) \times CMD,$$
$$= (14.29L + 36.90P + 34.03M + 13.51F + 55.85N) \times CMD. \quad (8.36)$$

Thus, given the quantitative software parameters and an average cost per man-day, it is possible to estimate the total cost for converting a non-DBMS system, assuming consistency in the planning ratios and the correlation between software characteristics and man-days required for conversion. Presumably, similar regularities exist for DBMS-oriented systems, but the one case available does not permit analysis.

As all the meager data available were used in estimating the parameters of equation (8.36), no data are left to which the estimating function can be applied in order to test its predictive ability. The collection of such data on the quantitative aspects of inventories of software to be converted, and a rigorous accounting of all costs incurred during the conversion process, is clearly called for.

8.7.6 Productivity Measurement

The ideas of productivity measurement are no different when used in the software context than elsewhere. Clearly, average and marginal physical productivities are available. It is also possible to use cost functions and their characteristics (e.g., scale economies). The most commonly used measure is to divide output by the quantity of labor used. This yields the average physical productivity of labor, and then this one measure becomes *the* measure of productivity. Basically, this is the practice in the software industry where productivity is frequently measured by the number of instructions delivered divided by the total man-months needed to produce the product. The following exercises permit a thoughtful consideration of productivity measurement using all the concepts developed to this point.

EXERCISE 8.14 The Usefulness of Productivity Measurement

Productivity, however measured, is a concept that is frequently said to be useful in managing a software activity. Explain the use of a productivity concept in managing a software activity.

EXERCISE 8.15 Software Activity Productivity Measurement

Given the answer to Exercise 8.14, suggest how productivity should be measured in a software activity.

8.8 Summary

The material in this chapter concerns the application of the basic analytical tools to a series of models of the software development and maintenance activity. The models are designed to provide insight into decisions concerning organization of the software activity and choice of type, level, and mix of resources and the appropriate software development technology. The scheduling of projects is also considered. The discussion of cost functions for individual projects and for the overall activity provides insight into the possibility of economies of scale. The use of this and other ideas in productivity measurement is also explained.

References

Boehm, Barry W. (1981) *Software Engineering Economics.* Englewood Cliffs, NJ: Prentice-Hall.

Brooks, Fred P. (1975) *The Mythical Man-Month,* Reading, MA: Addison-Wesley.

General Accounting Office. (1980) *Conversion: A Costly, Disruptive Process That Must Be Considered When Buying Computers.* Report to the Chairman, Committe on Appropriations, House of Representatives, by the Comptroller General of the United States. Washington, DC.

GSG Inc. (1980) *DPSC Experience Using the NAVDAC Conversion Management System.*

NAVDAC. (no date) *Project Management Control System.* DPSC Software Conversion Project, Management Support Section, Washington, DC.

Putnam, Larry H. (1978) "A General Empirical Solution to the Macro Software Sizing and Estimating Problem." *IEEE Transactions on Software Engineering* (July): 345–361.

Chapter 9
Information Users

9.1 Users and the Information Resource Management System

As we discussed in Chapter 5, users are managers of organizational units, which, for ease of exposition, are considered to be not directly involved in computer operations. A user may manage a production, financial, personnel, or any other functional unit. Whatever the specific function of the units, manager-users use information in making decisions. The information can be classified into that which is of a universal nature and is supplied by central management (e.g., balance sheets, income statements, policy guidelines), that which is routinely supplied as specific information services tailored to meet the units' needs (e.g., budget expenditure reports, personnel status), and that which is the result of specific action by users in the form of jobs submitted to the computer center in either batch or interactive mode (e.g., budget planning exercises, capital expenditure analysis). The creation and coordination of these information flows is the central issue of information resource management (IRM). It can only be solved by central management action in structuring the IRM system and then setting the transfer prices, output levels, and budgets so that system behavior is coordinated. In this chapter user decision problems will be studied within the context of a decision structure set by central management.

Each user, u, is assigned a life-cycle information budget $(B_{Iu}; u = 1 \cdots U)$ within which he or she is required to operate. This budget is designed for the entire planning period (i.e., time T_B to T_E) and is in present value units. This permits the user to trade off activity over time in consonance with the organization's rate of time tradeoff (the organization's discount rate r). Some information is supplied by central management without charge. This is the universal information $(I_v; v = 1 \cdots V)$. Use of information services in the form

9.1 Users and the Information Resource Management System

of standard reports is charged at the rate q_{Ik} at the time the services are used. In addition, users can initiate processing by submitting jobs to the computer center. For each of the jobs processed, j, computer capacity used is charged at the prevailing transfer price for each of the resources utilized (C_{Ej} at q_{CE}, M_{Ej} at q_{ME}, Y_{Ej} at q_{YE}; $j = 1 \cdots J$). Each job also requires labor L_{uj} to be expended at the prevailing wage rate (p_{Lu}). Table 9.1 displays the variables and their symbols.

The manager-user is also constrained to use the prevailing technology for composing and submitting jobs, and for processing information. This is a relationship based on technology that relates computer resources—CPU time, memory, and peripherals—and user information-processing labor to the amount of information produced. As with the technologies of the computer center software activity, central management is not necessarily conversant with the details of this technology, but the concept is understood. Central management is aware that this technology is an integral part of the manager-user's decision problem structure.

Organizational units are not necessarily required by central management to be profit or cost centers. Rather, central management recognizes that many

Table 9.1 The User Model: Variables and Symbols

Name	Symbol	
Information		
universal information	I_v	$v = 1 \cdots V$
specific information services	I_k	$k = 1 \cdots K$
user-generated information	I_{uj}	$j = 1 \cdots J$
		$u = 1 \cdots U$
Computer capacity		
CPU time	C_{Ej}	$j = 1 \cdots J$
memory	M_{Ej}	$j = 1 \cdots J$
inputs/outputs	Y_{Ej}	$j = 1 \cdots J$
Labor		
user information-processing labor	L_{uj}	$j = 1 \cdots J$
Transfer prices		
specific information services	q_{Ik}	$k = 1 \cdots K$
CPU time	q_{CE}	
memory	q_{ME}	
inputs/outputs	q_{YE}	
Market prices		
user information-processing labor	p_{Lu}	$u = 1 \cdots U$
User information budget	B_{Iu}	$u = 1 \cdots U$
Organizational rate of discount	r	

units do not readily lend themselves to such objective measures. There are many organizational units that are budget-constrained and managed by subjective judgment. In these cases, the manager-user's subjective judgments play a key role in understanding information resource management. This is the case assumed here and much of this chapter is devoted to modeling users' subjective judgments in the context of information collection.

9.2 User Information Generation Technology

If the user's unit management responsibilities were the topic of discussion, then the detailed process of composing and submitting jobs and returning results to the user would be necessary and of interest. Here, however, the focus is on the information system as a whole, so details of system components have been suppressed. Specifically, in the current context, details of individual jobs will be suppressed. Since in most information systems individual jobs are not control variables, it is not helpful to include them in detail, given the increase in complexity that inclusion entails. While the computer system cannot provide services without specific jobs being submitted, the focus is on total computer capacity made externally available (C_E, M_E, Y_E), and the details of specific jobs are not necessary. Central management controls and coordinates by setting budgets, transfer prices, and software outputs so that the demand for and supply of computer capacity is in balance. Hence, in the user context, the overall relationship between specific jobs (denoted j) and the information-generating resources (CPU time, memory, peripherals, labor) is all that need be articulated. This relationship is the function for information production by a user. The relationship can be written as

$$I_{uj} = f^{Iuj}(C_{Ej}, M_{Ej}, Y_{Ej}, L_{uj}), \qquad j = 1 \cdots J, \quad u = 1 \cdots U. \qquad (9.1)$$

This relationship has not been studied empirically, but observation suggests that it exhibits decreasing marginal physical productivities to each resource and also decreasing physical returns to scale. There is another resource that may appear in this relationship, namely, application software available in the computer center library. Managerial analyses or "what-if" questions frequently involve statistical analysis, linear programming, or other standard applications programs. In the information system described here, this has not been made explicit, in order to reduce the complexity of the model. A number of modifications may be introduced into the model to account for more complex control mechanisms. Some of these are discussed throughout the chapter, following their presentation as exercises. It is suggested that readers test their grasp of the material by doing the exercises before reading the discussion. The next exercise involves modifying the models to include users being charged for the use of computer library application programs.

9.2.1 Applications Programs as an Information Resource

EXERCISE 9.1 Applications Programs as an Information Resource

Modify the models in Chapters 5, 6, and 7 as necessary to permit the development and use of applications software to be controlled by a price mechanism in all its uses. How is its development and use controlled in the models included in Chapters 5 through 7.

Exercise 9.1 Discussion. Clearly this requires significant restructuring of the model. In the model used so far, applications software is "owned" by the software activity and exclusively rented by the computer center. Control is obtained through a software requirements determination process, the marginal cost of software products generated by the software activity, and a rental price for software paid by the computer center to the information systems manager. These structural elements are embedded in an iterative process among central management, the software activity, the computer center and the users. One possible change in the planning and control system is to permit software to be rented directly by the users as well as by the computer center. Central management then has two methods of obtaining the equilibrium services for users—by users' own production and by computer center production. These alternative methods permit a comparison, analogous to competition in the private sector, that ameliorates the monopolistic tendencies of a single computer center. In the final equilibrium one would expect the lowest-cost alternative to dominate entirely unless central management chooses to maintain a higher-cost method to provide a "disciplining" of the process. It might also happen that computer center production was cheapest for some types of software, while functional units could produce other types more efficiently themselves.

9.3. The Information Expenditure Budget

Users expend budgets both for the resources necessary to produce information themselves ($I_{uj}: j = 1 \cdots J, u = 1 \cdots U$) and for routinely supplied information products ($I_k: k = 1 \cdots K$). Each of these expenditures occurs at the time the information is provided to the user. Thus the present life-cycle expenditure by each user for information is

$$\sum_{j=1}^{J} \int_{T_B}^{T_E} [(q_{CE}C_{Ej} + q_{ME}M_{Ej} + q_{YE}Y_{Ej} + p_{Lu})e^{-rt}] \, dt$$
$$+ \sum_{k=1}^{K} \int_{T_B}^{T_E} [(q_{Ik}I_k e^{-rt})] \, dt. \tag{9.2}$$

The budget (B_{Iu}) imposed by central management on each user (u) places an upper bound on this expenditure. Thus a user's budget constraint is

$$\int_{T_B}^{T_E} \left[\sum_{j=1}^{J} (q_{CE}C_{Ej} + q_{ME}M_{Ej} + q_{YEj}) + \sum_{k=1}^{K} (q_{Ik}I_k) \right] e^{-rt} \, dt \leq B_{Iu}. \tag{9.3}$$

Alternately, central management could impose budgets at each instant of time, the continuous time version of discrete yearly or quarterly budgets. In such circumstances, central management also has the option of permitting or denying time tradeoffs within the budget and then, if the time tradeoff is permitted, deciding whether abstaining from expenditure at one moment means the user has the amount of that nonexpenditure plus interest on it to use later. The following exercise deals with these more advanced budgetary control issues.

9.3.1 Advanced Budgetary Control Methods

EXERCISE 9.2 Advanced Budgetary Control Methods

Modify the users' expenditure-budget constraint of equation (9.3) to permit a budget to be imposed at each instant of time under each of the following conditions:

1. Complete time tradeoff permitted and interest credited using the organization's discount rate r.
2. No time tradeoff at all.
3. Time tradeoff permitted, but the unit cannot earn "interest."

What should be the effect of each of these on user behavior?

Exercise 9.2 Discussion.

1. Complete time tradeoff at rate r. Suppose a user's budget at time t is $B_{Iu}(t)$. More generally, the budget level is a function of time. The expenditure at time t is

$$\sum_{j=1}^{J} \int_{T_B}^{T_E} [(q_{CE}C_{Ej} + q_{ME}M_{Ej} + q_{YE}Y_{Ej} + p_{Lu}L_{uj})e^{-rt}] \, dt + \sum_{k=1}^{K} q_{Ik}I_k. \tag{9.4}$$

Discounting both the expenditures and the budget yields

$$\int_{T_B}^{T_E} \left[\sum_{j=1}^{J} \left\{ q_{CE} C_{Ej} + q_{ME} M_{Ej} + q_{YE} Y_{Ej} + p_{Lu} L_{uj} \right\} e^{-rt} \right] dt$$
$$+ \int_{T_B}^{T_E} \left[\left\{ \sum_{k=1}^{K} q_{Ik} I_k \right\} e^{-rt} \right] dt \leq \int_{T_B}^{T_E} [B_{Iu}(t) e^{-rt}] \, dt. \quad (9.5)$$

Notice that the left-hand side is the same as in the discussion, but the right-hand side makes explicit the relationship between a time sequence of budgets, appropriately discounted, and a single present value budget number. The implication for user control is that time tradeoff will occur and is intended as part of the planning and control system.

2. No time tradeoff. This means that budgets only apply at one moment of time and thus, at each moment, the budget constraint is

$$\sum_{j=1}^{J} (q_{CE} C_{Ej} + q_{ME} M_{Ej} + q_{YE} Y_{Ej} + p_{Lu} L_{uj}) + \sum_{k=1}^{K} q_{Ik} I_k \leq B_{Ju}(t). \quad (9.6)$$

The implication for user behavior is that time tradeoffs are not to occur.

3. No interest earned. Implied in any discounting process is the assumption that if expenditures are strictly less than the budget, then interest is earned on the difference at rate r. With no interest earned, the user will have no funds "next" year over and above the budget provided by central management plus the funds not expended in the previous year. While time tradeoff is possible and sanctioned, there is no economic incentive, in the form of interest income, to reduce expenditures now in order to have higher expenditures later. The user's behavior would be myopic compared to case 1. It is hoped that it will also have been noticed that the expenditures, as written, are not time-dependent. To make the expenditures time-specific, each of the variables $(C_j, M_{Ej}, Y_{Ej}, L_{uj}, I_k)$ must also be a function of time. The solution to such problems is beyond the scope of this book but not uncommon in managerial decision making.

9.4 The Information User's Decision Problem

The previous sections contain two components of the users' choice problem—the budget constraint, and the users' information generation technology model. The final component—the users' utility function—was discussed in section 5.4.3. It is assumed that users are given the universal information furnished by central management as well as the various transfer prices and the market price of labor. Forecasts and plans are made under the central management policy guideline that the future should be regarded as a replication of the present, but choices should be optimal over the entire planning period (T_B to T_E). In devising an optimal plan, the user can choose the level and mix of specific information services ($I_k, k = 1 \cdots K$) and unit-generated information ($I_{uj}, j = 1 \cdots J$), as well as the level and mix of resources used in the unit's information generation production functions ($C_{Ej}, M_{Ej}, Y_{Ej}, L_{uj}; j = 1 \cdots J$). The formal decision problem is as follows:

$$\max \int_{T_B}^{T_E} [\tilde{U}(I_k, I_{uj}, I_v)e^{-rt}]\, dt,$$

by choice of $I_k, I_{uj}, C_{Ej}, M_{Ej}, Y_{Ej}, L_{uj}$,
constrained by

$$I_{uj} = f^{Iuj}(C_{Ej}, M_{Ej}, Y_{Ej}, L_{uj}),$$

$$\sum_{j=1}^{J} \int_{T_B}^{T_E} [(q_{CE}C_{Ej} + q_{ME}M_{Ej} + q_{YE}Y_{Ej} + p_{Lu}L_{uj})e^{-rt}]\, dt$$

$$+ \sum_{k=1}^{K} \int_{T_B}^{T_E} [q_{Ik}I_k e^{-rt}]\, dt \leqq B_{Iu},$$

$$I_k, I_{uj}, C_{Ej}, M_{Ej}, Y_{Ej}, L_{uj} \geqq 0$$

$$j = 1 \cdots J; \quad k = 1 \cdots K; \quad v = 1 \cdots V. \tag{9.7}$$

9.5 The Information User's Decision Rules

9.5.1 The Mix of Specific Information Services and User-Generated Information

While the measurement of marginal utility is not possible in any meaningful way, the concept can be used to develop the decision rules using the now familiar profit-maximizing procedure. Constrained utility maximization is analogous to constrained profit maximization, so the idea of setting marginal profit equal to zero, that is, equating marginal revenue to marginal cost, can be modified to that of equating marginal utility with marginal cost. After putting the decision rule into an appropriate form, the ratio of marginal utilities can be recognized as the marginal rate of psychological substitution and the convenient fiction of a measurable marginal utility can be dropped.

If utility is to be maximized, then the marginal utility of computer-based information of a given type (I_k) must equal its marginal cost, *ceteris paribus*. Here *ceteris paribus* means that all other information mixes and levels and user information generating resource mixes and levels are at their utility-maximizing levels. That is, the net marginal utility must be zero. The marginal utility of I_k is denoted MRGUTIL(I_k). The MRGCOST(I_k) is the

9.5 The Information User's Decision Rules

marginal cash cost

$$\int_{T_B}^{T_E} ([q_{Ik}e^{-rt}]\, dt)$$

multiplied by the marginal utility of a budgetary dollar [MRGUTIL(B_{Iu})]. This contains the idea of an opportunity cost. If there were one more budgetary dollar, then the user's utility could be larger, so the budget constraint imposes an opportunity foregone, or a cost equal to the degree to which the user would be better off—in the user's own subjective judgment. Hence,

$$\text{MRGUTIL}(I_k) = \left(\int_{T_B}^{T_E} [q_{Ik}e^{-rt}]\, dt\right)\left(\text{MRGUTIL}(B_{Iu})\right). \tag{9.8}$$

Applying the same reasoning to user-generated information, I_{uj}, the marginal utility is written as MRGUTIL(I_{uj}). The MRGCOST(I_{uj}) is the increase in the numeraire resource, CPU time, due to an increase in I_{uj} [MPIR(I_{uj}, C_{Ej})] multiplied by the marginal cost of C_{Ej}. Again there is the opportunity cost equivalent to the utility of a budgetary dollar, so the result is

$$\text{MRGCOST}(C_{Ej}) = \left(\int_{T_B}^{T_E} [q_{CE}e^{-rt}]\, dt\right)[\text{MRGUTIL}(B_{Iu})]. \tag{9.9}$$

The overall outcome then is

$$\text{MRGUTIL}(I_{uj}) = \text{MPIR}(I_{uj}, C_{Ej})\left(\int_{T_B}^{T_E} [q_{CE}e^{-rt}]\, dt\right)[\text{MRGUTIL}(B_{Iu})]. \tag{9.10}$$

Solving equations (9.8) and (9.10) for MRGUTIL(B_{Iu}) and equating the result yields

$$\frac{\text{MRGUTIL}(I_k)}{\text{MRGUTIL}(I_{uj})} = \frac{\int_{T_B}^{T_E} [q_{Ik}e^{-rt}]\, dt}{\text{MPIR}(I_{uj}, C_{Ej})\int_{T_B}^{T_E} [q_{CE}e^{-rt}]\, dt}. \tag{9.11}$$

The left-hand side is the marginal rate of psychological substitution (MRPS), so the formal decision rule is as follows:

The information user will choose the most preferred mix of specific information services and unit-generated information, *ceteris paribus*, by equating the MRPS(I_k, I_{uj}) to the ratio of their marginal costs, that is,

$$\text{MRPS}(I_K, I_{uj}) = \frac{\int_{T_B}^{T_E} [q_{Ik}e^{-rt}]\, dt}{\text{MPIR}(I_{uj}, C_{Ej})\int_{T_B}^{T_E} [q_{CE}e^{-rt}]\, dt}. \tag{9.12}$$

The next exercise applies this logic to another case.

EXERCISE 9.3 The Optimal Mix of Two Specific Information Services

Develop and interpret the decision rule for the utility-maximizing mix of information services I_k and $I_{k'}$.

Exercise 9.3 Discussion. At the users' most preferred solution, the marginal rate of psychological substitution must equal the ratio of the marginal costs (i.e., the relative cost of the services to the user). Thus

$$\text{MRPS}(I_k, I_{k'}) = \frac{\int_{T_B}^{T_E} [q_{Ik} e^{-rt}] \, dt}{\int_{T_B}^{T_E} [q_{Ik'} e^{-rt}] \, dt} = \frac{q_{Ik}}{q_{Ik'}}. \tag{9.13}$$

9.5.2 The Mix of CPU Time and Memory in the Production of User-Generated Information

Using the usual logic holding all other mixes and levels constant at their utility-maximizing level, the result for the optimal mix of CPU time and memory for users generating information is given by

$$\text{MRGUTIL}(\hat{I}_{uj}) \text{MPP}(C_{Ej}, \hat{I}_{uj}) = \int_{T_B}^{T_E} [q_{CE} e^{-rt}] \, dt; \tag{9.14}$$

$$\text{MRGUTIL}(\hat{I}_{uj}) \text{MPP}(M_{Ej}, \hat{I}_{uj}) = \int_{T_B}^{T_E} [q_{ME} e^{-rt}] \, dt. \tag{9.15}$$

Solving for $\text{MRGUTIL}(I_{uj})$ and combining these equations yields

$$\frac{\text{MPP}(C_{Ej}, \hat{I}_{uj})}{\text{MPP}(M_{Ej}, \hat{I}_{uj})} = \frac{\int_{T_B}^{T_E} [q_{CE} e^{-rt}] \, dt}{\int_{T_B}^{T_E} [q_{ME} e^{-rt}] \, dt}. \tag{9.16}$$

9.5 The Information User's Decision Rules

The left-hand side is the MRTS(C_{Ej}, M_{Ej}) so the formal decision rule is as follows:

The information user should choose the most preferred mix of CPU time and memory in the unit's generation of information, *ceteris paribus*, by equating the MRTS(C_{Ej}, M_{Ej}) to the ratio of the marginal costs, that is,

$$\text{MRTS}(C_{Ej}, M_{Ej}) = \frac{\int_{T_B}^{T_E} [q_{CE} e^{-rt}] \, dt}{\int_{T_B}^{T_E} [q_{ME} e^{-rt}] \, dt}. \tag{9.17}$$

Notice that this last decision rule is implicitly based on minimizing the cost of producing the information needed. Thus, information users applying the decision rule are also efficient users of resources.

9.5.3 The Quantity of CPU Time to Rent

The quantity of CPU time to rent can be found from equation (9.11). The usual logic requires that all mixes and levels be at their optimal values. So (9.16) becomes

$$\text{MPP}(C_{Ej}, \hat{I}_{uj}) = \text{MPP}(\hat{M}_{Ej}, \hat{I}_{uj}) \frac{\int_{T_B}^{T_E} [q_{CE} e^{-rt}] \, dt}{\int_{T_B}^{T_E} [q_{ME} e^{-rt}] \, dt}, \tag{9.18}$$

where there is only one variable unknown, C_{Ej}. Notice that equation (9.18) is used rather than equation (9.14) with its nonmeasurable marginal utility. This is analogous to choosing quantities in a cost-minimizing or revenue-maximizing production situation. Thus the formal decision rule is as follows:

The information user will rent CPU time, *ceteris paribus*, by applying the decision rule

$$\text{MPP}(C_{Ej}, \hat{I}_{uj}) = \text{MPP}(\hat{M}_{Ej}, \hat{I}_{uj}) \frac{\int_{T_B}^{T_E} [q_{CE} e^{-rt}] \, dt}{\int_{T_B}^{T_E} [q_{ME} e^{-rt}] \, dt}. \tag{9.19}$$

A similar procedure applies for the other inputs.

EXERCISE 9.4 The Quantity of Peripherals to Rent

Develop and interpret the decision rule for the quantity of peripherals (Y_{Ej}) for a user to rent.

Exercise 9.4 Discussion. The information user should rent peripheral time, *ceteris paribus*, by applying the decision rule

$$\text{MPP}(Y_{Ej}, \hat{I}_{uj}) = \text{MPP}(\hat{M}_{Ej}, \hat{I}_{uj}) \frac{\int_{T_B}^{T_E} [q_{YE} e^{-rt}]\, dt}{\int_{T_B}^{T_E} [q_{ME} e^{-rt}]\, dt}. \tag{9.20}$$

9.5.4 The Quantity to Use of a Specific Information Service

This decision rule is developed holding all other levels and mixes constant at their utility-maximizing levels. The $\text{MRPS}(I_k, I_{uj})$ is the slope of an indifference curve and has a numerical value that depends on the quantities of I_k and I_{uj} used. Thus, when seeking I_k, given I_{uj}, equation (9.12) can be used. Hence the formal decision rule:

The information user should choose the most preferred level of specific information service to use, *ceteris paribus*, by applying the following relationship:

$$\text{MRPS}(I_k, \hat{I}_{uj}) = \frac{\int_{T_B}^{T_E} [q_{Ik} e^{-rt}]\, dt}{\text{MPIR}(I_{uj}, C_{Ej}) \int_{T_B}^{T_E} [q_{CE} e^{-rt}]\, dt}. \tag{9.21}$$

9.6 The Demand for Specific Information Services, Computer Capacity, and Labor

The decision rules for the quantity of specific information services, computer capacity, and labor to be used can be seen from the central management perspective by studying the demand schedules for these items. For example,

9.6 The Demand for Specific Information Services

consider equation (9.21). It can be solved for I_k, that is, it can be used to find the level of I_k given the other variables, yielding

$$I_k = f^{Ik}(\hat{I}_{uj}, \hat{C}_{Ej}, q_{CE}, r, T_B, T_E). \tag{9.22}$$

If all such relationships for the decision variables were written, there would be $K + 5UJ$ equations in the same number of unknowns. These can then be solved for the decision variables in terms of the transfer prices, discount rate, and life cycle, yielding

$$I_k = f^{Ik}(q_{Ik}, q_{CE}, r, T_B, T_E),$$

$$I_{uj} = f^{Iuj}(q_{Ik}, q_{CE}, r, T_B, T_E),$$

$$C_{Euj} = f^{CEuj}(q_{Ik}, q_{CE}, r, T_B, T_E),$$

$$M_{Euj} = f^{MEuj}(q_{Ik}, q_{ME}, r, T_B, T_E),$$

$$Y_{Euj} = f^{YEuj}(q_{Ik}, q_{YE}, r, T_B, T_E),$$

$$L_{uj} = L_{uj}(q_{Ik}, q_{CE}, r, T_B, T_E),$$

$$(j = 1 \cdots J; \quad k = 1 \cdots K; \quad u = 1 \cdots U). \tag{9.23}$$

Each of these equations is a demand function for a given resource. As intuition suggests, if the price of a resource increases, the quantity demanded generally decreases, but not always. The exceptions are beyond the scope of this book and seem unlikely to apply to information systems analysis. Note also that the latter five equations can be summed over the number of unit information types (uj) to get the overall user demand for computer capacity and labor. The variation of the quantity demanded with the other prices, the discount rate, and so on, are less intuitive and ultimately rest on empirical estimation of the functions. These demand functions can be statistically estimated for computer services, telecommunication services, and other goods and services.

9.6.1 Manpower and Financial Budgets

Suppose that central management chose to budget information processing labor (in man-years) as well as overall information expenditures. Each user would then face a labor constraint, $\sum_{j=1}^{J} L_{uj} \leq \bar{L}$, in addition to the budget constraint. The user must still pay from the budget for the labor used. The next exercise deals with this advanced model.

EXERCISE 9.5 The Modified User Decision Problem

Define the formal decision problem when users face a manpower constraint as well as a financial budget.

Exercise 9.5 Discussion. The solution is to add the constraint $\sum_{j=1}^{J} L_j \leq \bar{L}$ to the decision problem shown in equation (9.7) and to drop the later expenditure term $p_{Lu} L_{uj}$ from the budgetary constraint.

Exercise 9.6 asks for the decision rules. In doing this exercise note that there are two constraints that place an upper bound on actions: these are the information expenditure budget and the labor budget. Thus there are two opportunity costs imposed with a MRGUTIL(B_{Iu}) and a MRGUTIL($\bar{L}_u$).

EXERCISE 9.6 The Modified Decision Problem Decision Rule

Develop and interpret the decision rules for the user decision problem with both manpower and budget constraints. Be sure to consider the implicit MRPS(B_{Iu}, L_u).

Exercise 9.6 Discussion. For the mix of I_k and I_{uj}: The marginal rate of psychological substitution must equal the relative cost of I_k and I_{uj}. Since I_{uj} is user-produced, it is necessary to measure its cost in terms of one of the production resources as an arbitrary cost measure. Suppose this cost measure is CPU time. Then

$$\text{MRPS}(I_k, I_{uj}) = \text{MPP}(C_E) \frac{\int_{T_B}^{T_E} [q_{Ik} e^{-rt}] \, dt}{\int_{T_B}^{T_E} [q_{CE} e^{-rt}] \, dt}. \quad (9.24)$$

For the mix of L_{uj} and C_{Ej}: Since these resources are used in the production of I_{uj}, the least-cost mix relates the MRTS to the price ratio. With a man-year constraint on labor imposed by central management, it only has a "price" in terms of a specific user's subjective tradeoff with budget dollars. So

$$\text{MRTS}(C_{Ej}, L_{uj}) = \text{MRPS}(B_{Iu}, \bar{L}_u) \int_{T_B}^{T_E} [q_{CE} e^{-rt}] \, dt. \quad (9.25)$$

The other decision rules follow in this vein.

9.7 Implications for Requirements Determination

EXERCISE 9.7 Requirements Determination

What are the implications of user behavior for determining the requirements for a user's information and computer needs?

Exercise 9.7 Discussion. First, note that users subjectively trade off sources of information and thus can be expected to differ among themselves. The diversity of the differences depends greatly on the strength of the organization's culture in socializing users toward common values. Second, the tradeoffs are very dependent on the specifics of the circumstance, that is, the budget level, manpower level, prices, and discount rates. Thus, requirements determination without consideration of these factors is bound to lead to incorrect specification of services and hence incorrect choice of hardware and software. The dependence of user behavior on budgets and other variables suggests that requirements determination is dependent on the planning and control system. This further suggests that requirements determination must be done using tradeoff analysis with a variety of budgets and other parameters. This tradeoff analysis should seek to measure the elasticity of user response to changes in the planning parameters. All of this is a far cry from the "what do you need" approach.

9.8 Implications for Cost Performance Analysis

EXERCISE 9.8 Cost Performance Analysis

Given a cost performance curve as shown below, what are the implications of the ideas in the user model for choice in this situation?

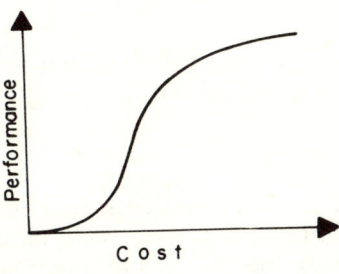

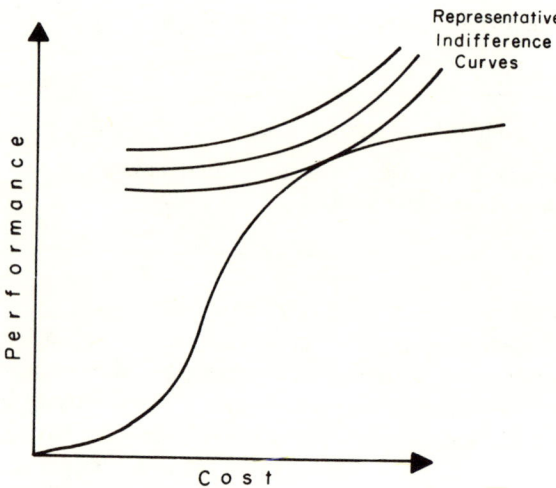

Figure 9.1 User's subjective choice of optimal cost/performance.

Exercise 9.8 Discussion. The user model suggests that individuals vary in their subjective tradeoff of cost and performance. Analytically there are indifference curves relating cost and performance based on the specific user's preferences. The best of all worlds is zero cost and infinite performance. So in general the picture is as in Figure 9.1.

9.9 Implications for Performance Measurement

EXERCISE 9.9 Performance Measurement

A number of indices have been developed for measuring computer system performance. One of these is analytical modelling, and one such model, due to Knight (1966), is

$$\text{PERFORMANCE} = \left[\frac{10^6 \times \text{MEMORY FACTOR}}{\text{PROCESSOR TIME PER MILLION OPERATIONS}} \right].$$

(9.26)

The memory factor is itself an index composed of word length, memory size, and other factors. The processor time per million operations is the time in seconds required to perform a million operations. This time, in turn, is itself an index. There are different indices of computer system performance for scientific and commercial operation.

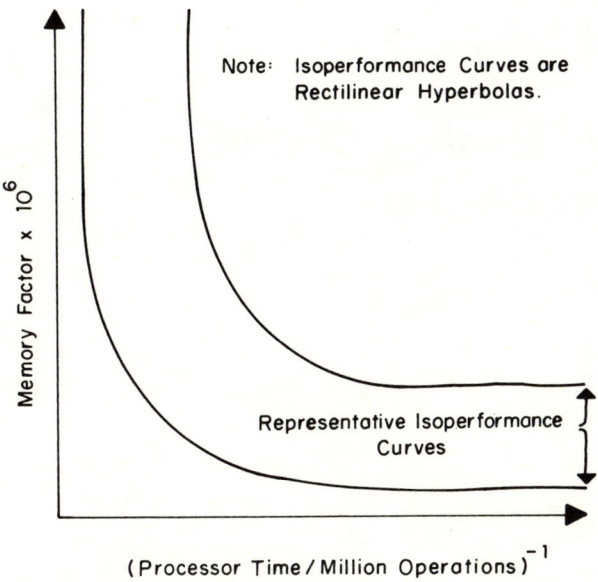

Figure 9.2 Knight isoperformance curves.

Without going into any details beyond those in equation (9.26), the performance measure can be thought of as a numerical representation of multiple factors (two in this case). Use the idea of utility as a numerical measure of preference to discuss Knight's performance index.

Exercise 9.9 Discussion. Memory factor and processor time are the basis for an index of performance. This is exhibited graphically in Figure 9.2. The interesting aspect is the subjective nature of much of index construction. Except where the physical system provides an objective production function view of an index, all indices contain the developer's subjective view of the relative weights of the factors (as refined in interactions with others). Thus, when any index is proposed it is useful to consider the isoperformance lines as indifference curves and to compare one's subjective tradeoffs with those of the author of the index.

Reference

Knight, Kenneth, E. (1966) "Changes in Computer Performance." *Datamation* (September): 40–54.

Chapter 10
System Planning, Control, and Coordination

In the previous chapters a generic information system was described and then analyzed. It is now appropriate to consider some global issues in planning, controlling, and coordinating information systems that encapsulate the major themes discussed. First, the design issue is addressed, with particular emphasis on some advanced ideas of control. This is followed by a discussion of the utilization of an existing system and of identifying the conditions of system equilibrium; the role of management in response to organizational disequilibrium is analyzed. Finally, we look at the interface between the information system and the extraorganizational environment. This discussion concentrates mainly on the industries that supply information system resources and on the strategic response to such institutional changes as the recent divestiture of the Bell System and technological changes in services offered by communications companies.

10.1 The Design Issue

A summary of the step-by-step design process for an information system is given in Chapter 5. For the reader's convenience it is repeated in Figure 10.1.

As the reader will recall, the management process is discussed in terms of routine as well as nonroutine processes. Basically, the nonroutine aspects of the system relate to the identification and analysis of new products that could provide the user with better information for decision making. In essence, the difference relates to the inherent uncertainty in new product creation compared to routine operation of the system. Let us explore the impact of uncertainty on control.

10.1 The Design Issue

Figure 10.1 The information system design process.

1. State the technology-physical flow schema.
2. State the desired system behavior:
   A. Nature of the system equilibrium
   B. Time constraints on reaching equilibrium
3. Design an organizational structure with the associated incentive (reward-penalty) structure.
4. Design the information system management process.
5. Study the system's behavior (by actually operating the information system if necessary):
   A. Does the system seek an equilibrium?
   B. How fast does the system approach equilibrium?
   C. What are the characteristics of the equilibrium?
6. Compare system behavior with the desired behavior and the cost with the budget.
7. Loop back through steps 3 through 6 as necessary to achieve the desired result. The criterion should be one that creates the least-cost system that is technically, physically, financially feasible.

First, in the generic system the interfaces between the organizational units are reasonably well defined—products are physically defined, schedules for delivery are set, budgets are planned, and transfer prices established and acted upon. In other words, the situation is equipped for output control. Ouchi (1979) suggests that there are two other types of control. In situations in which output cannot be well specified, it is possible to substitute behavioral control if the input-output process can be well described. Thus, supervisors and managers are able to monitor the details of the input-output process to ensure that services, however defined, are in fact being provided. Finally, there is the possibility that neither the process nor the output can be well described. In that case, the situation calls for clan control. In clan control, traditions and rituals (i.e., standard operating procedures developed over the years to deal with situations) are used to control both the process and the output. This type of system is typical of most research laboratories.

The history of software development illustrates the shift from clan control to output control as structured programming, program libraries, and other forms of software tools were invented and put to use. However, since the process and output description of new software products is still not well defined, one would assume that the natural control mechanism for specifying requirements for new software is inherently closer to clan control than to the output or behavioral models of control.

In fact, managers continue to engage in an interesting, perhaps even emotional, debate as to how to organize and manage the software requirements determination process. On the one hand, there are those who argue for making it part of the software development and maintenance effort. This position assumes that the requirements process is well described, that is, that the user-producer dialogue is well understood by both parties and that the user can state the nature of the information product needed. To the extent that this is true, this control mechanism works well. If the assumptions are not met, problems of control will arise, that is, cost and performance may deviate from the norm. Certainly the software industry is well known for crises of such proportion as to suggest that certain situations demand a different form of control. The rise of the information center concept of end-user computing appears to be an effective means of developing an organizational clan trained to control the process.

The creation of a group of user-oriented software specialists and the development of a language tailored to achieve good communication between the user and specialist is a major clue to the development of a clan form of organizational control. User and specialist work as a team. There is, of course, no universal method that can be applied to control the process of software requirements definition. Consequently, the overall design process must include the option to choose a cost-effective control mechanism based on the degree to which design in a particular organization is subject to output and process uncertainty.

Another aspect of the design issue is the never-ending debate over centralization versus decentralization. If these terms were not subject to interpretation, analysis of an information system on the basis of such a strict binary concept would be simple. However, different experts use these terms in different ways. For the purposes of the present discussion, rather than entering into the debate over the true meaning of centralization and decentralization —however important this distinction may be for research and for our future understanding of information systems management—we shall discuss a few relevant points in somewhat more detail.

Pure centralization is not possible because the necessary data cannot be centrally assembled and because human information processing capability is insufficient—nor is it economically feasible. Thus, the designer of an information system must recognize that each participant in the system may have a different set of data, a different method of organizing those data, and, depending on the organizational structure and its incentive scheme, different motivation for interacting with other participants. In effect, the system contains (1) a set of data organized in association with each participant, and (2) an organizational incentive scheme designed to encourage organizational cooperation. The overall system designer can vary both factors to develop the most effective information system. A system choice variable that can be adapted to human information-processing capabilities is the size, composition, and organization of each participant's data set. This is not to say that informal data that affect system performance are not collected, but rather that the basic role played by each participant is a choice variable. A second system choice variable is the organizational incentive scheme. In addition, the system designer can vary the composition and timing of administrative data flows in an effort to bring about the desired information system behavior.

In summary, rather than focusing on centralized versus decentralized designs, the system designer needs to concentrate on (1) the composition and organization of individual participant's data sets, (2) the organizational reward and penalty scheme, and (3) the composition and timing of the administrative data flow between participants. Despite the constraints of a given level of performance and the available technology, this approach can solve the information system design problem of minimizing life-cycle cost.

10.2 The Utilization of an Existing System

Performance evaluation of information systems has had a long and checkered career. At the risk of sounding overly casual, one might say that the focus has generally been on specific hardware and software measures of system performance, such as those described in previous chapters, rather than on overall information system performance. For the purposes of analyzing technical efficiency, this attention is not misplaced. Clearly, the software development and maintenance activity and the computer center must be technically efficient if the information system is to be technically efficient. But there is more to performance evaluation.

It is known that the organizational incentive scheme is geared to get the managers of the software activity and of the computer center to use the traditional hardware and software measures in order to ensure the technical efficiency of their operations. In particular, it is the cost center and profit center structures that induce this behavior. Thus, overall system performance is to be judged in terms of an audit of whether the cost and profit centers are in fact behaving as such.

An often overlooked aspect of performance evaluation, alluded to above, is whether the overall system is in balance, that is, in equilibrium. The system's balance, or equilibrium, can be measured by comparing the demand and supply for each product or item exchanged between or among the organizational units, provided that output measurement is feasible and used for all the interactions between and among the organizational units. The generic information system developed in this book makes this process rather straightforward for system management. If the system is not in equilibrium, the procedures described here can be implemented in order to bring the system closer to equilibrium. While real-world systems with complete output control may be more complex than the textbook analysis, the basic principles still apply. Nevertheless, a few subtleties should be considered.

For the equilibrating process to work in an output-controlled generic information system, the system itself must be stable. That is, the use of the process to bring the system to equilibrium must indeed move the system closer to that state and not further from it. Only experience with the actual system will provide the data with which to determine whether the system is stable. If, over time, there is no indication of stability in the system, it is clear that the organizational structure and the composition and timing of the administrative data flow are in need of change.

The appropriate action is to redesign the system's control aspects. It is reasonable to begin by adjusting the administrative data flows. The details of the system management decisions should also be carefully considered in terms of a need for change. Frequently, stability can be improved by manipulating the magnitude of the adjustments in transfer prices, budgets, and schedules, that is, by reducing the shock of any such changes. Improving stability leads to an associated change in the behavior of the system over time. In general, the more stable the system, the more smooth and even the approach to equilibrium. The designer seeking a faster approach to equilibrium must bear in mind the tendency for the time path to exhibit an oscillating behavior that overshoots the desired equilibrium.

Finally, there is the question of whether the equilibrium exhibited is the right one. It is the responsibility of management to select a level of equilibrium that is both feasible, given the available technology and the system budget, and in its judgment organizationally most effective. The only way to do this is for management to acquire some sense of alternative feasible equilibria through a feel for the system. Although it is both possible and useful to compute such things along with some analysis, the state of the art demands reliance on managerial judgment as to just what constitutes feasible equilibria. In most cases, it is assumed that considerable experience with the system is needed in order to understand it. After analyzing the feasible equilibria, management decides which equilibrium will provide the greatest organizational effectiveness. Once this judgment is made, the price-budget mechanism can be used to adjust the system to that equilibrium.

The above approach is predicated on the use of output control. If instead behavioral control is used to change the system, then in place of price-budget control, participants' jobs must be revised in some manner. In particular, the system manager must monitor the job performance of the participants and adjust the nature of those jobs by direct supervision of the details. Obviously, the workload of the system manager will increase. It may increase to the point where additional layers of managers are required to monitor and change behavior. The use of additional layers of management implies an increase in the administrative data flows to plan, coordinate, and control these additional managers. In general, there will be a larger transactions cost in operating a system in which behavioral control is used rather than output control. If the state of knowledge of system details is such that outputs cannot be described and measured in detail, this increased transactions cost must be incurred.

When the state of knowledge of the system does not permit the use of either output or behavioral control, clan control must be adopted. In this case, the transactions cost is even larger than in the behavioral case.

Clearly, the less that is known about the system, the higher the system transactions cost. In general, then, the least-cost method of control should be chosen. Toward that end, it is useful for managers to invest in a better understanding of the system in an effort to employ output control. Such an investment should occur up to the point where the investment cost equals the decrease in the transactions cost of operating the system. Whatever the state of system knowledge, the management process selected will be used to bring the system to equilibrium. Readjustment to a new and better equilibrium will probably be required at a later time when the need again arises.

10.3 Extraorganizational Impacts

Information systems interface with a variety of industries external to the organizations that use them. In general, these interfaces relate to the organization's competitors, suppliers, and buyers of its products and/or services. In all cases, management must use information to evaluate possible actions by these other organizations. In particular, the impact of such actions on its own organization is the ultimate criterion with which management is concerned. The information product that provides the basis for evaluating these criteria includes what is called an industry analysis. Although the focus of this book is the internal management issues—and not such external interactions—a brief description of the general nature of industry analysis as well as an overview of the management decisions involved are germane to this discussion.

One of the main determinants of an industry's behavior is its structure. For example, the mainframe computer market is dominated by a single firm, IBM, against which several peripheral firms compete. By contrast, the applications software market does not have such a dominant firm. Some industries experience major upheavals. The best example is the recent divestiture of AT&T. Not only is the long-haul telecommunications market no longer regulated, but there is intense competition for customers, resulting in new services and lower prices. In the case of labor markets, individual participants in the market usually perceive that they have no influence on the market price: consequently, they consider the market price to be fixed.

The use of such forms of industry analysis as the effects of market structure enables management to develop several scenarios for how each specific external interaction will evolve. These scenarios include the time path of prices and products and services that are or will be offered and can then be used to generate several new scenarios vis à vis the evolution of the information system as a whole. One of the important issues to be assessed by management is the likelihood that a particular scenario will actually occur. Despite techniques involving a combination of expert opinion and objective probabilities, in general such judgments are made in conditions of uncertainty, so there is no guarantee that reasonable managers will agree. In any case, the outcome of this procees is the adoption of a specific strategy for developing the information system over time.

The chosen strategy will have characteristics that imply a hedge against other scenarios occurring rather than the one considered most likely. For example, consider again the rapid changes occurring in the telecommunications industry. Now that customers must lease or buy the equipment used on their premises, many companies are competing for the business with a variety of products. Or consider the fact that local area networks are now a major field of development. Is it preferable to purchase computers from IBM, which is moving into the communications field in order to provide complete network facilities? Or is AT&T, with its established communications abilities and recent entry into the computer field, the better choice? The information system strategy that is selected will assume a sequence of new products as well as a decision as to optimal timing and purchase of equipment. Depending on management's attitude toward risk taking, there will be a tendency to delay the acquisition of new equipment until additional information is available on the evolution of the market. The lease or buy decision should tend toward a preference for leasing.

Another example of extraorganizational impact is the price for telecommunications services. At this writing there is every indication that such prices will decline over time. As prices decline, it is relatively more advantageous to use more and smaller computer systems to take advantage of the economies of scale and scope discussed earlier. As this will take some time to accomplish, the hedge is to select smaller systems, as they can be more easily distributed than larger ones yet can still perform well in the event that telecommunications prices do not decline as anticipated.

Such decisions are unique to each organization, depending on management's assessment of the future and of the organization's assets and liabilities at a particular point in time. Nevertheless, the basic ideas learned in this book will permit the structuring of these decisions as well as the careful, logical analysis that supports sound management decisions.

Reference

Ouchi, William G. (1979) "A Conceptual Framework for the Design of Organizational Control Mechanisms." *Management Science* 25, 9 (September): 838–848.

Index

Acquisition,
   alternatives, 138–140
   marginal cost of, 150
Administrative data, 84, 87, 93–95t, 106, 219–220
Analogy, 31, 33–34
Analytical approach, overview of, 3–11
Applications programs, 5, 79
   as collective (public) good, 123–124
   as information resource, 203
Arbuckle's standard instruction mix, 153
AT&T, 221–222

Balance, 10–11, 31, 92–93, 148, 219
   choice of, 157
   measure of, 149–150
BASIC, 144
Bayes' theorem, 18
Baumol, W., 76
Boehm, B. W., 175, 177–178, 189, 193
Borovits, I., 147
Brooks, F. P., 178–179, 193–194
Budget, 10, 163
   adjustment, 97–98, 220
   as integrating mechanism, 93
   financial, 211
   information, 8–9, 103, 163, 203–205
   life-cycle, 211–212
   manpower, 211–212

Cale, E. G., 155
Capacity
   decision problem, 9
   management, 165–170

Capital budgeting system, 5
   for nonroutine activities, 100–103
Central management, 2, 6–11, 14, 31–32, 75, 83–84, 87, 92–93, 163
   decision problem, 8, 95–96
   software issues, 190–191
Central processor time, 5
Centralization and dispersion, 218
   cost of, 159
   economics of, 156–162
   optimal, 157
Centralized structure, 9
COCOMO, 177, 189
Collective (public) resource, 72
   marginal revenue of, 124
Communications
   channels, 7–8
   costs, 156
      between installations, 158, 161
      user, 158, 161
   price, 222
Composite commodity, 61
   cost function, 62
   isoproduct line for, 61
   unit level of, 61, 65
   see also Ray
Computer capacity, 5, 166
   allocation, 109
   decentralization and distribution of, 156
   demand for, 210
   enhancement, 166
Computer center, 2, 4–5, 8, 83, 88–90, 163
   as central data processing capability, 105
   as profit center, 88, 106

Computer center (*continued*)
  decision problem, 112–116
  management problem
    variables in 106
  manager, 8–9
    evaluation of, 89–90
  production function, 88
  production model, 109–112
  production processes
    multiplicity of, 109
  profit and loss statement, 10
  role of, 106
Computer services, 4–5, 80
  allocation of, 6, 163
  charging for, 162
  demand and supply, 9
  external, 105, 109
  internal, 105
  supply, 140
  transfer prices, 9, 140
Computer system, 75
  capacity, 5, 159
    measure for, 152
  conversion costs, 194–198
  cost function, 151–157
  cost of, 32, 151
  efficiency of operations, 142
  production function, 152, 159
Computer technology, 8
Communications
  costs, 85
  industry, 222
  services, 85
Configuration
  evolution of, 169
  management, 147–151
Constraints, 114
Control
  behavioral, 217, 220
  budgetary, 204
  clan, 217–218, 220
  effect of uncertainty on, 216–217
  mechanisms, 8
  output, 217, 220
  types of, 8
Control Data—Scope, 148
Control structure, 7, 83–93
Costs, short-run, 128
Cost center, 8
Cost complementarity, 71
Cost curves, 152
Cost estimation methods, 32–34

Cost function, 60, 76
  two-product, 53
  multiple-product, 58–76
  shape of, 76
Cost of information, incremental, 67–68
Cost/performance, 152, 213
Cost/utilization technique, 147–151
  uses of, 151
Coyne, T. J., 36

Decentralized structure, 9–10, 31
Decision making, 14
  under risk and uncertainty, 15–16
Decision point, 28–29
Decision processes, 8
Decision problem, 9–10, 15, 34
  computer center, 109, 115
  parameters, 9
  product mix, 55
  profit maximizing, 75
  rent or buy, 139
  replacement, 137
  scale of operations, 43–49
  short-run utilization, 128–132
  software manager's
    long-run, 180–181
    short-run, 186
  structure of, 9
  two-resource, 49–52
  user's, 91, 205–206
Decision rules, 9, 24, 32, 34
  allocation, 126–128, 184
  change in, 29
  choice of technology (resource mix), 121–125
  computer center, 116–128
  computer system capacity, 116–118
  myopic, 135
  product levels, 118–120
  product mix, 55–57, 125–126
  rent or buy, 139
  replacement, 137–138
    of components, 138
  resource levels, 184–186
  resource mix, 181–183
  scale of operations, 43–49
  short-run, 130–132
  software manager's
    long-run, 181–186
    short-run, 186–187
  two-resource, 49–52

Index

user's, 206–210
  mix, 206–209
  quantity, 209–210
  with budget constraint, 212
Decision support systems (DSS), 14
Decision tree, 15, 18, 20
  phases of, 18
Decision variables, 75, 114
Decisions
  initiation, termination and replacement, 133–138
  interdependence of, 116
  make or buy, 140, 190–191
  nonroutine, 5
  optimal, 10
  outcomes of, 15
  scale of operations, 40
  timing, 133
Delphi method, 31, 33–34
Demand, optimal, 10
Depreciation, 140
Design, 216–219
Diseconomies of scale, 163
Diseconomies of scope, 70, 72, 163
Discount rate (or factor), 38–39, 169
  as cost of capital, 39
  as opportunity cost, 39
  as standard rate, 39
Distributed systems, communication cost in, 156
DYNAMO, 28–29

Economies of scale, 151, 157, 163,
  of software activity, 193
  of software projects, 192
  see also Returns to scale
Economies of scope, 59–60, 69–72, 192
  degree of, 70–71
Effort multiplier, 194
Ein-Dor, P., 147, 155, 165
Equilibrating process, 219
Equilibrium, 10, 31–32, 84, 103–104, 219–221
  search procedure, 96–100
Expansion path
  cost minimizing, 57
  revenue maximizing, 57
Extraorganizational impacts, 221–222

Feasibility, 101
Federal Government, 11

Financing considerations, 141
Forecasts, 17–18, 20
Forrester, J., 28–29

General Accounting Office (GAO), 194–195
Goals, vision of, 3, 11
Gremillion, L. L., 170
Grosch, H., 151
Grosch's law, 151–152, 156–157, 160
Growth pat, 168–169

Hansen, J. V., 164
Hardware, 5
  acquired from external markets, 4
  acquisition
    cost, 88–89
    source of funds for, 141
  cost, 159
  increments to, 165
  investment cost, 113
  maintenance cost, 88–89
  managers, 8
  marginal physical productivity, 111
  monitors, 142–143
  production function, 151
  salvage value, 89
Heitzer, L. E., 164
Human information processing capabilities, 218

IBM, 11, 221–222
  MSF, 148
  System/360, 152
Incentive structure, 2, 8, 11, 75, 84, 103, 219
Incentives, 7, 34
Individual data sets, 218–219
Industrial Dynamics, 28–30, 80
Industry analysis, 221
Information, 34
  amount to produce, 51
  as organizational resource, 1
  cost of, 32–34
  importance of, 1
  in decision making, 1, 14, 29
  perfect, 17
  physical flows of, 28–29
  representing physical values, 28–29
  structures, 34
  use of, 13
  user created, 80, 202
  value of, 1, 8, 13–15, 31–32, 34, 75

Information management system, structure of, 9
Information processing
  as production process, 13
  expenditure on, 1
Information products, 4–6
  demand for, 4
  mix of, 6
  new, 5
  profitability study, 101
  specific, 5
  supply of, 4
Information resource, 2
  cost of, 34
  management, 31
  management system, 2
  manager of, 8
Information services
  demand for, 210
  production model, 111
  specific, 80, 105
  universal, 80, 105
Information system, 34
  amount of service provided by, 142
  behavior, 85–100
  as communications network, 26
  components
    communications between, 31
    decision problems, 9
    managers of, 8–9
    relationships between, 4
  computerized, 6
  defined, 2
  describing, 4–6
  economic feasibility of, 20
  elements of, 4
  evaluation of, 34
    subjective, 30–32
  good decisions about, attributes of, 2–3
  life-cycle, 37–38
  management process, 103
  manager, 8, 11, 34
  managerial view of, 3
  null, 25
  perfect, 24–26
  role of, 28
  status of, 92
  structure of, 21, 26, 34
  value of, 20, 28, 30
Information system management, 2, 8, 11, 83–84
  concept of, 8
  organizational structure for, 14
  structure of, 6–10
  see also Central management
Input-output services, 5
Isocost
  contour, 72
  curve, 60
Isoperformance lines, 215
Isoquant, 47
  slope of, 48
Iterative process (or procedure), 9, 97–100, 163
  for communicating about information resources, 2
  for planning, coordination, and control, 2
  iteration of, 10

Job requests, 5, 79
Joint production, cost of, 59

Kanter, H. M., 163, 164 t
Kiviat charts, 146–147
Knight, K. E., 152–155

Labor, 5
  demand for, 210
  experience, 188–189
  markets, 174
  specialization, 187
Learning curve, 188
Life-cycle
  cost, 8
  of computer hardware, 37
  of information system, 37–38
  of software, 37
  profit, 8
  sequence of, 137
  set by central management, 106
Local area networks, 222

MacCrimmon, K. R., 28
Mainframes, 155
Management control, 8
  criterion for, 92
Management information systems (MIS), 14
Management process, 11
Managerial work, nature of, 3
Managers, 9
  lower level, 7
  performance evaluation, 84
Marchand, M., 163, 164 t
Marginal cost, 9, 46–47, 163

Index

approximation to, 141
measurement problems, 163
Marginal life-cycle profit, 51
  maximized, 44
Marginal physical input requirement, 45, 54
Marginal physical schedule productivity, 178
Marginal present life-cycle value of information, 52
Marginal rate of technical substitution (marginal technical tradeoff), 48, 54
Marginal rate of product transformation, 54
Marginal revenue, 163
Market-based pricing, 163
Markets, 10
  external, 11
  input, 10–11
  pure and perfect, 11
Market prices, 9–11, 106, 165
Marschak, J., 21, 26
Massé, P., 39
McKell, L. J., 163, 165
McKinney, J. L., 170
Memory, 5
Microcomputers, 155–157
Microeconomics, 3
Minicomputers, 155–157
Mintzberg, H., 3
MIPS (millions of instructions per second), 155–156
MIS (management information system), 14
Mix, 6
  decision, 9, 40, 50–52, 131
  of components, 151
Multiple-product production, 111
  feasibility of, 66

Naval Data Automation Command (NAVDAC), 194
Nielsen, R., 163, 164t
Noise, 20

Operating profit, 113
Opportunity cost, 130, 191, 207
  of acquisition pre change, 134–135
  of alternative investments, 134–135
  of salvage value, 136
Organization, 34
  design of, 65, 81, 83
  for planning, coordination and control, 80–81

performance of, 14
procedures, 6
representation of, 28
structure of, 6, 11, 21, 34, 80–83, 103, 220
Ouchi, W. G., 217
Output, accuracy of, 20

Panzer, J. C., 76
Parallel operation, 138
Parametric cost estimation, 33, 157
Penalties, 7
Performance
  evaluation, 142–151
  index of, 215
  measurement, 214, 219
Perrow, C., 82
Personnel or personnel resources
  acquisition from external markets, 4–5
Peters, T. J., 3
Physical flows, 5, 28–29, 34, 77–80, 103
Physical productivity
  average, 42–43
  marginal, 42–43, 45, 47, 75, 110
  positive, 43
  total, 42–43
Physical resources, 5
Planning, coordination and control, 8, 11, 75
  choice of system for, 157
  complexity of, 6
  data flows, 93–95
  perfect, 9
  procedure, 84
Present value, 38
  of life-cycle cost
    of information, 46
    of operations, 75
  of life-cycle marginal cost, 45
  of life-cycle profit, 44, 46, 49, 55, 113
  of life-cycle revenue, 75
Price projection
  change over time, 189
  relationship, 112–113, 134
Probabilities, 15, 18, 23–24
  conditional, 18, 20
  unconditional, 18
Procedure, decentralized, 9
Processes, routine and nonroutine, 216
Product cost, incremental, 60, 67–68, 71
Product mix, 53
Product transformation curves, 53–54

Production
  function, 42–43, 53–60
    as seen by central management, 95
    multiple-resource, 47–48
    independent, 70
    joint, 70
      cost of, 71
Production plan, 40–43
  defined, 40
  profit maximizing, 45, 56, 75
  revenue maximizing, 57
  technically efficient, 40
  technically feasible, 43, 47
  technology-constrained, 75–76
Productivity
  average, 40–41
  marginal, 40–41
  total, 40
Products
  mix of, 6, 9
  physical flow of, 11
Profit and loss statement, 9–10, 89–90
Profit center, 8, 162, 165
Profit, components of, 112
Profit function, 75
  short-run, 128–129
Programming costs, 33
Project teams, 172
Putnam, L. H., 175, 177–178, 189, 193–194

Quantities demanded, 9–10
Quantities supplied, 9–10
Queries, 5

Ray
  average cost, 62–66
    characteristics, 63–64
    defined, 62
    elasticity of, 64
    minimum, 65
  cost behavior, 60, 62
  marginal cost, 66
    defined, 62–63
  index for locating, 61
  see also Composite commodity
Rayleigh curve, 189
Rent or buy decisions, 138–140
  as minimum cost problem, 139
Requirement determination, 5, 176, 213, 217
Resource productivity surface, 54
Resource requirement function, 45, 53

Resources
  demand for, 4
  devoted to information systems, 5
  mix of, 6, 9, 47–49
    profit maximizing, 121
  physical flow of, 11
  supply of, 4
Returns to scale, 48–49, 75
  constant, 40, 43
  diminishing (decreasing), 40, 110, 151
  increasing, 40
  multiple product, 64–67
  see also Economies of scale
Rewards, 7, 103
Routinizing, 100–103

Scale of operations, 5–6, 9, 43–49
Schedules, adjustment, 220
Selwyn, L. L., 163, 164 t
Seo, K. K., 36
Service interruption costs, 159, 161
Sharkey, W. W., 76
Short run
  constraints, 129–130
  decision variables, 129
  defined, 128
Simon, H. A., 82
Simulation, 28–30, 34
Small mainframes, 155
Smidt, S., 163, 164 t
Software, 5, 83
  acquisition from external markets, 4
  conversion, 194–195
  cost estimation, 177
  delivery dates, 9–10, 176, 193
  demand and supply, 9
  for information service production, 111
  maintenance, 176
  make or buy decision, 190–191
  manager, 8–9, 87
    performance of, 174
  marginal cost of, 10, 102
  monitors, 143–144
  nature of, 176
  optimizers, 144–145
  specification, 84, 100
  see also Software products
Software development and maintenance
  activity, 2, 4–5, 8, 84–87, 163
  as cost center, 8, 84, 173
  cost function, 192
  described, 172–174

Index

Software development (production) and maintenance, 79
  capacity, 5
  cost function, 191–193
  cost of, 32, 177
    estimating relationship, 86
  life-cycle, 175
  present life-cycle cost of, 85
  production function, 79, 86, 177–180
  productivity measurement, 198–199
  resources in, 85
  technology, 8, 79, 174–180, 189
  tools, 172–173
    cost of, 181
Software products, 5, 8
  delivery and maintenance schedules, 8
  development and maintenance, 6
  development time, 178
  introduction, 100
  size of, 86
  see also Software
Software schedules, 9
  delivery dates, 8
Software specifications, 9–10
Solomon, M. B., 152–155
Stability, 220
Statistical decision theory, 15–21, 28, 34
Starting date, 133
  marginal present value of profit for, 134
  profit-maximizing, 136
    decision on, 135
Streeter, D. N., 157, 159, 161
Subadditivity, 70
Subsidy, 163
Supercomputers, 155
Supply, optimal, 10
System accounting, 145–146
System analysis, 101
System components. *See* Information system
System manager. *See* Central management; Information system management
System programs, 79
System utilization, 219–221
  measures of, 149
Systemic behavior, 11, 104
Systems analysts and programmers, 174

Task
  coping difficulty, 82
  interdependence, 81–82
    pooled, 82
    reciprocal, 82
    sequential, 81–82
  variability, 82
Team
  decisions, 22
  defined, 21
  examples of, 22
  members, 22–24, 26
  organization, 22
  problem, 22
Team theory, 21–28, 34
Technical analysis, 101
Technology, 6, 9, 34, 103
  available, 32
  change in, 43, 111, 152, 156, 161
  choice of, 50
  constraint, 201
  decision, 40
  employed, 10, 75
  organizational, 9
  physical, 9
  projection, 189
  trends, 155
  user information generation, 202–203
  zones, 83
  see also Computer technology
Telecommunications. *See* Communications
Termination decision, 136
Thompson, J. D., 81
Time
  continuous, 113
  role of, in economic decisions, 37–39
Tradeoffs, 121
  cost and performance, 214
  economic (external), 45, 75, 121, 123, 125
  sources of information, 213
  technological (internal), 45, 121, 123, 125
  time, 204–205
Transaction costs, 10, 220–221
Transaction processing systems, 13–14
  value of, 14
Transfer prices, 9–10, 14, 31, 93, 97–98, 173
  adjustment, 220
  establishing, 162–165
  set by central management, 106, 140, 162
  software, 191
Transformation, technological, 11
Truett, D. B., 36
Truett, L. J., 36

Units, organizational, 11, 35
User (or user-manager), 2, 4–5, 8–9, 80, 83, 90–92, 163
   and information resource management system, 200–202
   budgets, 9–10
   charges to, 141
   coordination and control of, 91
   demand, 10, 91–92
   program development and maintenance, 80
      production function, 90
      sources of information for, 90
      subjective judgment, 203, 213
      time preference, 90
      utility function, 90

Value Computing—Comput-a-charge, 148
Values, expected, 15–16, 24, 26
Vendors, 168–169

Wages and salaries, 174
Waterman, R. H., 3
Willig, R. D., 76
Workload, 157, 161, 165–170